T0270959

Public Management and Performance

Public services touch the majority of people in advanced and developing economies on a daily basis: children require schooling, the elderly need personal care and assistance, rubbish needs collecting, water must be safe to drink and the streets need policing. In short, there is practically no area of our lives that isn't touched in some way by public services. As such, knowledge about strategies to improve their performance is central to the good of society. In this book, a group of leading scholars examine some of the most pressing issues in public administration, political science and public policy by undertaking a systematic review of the research literature on public management and the performance of public agencies. It is an important resource for public management researchers, policy-makers and practitioners who wish to understand the current state of the field and the challenges that lie ahead.

Richard M. Walker is Professor of Public Management and Policy at the University of Hong Kong, and Senior Research Associate in the Department of Public Administration and Policy at Xi'an Jiaotong University.

George A. Boyne is Professor of Public Sector Management at Cardiff University.

Gene A. Brewer is Associate Professor of Public Administration and Policy at the University of Georgia School of Public and International Affairs, and Visiting Professor of Public Management at the Utrecht University School of Governance in the Netherlands.

Public Management and Performance

Research Directions

Edited by

Richard M. Walker

University of Hong Kong

George A. Boyne

Cardiff University

Gene A. Brewer

University of Georgia

CAMBRIDGE
UNIVERSITY PRESS

University Printing House, Cambridge CB2 8BS, United Kingdom

One Liberty Plaza, 20th Floor, New York, NY 10006, USA

477 Williamstown Road, Port Melbourne, VIC 3207, Australia

4843/24, 2nd Floor, Ansari Road, Daryaganj, Delhi - 110002, India

79 Anson Road, #06-04/06, Singapore 079906

Cambridge University Press is part of the University of Cambridge.

It furthers the University's mission by disseminating knowledge in the pursuit of education, learning and research at the highest international levels of excellence.

www.cambridge.org
Information on this title: www.cambridge.org/9780521116633

© Cambridge University Press 2010

First published 2010

A catalogue record for this publication is available from the British Library

Library of Congress Cataloging in Publication data
Public management and performance : research directions / [edited by]
    Richard M. Walker, George A. Boyne, Gene A. Brewer.
        p.   cm.
    Includes bibliographical references and index.
    ISBN 978-0-521-11663-3
    1. Municipal services–Management–Research.   2. Public administration–Research.
    I. Walker, Richard M.   II. Boyne, George A.   III. Brewer, Gene A.   IV. Title.
    HD4431.P815 2010
    351–dc22
    2010022032

ISBN 978-0-521-11663-3 Hardback
ISBN 978-1-107-41167-8 Paperback

Contents

Figures

Tables

Contributors

Matt Andrews is Assistant Professor of Public Policy at Harvard University's Kennedy School of Government. A South African, he has worked in over twenty developing countries and writes on governance and management issues in these settings.

Dr Rhys Andrews is a Senior Research Fellow in Cardiff Business School, Cardiff University. His primary research interests are in strategic management, organizational environments and public service performance. He is a contributor to *Public Service Performance: Perspectives on Measurement and Management*, Cambridge University Press, 2006 and has published articles in *Journal of Public Administration Research and Theory, Public Administration Review* and other journals.

George Boyne is Professor of Public Sector Management at Cardiff Business School, Cardiff University. His main current research interests are organizational performance, executive succession and structural change in public services. He has published 7 books and 115 articles in academic journals that include the *Journal of Management Studies*, the *Journal of Public Administration Research and Theory, Public Administration* and *Public Administration Review*. His recent books include *Public Service Performance: Perspectives on Measurement and Management* (Cambridge University Press, 2006) and *Theories of Public Service Improvement* (2009). He is President of the Public Management Research Association, co-editor of the *Journal of Public Administration Research and Theory* and a member of the UK ESRC Research Grants Board.

Gene A. Brewer is Associate Professor of Public Administration and Policy at the University of Georgia School of Public and International Affairs, an International Scholar at the Georgian Institute of Public Administration (former Soviet-bloc country), and Visiting Professor of Public Management at the Utrecht University School of Governance in the Netherlands. He is case editor of the Public Administration Review and sits on the editorial boards of several journals. His research interests include public sector reform, governmental performance, policy implementation, comparative and international administration, employee motivation and behavior, and bureaucratic accountability in democratic political systems. He actively lectures for and consults with various universities, governments, and nongovernmental organizations internationally.

Alisa Hicklin an Assistant Professor in the Department of Political Science at the University of Oklahoma: her research interests include public management, higher education policy and minority representation. Her most recent work focuses on how policy-makers and public managers can affect African American and Latino student access to American public universities.

Chan Su Jung is a Research Associate in the School of Public and International Affairs at the University of Georgia. His research interests include organizational goal properties such as goal ambiguity, performance measurement and management, turnover, motivation and leadership in public organizations. His papers were included in the 2008 and 2009 Academy of Management Best Paper Proceedings. He was nominated for the William H. Newman Award at the 2009 Academy of Management Conference.

Kenneth J. Meier is the Charles H. Gregory Chair in Liberal Arts and Distinguished Professor of Political Science at Texas A&M University (USA) and Professor of Public Management at Cardiff School of Business, Cardiff University (UK). His research agenda focuses on how public organizations interface with political institutions and influence public policy via the implementation process. He is acknowledged to be the best shot putter working in public management and the leading scholar of public management among all former shot putters.

Donald Moynihan is Associate Professor of Public Affairs at the University of Wisconsin-Madison. He is the author of numerous articles on topics including performance management, organizational change, homeland security and organizational behaviour, in journals such as *Public Administration Review*, *Journal of Public Administration Research and Theory*, and *Governance*. His book, *The Dynamics of Performance Management: Constructing Information and Reform*, was published in 2008.

Laurence J. O'Toole, Jr. is the Margaret Hughes and Robert T. Golembiewski Professor of Public Administration, Department of Public Administration and Policy, School of Public and International Affairs, The University of Georgia (USA). He is also Professor of Comparative Sustainability Policy Studies at the Center for Clean Technology and Environmental Policy, Faculty of Management and Governance, The University of Twente (The Netherlands). He is the author or co-author of many studies on networks, public management and performance.

David Pitts is Assistant Professor of Public Administration and Policy at American University. His research concentrates on public management, with a particular focus on workforce diversity and representative bureaucracy. His work has appeared in a number of public administration journals, including the *Journal of Public Administration Research and Theory, Public Administration Review,* and *Public Administration.*

Hal G. Rainey is Alumni Foundation Distinguished Professor in the School of Public and International Affairs at the University of Georgia. His research concentrates on organizations and management in government, with emphasis on performance, change, leadership, privatization, and comparisons of governmental management to management in the business and nonprofit sectors. The fourth edition of his book, *Understanding and Managing Public Organizations,* was published in 2010. He serves as a Fellow of the National Academy of Public Administration. In 2009, he received the American Society for Public Administration's Dwight Waldo Award for career scholarly contributions to public administration.

Richard M. Walker is Professor of Public Management and Policy at the University of Hong Kong in the Department of Sociology and the Kadoorie Institute. He is a Senior Research Associate at Xi'an Jiaotong University, and a Fellow of the Advanced Institute for Management Research. His research interests are in the determinants of performance in public organizations, innovation, management reform and red tape, and he also focuses on urban management and environmental policy and sustainable development.

1 Introduction

Richard M. Walker, George A. Boyne and Gene A. Brewer

Introduction

The performance of public services is one of the central policy issues across the globe. Response to the global financial crisis during the late 2000s was typically led by government – in the UK and USA governments stepped into the banking system and either shored up these institutions or nationalized them, whereas in China the Communist Party sought to spend its way out of recession. The emergence of SARS in the early 2000s and the subsequent swine flu epidemic were public health crises managed and coordinated by public organizations: some of these were international agencies, such as the World Health Organization, but the majority of the heavy lifting was done at the coal face by public organizations and health agencies. The majority of crises, whether they are perpetrated by people (e.g. terrorist attacks, mass genocide or nuclear accidents) or result from natural catastrophes (e.g. earthquakes, tsunamis or famine), require public action. These global and high-impact examples are the tip of the iceberg – public services touch the majority of people in advanced and developing economies on a daily basis: children require schooling, the elderly need personal care and assistance, rubbish needs collecting to prevent public health incidents and the public needs to be confident that the water they drink is potable and the food they eat is safe. Moreover, government must protect its people from internal and external threats such as civil war and foreign invasion. In short, public services shore up our world and therefore knowledge about strategies to improve their performance is central to the good of society.

A growing body of evidence is being accumulated on the management practices and organizational arrangements that may lead to higher levels of performance in public organizations. This evidence suggests that a range of factors may be important. These factors include: instilling a developmental culture steeped in public service motivation, learning to concert action through inter- and intra-organizational relationships, sound resource management, setting and fulfilling organizational goals, minimizing harmful red tape, pursing viable management strategies, adopting appropriate organizational structures, and adapting public service organizations to their context and environment. In this edited volume we will, therefore, contribute to this growing body of knowledge by seeking to bring some coherence to the field. The aim is to establish not only *what is known* but also *what we need to know* to improve public service performance.

The need for evaluation and integration of knowledge is important as any field of academic endeavour grows. Though research on public management and performance is rapidly developing, the field is still in its infancy. However, the volume of published work is now sufficient for us to take stock of what is known and offer readers a review, synthesis and set of research directions on management and performance. This will hopefully make the research process more efficient, and help inch knowledge forward. We hope that by clearly specifying what we need to know, others can join in the effort, challenge this research agenda, or spawn their own agendas to complement and contrast with this work. The development of a research agenda for future work is just as important as evaluating and synthesizing current knowledge. For example, little work has been undertaken on the performance effects of finance, information and political support. We therefore supplement our coverage by sketching out new research agendas in areas where public management scholars have given only limited attention.

Comprehensive and robust knowledge on the impact of management on public services has important application to the world of policy and practice. The performance of supra-national, central, regional and local governments is hotly debated by politicians, policy-makers, pressure groups and the wider public. They are also concerned about the performance of the sprawling number of quasi-governmental organizations and private sector contractors doing public sector work: for example, we note the recent controversy surrounding the Blackwater Worldwide international security firm and its role in providing security services following the US invasion of Iraq. By bringing together knowledge to date, we hope to offer crisper advice to governments on where and when management matters for government performance.

The aim of this book is to fill an important gap in the public service performance literature by providing an assessment of the state of the art and mapping out what remains to be done. We hope that it will be an important resource for public management researchers, policy-makers and practitioners interested in improving public sector performance.

In order to meet these aims each contributing author was asked to review the main questions and concerns related to the topics of goal ambiguity, public service motivation, performance management, structure, networking, diversity, strategy content, red tape, budgetary and financial management and appropriate methods for research. The authors were asked to inventory what has been done in their field. The main questions were: Why does management matter? What has been found in empirical studies and how were these studies conducted? What are the implications for researchers, policy-makers and practitioners? What remains to be done? Clarity is brought to these questions in each chapter by way of the contributor's identification of propositions on what we know and what needs to be done. Each chapter offers the most comprehensive treatment possible on the topic of performance in public organizations, taking stock of current knowledge and laying out future directions.

In the remainder of this chapter we provide answers to two important questions: first, what is meant by 'public service performance'? Second, what has been done in the field to date? In relation to the latter question we sketch an update to Boyne's (2003) *Journal of Public Administration Research and Theory* review of the field by identifying studies published in the ensuing years and assessing how well they conform to the agenda previously set out. Many of the contributions in this book tackle this very issue, so our introduction will offer a summary of the direction of research in the field of public management performance.

Impetus for the book

The impetus for this book comes from two meetings co-sponsored by the *Public Management Research Association* (www.pmranet.org/index.html) in different parts of the world, two large-scale empirical research projects and substantial academic endeavour from a number of scholars around the globe.

In May 2004 the 'Determinants of Performance in Public Organizations I' seminar was held at Cardiff University (led by Boyne and Walker). In addition to being sponsored by the *Public Management Research Association* the meeting was supported by the *Advanced Institute for Management*

Rhys Andrews (Cardiff Business School, Cardiff University)
George A. Boyne (Cardiff Business School, Cardiff University)
Size, Structure and Administrative Overheads: An Empirical Analysis of English Local Authorities

Rhys Andrews (Cardiff Business School, Cardiff University)
George A. Boyne (Cardiff Business School, Cardiff University)
M. Jae Moon (Department of Political Science, Korea University)
Richard M. Walker (Centre of Urban Planning and Environmental Management, University of Hong Kong and Cardiff University)
Measuring Organizational Performance: Reliability and Overestimation of Performance Measurement
Gene A. Brewer (Department of Public Administration and Policy, University of Georgia)
George A. Boyne (Cardiff Business School, Cardiff University)
Richard M. Walker (Centre of Urban Planning and Environmental Management, University of Hong Kong)
Market Orientation and Public Service Performance: NPM Gone Mad?

Gene A. Brewer (Department of Public Administration and Policy, University of Georgia)
Alisa Hicklin (Department of Political Science, University of Okalahoma)
Richard M. Walker (Centre of Urban Planning and Environmental Management, University of Hong Kong and Cardiff University)
Layers of Red Tap: Using Multilevel Modelling to Study the Effects of Red Tape, Management, and the Environment on Performance

Robert Christensen (Department of Political Science, University of North Carolina at Charlotte)
Beth Gazley (School of Public and Environmental Affairs, Indiana University)
What's Capacity Got to Do With It: A Review of the Capacity and Performance Research

Melissa Forbes (Ford School of Public Policy and Department of Sociology, University of Michigan)
Laurence E Lynn Jr. (George Bush School of Government and Public Service, Texas A&M University)
Organizational Effectiveness and Government Performance: A New Look at the Empirical Literature

Ahmed Shafiqul Huque (Department of Political Science, McMaster University)
Ideology and Autonomy as the Determinants of Performance in Public Organizations

Kyu-Nahm Jun (School of Policy, Planning, and Development, Univ. of Southern California)
Ellen Shiau (School of Policy, Planning, and Development, Univ. of Southern California)
Christopher Weare (School of Policy, Planning, and Development, Univ. of Southern California)
Determinants of Department Responsiveness as a Local Government Performance Measure: The Case of the Los Angeles Neighborhood Council System

Patrick Kenis (Department of Organization Studies, Tilburg University)
Keith Provan (School of Public Administration and Policy, University of Arizona)
Causes and Consequences of the Use of Evaluation Criteria for Public Service Networks

Kenneth J. Meier *(Department of Political Science, Texas A&M Univeristy and Cardiff School of Business, Cardiff University)*
Laurence J. O'Toole, Jr. *(Department of Public Administration and Policy, The University of Georgia)*
The Dog that Didn't Bark: How Public Managers Handle Environmental Shocks

David Pitts (Andrew Young School of Policy Studies, Georgia State University)
Elizabeth Jarry (Andrew Young School of Policy Studies, Georgia State University)
Getting to Know You: Diversity, Time, and Performance in Public Organizations

Denise van Raaij *(Department of Organization Studies, Tilburg University)*
Patrick Kenis *(Department of Organization Studies, Tilburg University)*
How Networks Know How They Are Doing Intention versus Realization Oriented Evaluation in Different Types of Networks

Hal G. Rainey (Department of Public Administration and Policy, School of Public and International Affairs, The University of Georgia)

Figure 1.1:   Papers and presenters at the Determinants of Performance in Public Organizations II

Jung Wook Lee (University of Illinois at Springfield)
Of Politics and Purpose: Political Salience, Structural Insulation, and Goal Ambiguity of US Federal Agencies

Anne Rouse (Deakin Business School, Deakin University)
Graeme Hodge (Centre for Regulatory Studies, Faculty of Law, Monash University)
Rethinking Risk to Improve Public Sector Sourcing Performance

Eric Welch (Graduate Program in Public Administration, University of Illinois at Chicago)
Sanjay K. Pandey (Department of Public Administration, University of Kansas)
Wilson Wong (Department of Government and Public Administration, The Chinese University of Hong Kong)
Beyond Pure Efficiency and Technological Features: Developing a Model of Measuring E-Governance and Exploring its Performance

Amber Wichowsky (Department of Political Science, University of Wisconsin-Madison)
Donald P. Moynihan (La Follette School of Public Affairs, University of Wisconsin-Madison)
Public Policies, Citizenship Outcomes and the Implications for Performance Measurement: An Analysis of the Program Assessment Rating Tool

Figure 1.1:   *(cont.)*

Research (an Economic and Social Research Council and Engineering and Physical Sciences Research Council initiative to enhance the quality of management research in the UK). This first international conference was dedicated to questions of public service performance and led to an edited Cambridge University Press book *Public Service Performance: Perspectives on Measurement and Management* (Boyne *et al.* 2006) and to a symposium edition of *Journal of Public Administration Research and Theory* (Boyne and Walker 2005).

The 'Determinants of Performance in Public Organizations II' was held at the University of Hong Kong in December 2006 (led by Walker). This was again a productive event and led to a symposium in *Public Administration* (Walker and Boyne 2009) and this book. Figure 1.1 lists the authors and papers presented at this conference. Our thanks go to them for their contribution to the conference and the stimulation they offered which helped to inspire this book. The Hong Kong conference was supported by the University of Hong Kong's *Strategic Research Theme on Social and Public Policy* (now *Policy, Law and Development*) and the then *Centre of Urban Planning and Environmental Management* (now the *Kadoorie Institute*).

The two large-scale empirical projects on performance in public organizations are based on either side of the Atlantic Ocean. In the UK the ESRC-funded 'How Public Management Matters' project at Cardiff University brings together Andrews, Boyne, Meier, O'Toole and Walker (www.clrgr.cf.ac.uk/research/managementmatters.html). It seeks to develop new theoretical perspectives on the impact of strategy and networking on public service performance and make methodological contributions to this study. In the USA the Project for Equity, Representation and Governance (http://perg.tamu.edu/) (including the Texas Educational Excellence Project http://teep.tamu.edu/) is led by Meier and focuses upon the quality and equity of education in Texas. These projects and events, alongside the work of a growing band of scholars, have assisted in raising the quality and level of output on the determinants of performance in public organizations, and they have assisted in creating an international academic research community interested in ongoing work on the topic. To this end, this book on public management and performance feeds off these synergistic relationships.

On public service performance

It is only in recent years that public administration scholars have turned their attention to systematically conceptualizing and theorizing the performance of public agencies. This is in part a product of the main theoretical and empirical questions posed by the discipline, which were traditionally about organizational processes and administration of public policies and programmes without a clear focus on outputs and outcomes, and also because of the paucity of data on the performance of public agencies.

The more recent growth of theoretical and empirical studies of the performance of public organizations can be traced to the groundbreaking theoretical work of O'Toole and Meier (1999). They argue that managers contribute to performance through their impact on organizational stability, and by buffering and exploiting events in the external environment. A series of empirical tests of this model has clearly pointed towards the contribution that managers and management can make to the performance of public agencies, including networking, managerial quality and organizational stability (Meier and O'Toole 2002, 2003; Meier *et al.* 2004). A second model has been developed that has implicit links to the performance of public organizations. The Government Performance Project, led by Ingraham (Ingraham *et al.* 2003), examines the management capacity of public agencies. The public management variables examined in the project include finance, human resources and information technology.

These two frameworks emphasize the importance of management processes in organizations and how public agencies can enhance their ability to manage. What these approaches to the performance of public organizations have in common is their emphasis on viewing the performance of public organizations as a 'service production' function.

A further model found in the management literature likewise emphasizes service production, but also considers the wider context within which public organizations operate. The 'logic of governance' framework, developed by Lynn and others (Heinrich and Lynn 2000; Lynn *et al.* 2001), runs from public demands at the front end to stakeholder satisfaction at the other. The management elements in this framework include organizational structures and technological processes, while also capturing the political aspects of public management that are omitted from many models.

Rainey and Steinbauer (1999) proposed a theory of effective public organizations based on theoretical assertions and empirical evidence drawn from the public management literature. The authors began by arguing that elephants and public organizations have something in common: both are saddled with inaccurate stereotypes. Elephants are believed to be slow and insensitive creatures, when in fact they can run very fast and are quite sensitive and altruistic. Similarly, public organizations are believed to be low performing and unresponsive, when in fact many public organizations perform very well and are models of responsiveness. After making the crucial point that some public organizations are high performers, the authors laid out their theory and encouraged researchers to test it empirically. Brewer and Selden (2000) followed up on Rainey and Steinbauer's work by elaborating and adapting their model to fit the twenty-three largest US federal government agencies. The authors then tested the model. They found that federal agencies varied significantly in their levels of performance, with some agencies ranking very high and some very low. This finding called into question the New Public Management (NPM) assertion that civil service systems are a major impediment to high performance, since all of the agencies were operating under the same civil service system. Brewer and Selden (2000) did, however, determine that the following variables were related to high performance in public organizations: high levels of employee efficacy and teamwork, efforts to build human capital, structuring work tasks in interesting and challenging ways, protecting employees from political interference and unfair management practices, fostering concern for the public interest, high levels of employee task motivation and public service motivation, and low workforce turnover. These findings were largely consistent with Rainey and Steinbauer's model.

The service production function approach breaks down the activities of a public agency into a smaller number of steps, each of which is associated with a particular aspect of organizational performance. Performance is seen as the result of various inputs, organizational processes or management practices, outputs and longer-term impacts or outcomes, and the organizational environment. The multidimensional and multilevel nature of governmental performance means that the operationalization of this model is highly complex. The growing body of research on the determinants of performance shows that a range of management practices and external constraints affect different dimensions of performance in different ways, and evidence on this variation is presented throughout the chapters in this volume.

The various ways in which management interacts with the environment to influence organizational performance has led to an interest in contingency theory in many studies. This reflects the complexity of management in public organizations and the wide variety of tasks performed by public managers who are involved in buffering and exploiting the organizational environment, managing people inside and outside the organization, and structuring the organization and delivering services. Furthermore, public managers will simultaneously have to trade off the attainment of different dimensions of performance – making decisions to achieve effectiveness and equity while seeking to ensure that services are delivered efficiently in order to attain value for money. While some progress is being made in understanding the contingent nature of these relationships, much more remains to be explained and understood. Contingency theory promises much in our search for a more detailed understanding of the effects of management, organization and environment on public service performance.

Turning to the nature of the dependent variable, a number of models have been widely used in the academic and practitioner literature, and they inform many measures of performance used by governments and researchers (see for example, Boyne 2002; OECD 2005). One model is the '3Es', and a second is the 'IOO' model. The 3Es model focuses upon the economy, efficiency and effectiveness of public services. Economy is the cost of procuring specific service inputs (facilities, staff, equipment) of a given quality. This is typically equated with the level of spending on a service. Efficiency is defined in two ways (Jackson 1982): (1) technical efficiency refers to the cost per unit of output, and (2) allocative efficiency refers to the responsiveness of the service to public preferences. Effectiveness is the actual achievement of the formal objectives of services.

The IOO model offers a different set of criteria by which the performance of public organizations can be measured and evaluated by examining the sequence of inputs–outputs–outcomes. Inputs include expenditure and are comparable with economy. Outputs include a number of categories: quantity of service and service quality (speed of service delivery, accessibility of provision, etc.). The ratio of outputs to inputs is one way to define efficiency. Outcomes include effectiveness from the 3Es model but also impact (which include positive and negative impacts) and equity or fairness of service provision (for example, how services are distributed by gender, race, income, geographical area, etc.). The ratio of outcomes to inputs is the cost per unit of outcome or 'value for money': for example, how much spending is required to achieve clean drinking water or to save a life on the highways. These two models provide a number of measures of organizational performance. However, they also suffer from a number of weaknesses.

First, both the 3Es and IOO models include a strong emphasis upon economy or inputs. While costs may seem relatively straightforward, they are a highly controversial topic (Boyne 2002). The first problem is of an administrative nature: is high or low expenditure good? What does expenditure reveal about performance, and does it matter whether expenditure is high or low in the hunt for higher performance? We suspect that neither high nor low expenditure or expenditure in itself is a predictor of performance achievements. The political problem typically relates to the nature of the public service production function: the majority of the costs often fall on labour and wage reductions and this does not necessarily equate with good performance. These concerns are reflected in the current recommendations on performance measurement. The OECD (2005: 58), discussing performance management, argues that 'input controls are relaxed and managers and/or organizations are given flexibility to improve performance. In return they are held accountable for results measured in the form of outputs and/or outcomes'.

Second, the 3Es model usually emphasizes technical efficiency over allocative efficiency (see Boyne *et al.* 2003). However, responsiveness is a key characteristic of the performance of public organizations and should be at the centre of any measures of performance (Boyne 2002). Measures of responsiveness should consider direct service users or their representatives (Symon and Walker 1995), and citizens who may not be direct consumers of services. Associated with this point is the focus of the 3Es and IOO models upon external stakeholders, to the detriment of internal stakeholders. The performance management literature points towards the need for motivated public servants; consequently, they must be brought into the equation.

Third, the models are overly service-delivery or management oriented and overlook some of the key issues associated with the public sector. Given the shift towards governance, a range of issues associated with the way states service their citizens needs to be included, such as human rights, democratization and self-determination. The United Nations Development Programme (UNDP) defines governance thus:

Governance is the system of values, policies and institutions by which a society manages its economic, political and social affairs through interactions within and among the state, civil society and private sector. It is the way a society organizes itself to make and implement decisions – achieving mutual understanding, agreement and action. It comprises the mechanisms and processes for citizens and groups to articulate their interests, mediate their differences and exercise their legal rights and obligations. It is the rules, institutions and practices that set limits and provide incentives for individuals, organizations and firms. Governance, including its social, political and economic dimensions, operates at every level of human enterprise, be it the household, village, municipality, nation, region or globe. (UNDP 2004: 2)

The inclusion of governance within our discussion of the performance of public organizations indicates that a range of additional indicators needs to be added to the suite suggested thus far. Governance indicators to be considered could then include measures of democratic outcomes, participation in democratic processes, probity, accountability, political rights and civil rights. The inclusion of these measures also implies a new set of relationships between the different sets of criteria. Table 1.1 provides a list of the domains under which performance can be measured and gives key examples of sub-domain measures.

While progress has been made in understanding the impact of management and performance, the field is still relatively new – theoretical frameworks are still being advanced but have not been fully tested and, as we note below, the dependent variable is not clearly specified.

Judgements on organizational performance

A range of stakeholders can judge the performance of a public agency. A theory of stakeholders has been developed by Mitchell *et al.* (1997), who argue that attention should be focused on three characteristics. Power implies the ability of one actor to influence another actor, and to get that set of actors to do something they would otherwise not have done, by means that may be

Table 1.1: Dimensions of organizational performance

Performance domain	Sub-performance domain
Outputs	Quantity
	Quality
Efficiency	Cost per unit of output
Service Outcomes	Equity
	Formal effectiveness
	Impact
	Value for money (cost per unit of service outcome)
Responsiveness	Citizen satisfaction
	Consumer satisfaction
	Staff satisfaction
Governance	Accountability
	Civil rights
	Human rights
	Probity

Source: adapted from Boyne (2002)

coercive, normative or via incentives. Legitimacy derives from norms, values and beliefs in a social system and promotes the authority of some stakeholders over others. Finally, different stakeholders are able to confer urgency upon a public agency; urgency is likely to be measured by time sensitivity and the extent to which it is acceptable to delay responding to the stakeholder. Expressions of power, legitimacy and urgency are likely to be made by stakeholders internal and external to an organization.

External judgements are made by stakeholders in the environment of an organization and include service consumers, voters, citizens, regulators and other public, private and voluntary sector organizations. Internal measures of performance are based on the views of stakeholders within an organization, such as politicians, senior managers and front-line staff. Different types of data may be used when either internal or external actors make judgements. Data could be archival or perceptual. Archival data are collected by an organization and stored so that they can be checked or audited, while perceptual data consist of people's views about the performance of an organization. Perceptual measures are often based upon beliefs about the level of performance relative to similar organizations.

Internal stakeholders can make perceptual judgements about their services through staff surveys and other means. Internal stakeholders may also use archival data such as performance indicators that have been collected but not subjected to external verification. Another source of archival data might be information collected by internal auditors on the performance of the organization. Internal audit reports may in fact combine these two types of data. It is also possible to have external stakeholders make judgements on the performance of the organization using both perceptual and archival data. One example of this is scorecards, such as the Executive Branch Management Scorecard used by the US government during the Bush Administration (Government Executive 2004) or the Comprehensive Performance Assessment seen in English local government (Audit Commission 2002). Where performance indicators have been externally audited, they fall into the external stakeholder archival data category. Perceptual data can also be used where external stakeholders comment on the performance of an organization, such as in customer satisfaction surveys.

Performance measures that are external and archival have been viewed as the 'gold standard', typically because the data are verified and audited by other organizations (OECD 2005). One in five OECD countries have their performance data externally audited, one quarter have no data audited and the remaining have some programmes externally audited. Examples include the Best Value Performance Indicators in English and Welsh local government (Office of the Deputy Prime Minister 2000). Internal and perceptual measures, by contrast, are considered limited because they suffer from a number of flaws, of which common-source bias (Wall et al. 2004), alongside the systematic over-reporting of performance achievements, are believed to be the most serious. Furthermore, perceptual measures of performance often rely upon recall, which has been shown to compromise assessments of organizational achievements (Golden 1992). Furthermore, the uncertainty about informants' knowledge of actual performance may also undermine the accuracy of such measures. This technical evidence would suggest that judgements should be external and use archival data that has been audited: 'Having externally audited performance information would help to assure the public of the quality and accuracy of the information presented in government reports' (OECD 2005: 69).

However, serious questions have also been posed about the 'objectivity' of archival measures of performance. The major accounting scandals in private firms such as Exxon and World Com in the USA indicate that it is possible to manipulate externally audited data. In the public sector there is frequent evidence of 'cheating' on indicators – for example, excluding certain pupils from school rolls in order to boost examination pass rates (Bohte and Meier 2000). Furthermore, instrumentation is widely written about, where target setting focuses the organization's attention on certain activities while diverting attention from other activities. Finally, these so-called objective, external archival data are often politically and socially constructed. They are politically constructed in that powerful groups in society will determine what should be collected, perhaps at the expense of some measures. They are socially constructed in that decisions are made about what performance data should and should not be recorded. For example, scorecards are collated by officials of regulatory agencies through field visits.

There is, then, no clear consensus on what should be measured or who should make the judgement: perceptual measures from the staff of a public agency or users may suffer from problems of recall. Archival measures typically cover only a limited range of the dimensions of performance; indeed, in the growing research literature on the performance of public organizations, the limited range of dimensions of performance is frequently cited to justify the use of perceptual measures through which individuals scan the range of performance concerns and consolidate their opinions into one or more indicators. This suggests that it is appropriate to have performance measures from a number of different sources, implying that it might be possible to triangulate between these different sources to derive a judgement about an agency's performance.

Second, different groups of actors will assess the performance of public organizations, or use performance data, in different ways. Evidence presented from OECD (2005) countries suggests that performance data is increasingly being used in public agencies. Around 50 per cent of OECD countries have a system of performance management, though the nature and extent of the regimes varies widely. Performance data are used in nearly half of OECD countries to assist in the management and future planning of programme priorities and reforms to internal processes and systems. Data are also presented in most countries in the budget but typically performance budgeting systems have not been developed and politicians do not systematically use this data when making decisions. This reinforces the need to collect data from a number of sources, both internal and external to the organization.

The use of data from different sources should compensate for the deficiencies of using either in isolation. Research findings increasingly support this view – the evidence demonstrates that there are positive and statistically significant correlations between external and internal measures of overall performance, some in the region of $r = 0.8$ (Bommer *et al.* 1995). However, such findings are only achieved when measures of the same dimensions of

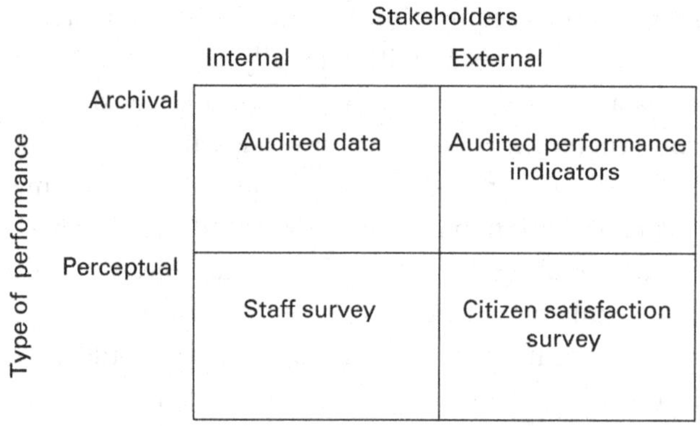

Stakeholders

	Internal	External
Archival	Audited data	Audited performance indicators
Perceptual	Staff survey	Citizen satisfaction survey

Type of performance

Figure 1.2:   Stakeholders and types of performance in public management research

performance are used; when the dimensions vary, it is not surprising to learn that weaker correlations are reported (Andrews *et al.* 2010).

Figure 1.2 depicts these relationships visually. Our contention is that a comprehensive study of the impact of management, organization and environment on performance should be populated with data from all four cells in the matrix. This would also help us move towards a more sophisticated understanding of the relative power, urgency and legitimacy conferred by internal and external stakeholders on alternative dimensions of performance – this evidence could then be used to weight dimensions of performance when a composite score is used.

Management and public service performance research

Resources, regulation, markets, organization and management were identified as variables used in the study of public service performance by Boyne (2003) in his critical review. At the time of his study, scholarly effort had been dedicated to the following explanatory variables: resources, market structure and organizational size, using a dependent variable that typically measured outcomes with some limited attention to quantity, quality, efficiency and consumer satisfaction. The topic of equity, which is arguably the central criterion of public provision, was not addressed. Based upon the evidence presented in these articles, Boyne concluded that improvements to public service performance would most likely come about through the provision of extra resources and better management. Though the evidence was patchy, it was possible to conclude that 'public service performance is subject to systematic influences' (Boyne 2003: 389).

As Boyne (2003) noted, in the main, scholars had offered five perspectives rather than hard-and-fast theoretical frameworks (for exceptions see above). Each of the five perspectives offered arguments in support of their effectiveness at driving up public service performance. The propositions can be summarized as follows:

Resources. Two competing positive views were offered: (1) higher public expenditure *is a sufficient condition* for improvement because it drives up quantity and quality, and (2) it *is not a sufficient condition* because the resources must be effectively managed.

Regulation. The impact of regulation on public service performance was argued to be uncertain. While regulation for the purposes of accountability etc. is a central feature of public management, too much regulation can harm performance, whereas regulation managed in appropriate ways can benefit organizations.

Market structure. The effect of market structure on performance is not likely to be uniform. In its simplest form, more competition is argued to improve efficiency, innovation and consumer satisfaction. This public choice framework has been questioned, and contingent relationships have been shown to have an important impact on this relationship. Notably, and based upon Williamson (1975), hierarchy may be an appropriate way to provide services when the number of supplies is low, and information costs and asset specificity are high – the converse would apply for a market form of organization.

Organization. Two facets of organization were identified in the 2003 review. Internal organization was concerned with debates about organizational size and structure. Size has been a constant theme in public administration research. However, theory and empirical evidence have been equivocal and at best point towards a non-linear relationship with performance. Structure, be it the level of formalization, centralization or specialization, is likely to be contingent on organizational context: turbulent environments are more likely to produce informal and decentralized organizations. External organization or external structure was linked to the emergence of the mixed economy of provision and in particular the growth of networks as means to coordinate and deliver services. While Boyne hypothesized that the network-performance hypothesis was contingent on management, the relationship is likely to be positive.

Management. The main management variables that Boyne isolated included leadership styles and expertise, organizational culture, human resource management (HRM) practice, strategy processes and strategy content. Arguments about leadership focused on stability and change and their relationship to service performance rather than the more elusive arguments found in the traits or transformational leadership studies. Organizational culture, while perhaps the glue of an organization, is a very broad subject. However, from time to time governments and reform movements promote particular norms and values that they would like to see imbued in the cultures of public agencies. Much of the rhetoric in recent years has been on the importance of results-oriented cultures, as opposed to procedure-dominated ones, as drivers of public service performance. Human resource management practices have been characterized as hard and soft. It has been argued that soft practices are more likely to satisfy and motivate staff and in turn result in public service improvement. The debate on strategy process has also been one of opposites: of incremental approaches to formulating and implementing strategies to more rational ones. Incremental approaches are seen as unlikely to damage performance because the purpose of a strategy is not clear and processes for organizational advancement uncertain. By contrast, planning is argued to assist by offering meaningful ways to move towards targets. Lastly, Boyne noted strategy content and the importance of the generic management literature. At the time of writing, Boyne was uncertain about the likely performance impacts of different strategic stances. Subsequent evidence indicates that proactive and outward-looking organizations are often more likely to be high achievers.

As we note below, some of these areas have been tackled whilst other remain untouched. While this list of variables was expansive, it was not comprehensive, and we can now include research on the environmental context within which organizations work. The argument here is that more complex, dynamic and turbulent environments will be harmful to public service performance. A further twist on culture has emerged in recent years and empirical tests of its effectiveness on performance have been undertaken: this is the literature on public service motivation which will be summarized later in this volume.

To chart progress since 2003, the editors undertook a review of the evidence. To illustrate the changing nature of the field, we limited our review to peer-reviewed journals listed in Thompson's *ISI Web of Science*. Within this scope, we examined articles defined by the Index as being in the field of public administration. The search was limited to journal articles in order to provide a rough quality control – the assumption is that peer-reviewed work is more likely to meet higher standards of theoretical development and methodological rigour. It is possible that there is selection bias in our sample: we ignore work published in books or by international organizations such as the

World Bank and unpublished work which may not contain statistically significant results and an 'interesting' story.

The final process of selecting articles included a number of decision rules. First, we only included articles published since Boyne undertook the review in 2002. Second, the articles needed to include a dependent variable that measured one or more facets of organizational performance (see above) and independent measures of management and organization, also as outlined above. Thus, in this book we do not address the effect of the environment per se on performance. This approach does exclude some scholars' work on questions of public service performance – for example, policy studies which examine the relationship between policy and performance which do not consider the role of public organizations in the implementation of policy (see Witte *et al.* 2007) or the examination of the determinants of citizen satisfaction (van Ryzin 2005)

The implementation of this search process resulted in the identification of seventy-five articles. The remaining articles were conceptual discussions of performance, case studies of particular organizations or policy analysis. A large number of these studies examined performance management rather than performance per se; some comment on the growth in target setting and others examine its empirical determinants (de Lancer Julnes and Holzer 2001); but few of these studies include it as an independent variable. The number of articles recorded in the seven years from 2002 to 2009 indicates that there has been a substantial increase in the attention focused on the determinants of performance by academic scholars.

In what follows, we review progress in empirical research on the sub-theme of management and performance and take the opportunity to introduce the chapters that will follow where they focus upon one of the domains noted above. Prior to this we note some of the characteristics of the sample that we selected.

The majority of the research has been published in *Journal of Public Administration Research and Theory* (twenty-five, a third of the articles), followed by *Public Administration Review* (with sixteen). Following some distance behind were *Public Administration* (seven), *Administration & Society* (five) and *American Review of Public Administration* (five), with the other articles scattered amongst other journals.

The vast majority of the research conducted over recent years has been based in the USA. Indeed all studies bar a dozen from the UK, or more precisely English and Welsh local government, and one each from Columbia, Denmark, Indonesia, Israel, Japan and Taiwan (Andersen and Blegvad 2006;

Avellaneda 2008; Carmeli 2006; Eckardt 2008; Yamamoto 2006; Yang *et al.* 2009) were based on US data – the preponderance of evidence from the USA is unchanged since 2002. Units of analysis vary somewhat but by no means capture the full variety of public organizations and their programmes. Topping this list are studies using school districts in the Equity, Representation and Governance project at Texas A&M University (with over twenty published journal articles) followed by the English and Welsh local government datasets and then secondary data from the US federal government and the NASP III project. In turn this means that much of our knowledge comes from schools – again similar to Boyne's earlier findings.

Regulation, markets and environments

Our focus in this volume is upon management and organization. To this end we have not included chapters that examine regulation and markets, which are more broadly associated with strategies to improve performance. Similarly, studies of the environment, while important, have not been singled out for attention, and the majority of the studies we examine in this book include external controls or examine relationships between a management or organizational variable and the environment (e.g. Boyne and Meier 2009). Thus, we are able to draw out some implications of the environment in our concluding chapter.

During the period 2003 to the time of writing in late 2009, only one study has included regulation as an independent variable. Andrews *et al.* (2008) note that regulation damages organizational performance unless it is perceived as supportive by those being audited and inspected. Markets have figured in the writings of public management scholars, who typically find mixed results at best for the effects of markets and contracting on performance. For example, O'Toole and Meier (2004) offer very interesting results: that contracting is not necessarily associated with higher levels of performance and also leads to more bureaucracy. Mixed findings are reported by Lukemeyer and McCorkle (2006) for the relative performance of public and private prisons in the USA, and by Yang *et al.* (2009) in their study of central government contracting in Taiwan and Heinrich and Choi (2007) in social welfare programmes.

As we noted above, many of the studies of management and performance now implement sophisticated research designs and include internal and external control variables. External control, usually operationalized as aspects of the organizational environment, has become a topic of interest in its own right for some scholars. A number of studies from English local government make this point eloquently – Andrews *et al.* (2005) note how the organizational context can account for up to a third of the variance when performance is measured by means of an aggregate index. Complex and dynamic organizational environments have been shown to be significant predictors of failure across a range of different types of public service organizations (Andrews and Boyne 2008; also see Meier and O'Toole 2009).

Goal ambiguity

The book kicks off with a topic longstanding in the public management field, but one only recently subjected to empirical investigation examining its relationship with organizational performance. Chapter 2 presents a discussion by Hal. G. Rainey and Chan Su Jung on one the main characteristics of public agencies, and a trait often associated with lowered performance: goal ambiguity. For years, a diverse literature has provided analyses and observations about the distinctive character of government organizations and their management, often as contrasted with business firms. In that literature, no observation appears more regularly and frequently than the claim that government organizations have distinctively vague goals. Yet, in spite of the near-ubiquity of observations about vague goals among authors writing about the nature of governmental organizations and management, one finds very little research that seeks to measure goal vagueness (or, conversely, goal clarity), not only in analysis of government organizations, but in the social sciences more generally.

To this end, Chapter 2 summarizes some recent studies that have sought to address this lack of empirical attention to the issue of vague goals. The scarcity of work on this topic raises the possibility that no one has conducted empirical analyses of goal ambiguity (or clarity) because of the difficulty or impossibility of defining and measuring goal ambiguity. A first challenge, then, is to develop a conception of goal ambiguity and measures of it. One of the studies reviewed developed measures of four concepts of organizational goal ambiguity and showed variations among federal agencies on these measures (Chun and Rainey 2005). The next challenge involves showing that these measures are related meaningfully to other organizational characteristics and Rainey and Jung walk us through the research that relates ambiguity to characteristics including 'financial publicness' (the level of funding public agencies receive from governmental budget allocations as opposed to user charges and fees), their responsibility for regulatory policy (since experts usually observe that regulatory agencies have vague mandates), work-related attitudes of employees, political 'salience' of the agency, and measures of employee perceptions of organizational performance. Having described and summarized this body of research, the chapter discusses remaining research challenges and next steps for this stream of research.

Resources

Resources figured strongly in work prior to 2002 on public management and performance. Much recent effort has not, however, kept up with this tradition and we identified very few new articles focusing on this topic in the public administration literature (for exceptions see Eckardt 2008). In this volume, Donald P. Moynihan and Matthew Andrews shift focus and tackle the question of budgets and financial management in Chapter 3. Because money is the lifeblood of public service provision, budgetary institutions offer a powerful means of directing bureaucratic behaviour. Indeed, resistance to reforms that seek to achieve higher levels of organizational performance often occurs because of disconnects with financial management practices. This chapter explores efforts to make budget systems more performance driven, and takes as its focus countries rather than organizations.

In recent decades, reformers have made the case that improving public service performance required changing budgetary incentives and constraints. One traditional criticism of the budget process was that it fostered consensus via incrementalism and inflexibility by focusing upon inputs for accountability, and did this at the expense of a strategic focus on performance. Responses to this have included adding performance information to the budgetary process, but implementation has been inconsistent and public officials have struggled to make use of this information because its addition does not overcome the problem that budgetary reform can be viewed as symbolic. Governments have sought to address this and increase performance by creating contract-like arrangements where the budget and/or bonuses are tied to performance indicators. Incomplete contract arrangements can lead to moral hazard on the part of contractors, leading to a performance paradox: agents work to improve measured performance in a way that is unrelated or deleterious to actual performance (as covered in Chapter 9).

Chapter 3 looks beyond the technical aspects of prior financial management work, and beyond reporting, budgeting and managing mechanisms, to the way these mechanisms impact incentives and an understanding of organizational mission and performance. Performance-related research has generally focused on the impact of reforms on the budget system and whether they impact fiscal constraint, allocative efficiency and technical efficiency. The findings have often been disappointing for the reasons outlined above, and some authors have argued that this shortcoming reflects a mixture of unrealistic expectations and a narrow focus on political decisions. The chapter concludes by presenting a more pragmatic research agenda that will look at how managers respond to budget reforms, and try to connect how budgetary rules relate to specific performance outcomes.

Internal organization

Structure

The relationship between form and function is an enduring concern across the social sciences. One of the key functions for public managers is the creation of structures that can provide system stability and institutional support for a host of other internal organizational elements, such as culture, values and routines. Structure is the topic examined in Chapter 4 by Rhys Andrews. Organizational structures provide the pervasive foundation for achieving coordination and control within an organization, influencing and being influenced by a host of different inputs, outputs and outcomes. The relationship between structure and performance, in particular, is therefore a timeless concern for students of public management.

Organizational structure comprises broad 'structural' features such as the overall physical size of an organization and the 'structuring' activities, such as the decentralization of decision making, that managers carry out. Organization theorists suggest that there are three key 'structuring' dimensions that are susceptible to managerial control, which in turn may influence performance: centralization, formalization and specialization. The distribution of decision-making power, the extent of procedural standardization and the degree of occupational specialism within an organization are all argued to be important determinants of its achievements. These arguments have had significant practical as well as theoretical import. The mantras of NPM, particularly its preference for decentralized organizational structures, have been reflected in the Reinventing Government movement in the USA, and more recently have formed an integral part of the public service reform agenda pursued in the UK.

While there is a wealth of material on organizational structure and performance in the private sector, there is still comparatively little research investigating the effects of the relative degree of centralization, formalization and specialization within public organizations – see for example work on the hierarchy of authority and participation in decision making (Andrews *et al.* 2009; Moynihan and Pandey 2005). This chapter critically reviews the existing evidence on organizational structure and performance in the public sector, covering both quantitative and qualitative studies. Evidence from the USA, UK and elsewhere is used to develop a better understanding of which organizational structures are most likely to be associated with higher performance and under what circumstances.

Red tape

Chapter 5 delves into the subject of formalization in greater detail and examines red tape. Red tape can result from over-formalization and consists of rules that were 'badly designed' in the first place and rules that were once functional but have since 'gone bad'. The term 'red tape' has distinctly negative connotations, which has important implications for the theoretical and empirical development of the concept as well as practice. As Bozeman explains, red tape is 'rules, regulations, and procedures that remain in force and entail a compliance burden but [do] not advance the legitimate purposes the rules were intended to serve'. Importantly, while several other bureaucratic maladies have attained mythical stature over the years, red tape is perhaps the most pervasive and damaging overall. This is because red tape has been alleged to make life hard for public employees and citizens alike, and take a heavy toll on organizational performance in the public sector. Indeed, if we take anecdotal reports and the academic literature seriously, red tape may be the most prevalent cause of failing organizational performance in government.

Despite these claims, scant empirical evidence on the effects of red tape has been published, and this did not figure as a topic in empirical performance research until recently (Brewer and Walker 2009; Pandey and Moynihan 2006). In Chapter 5, Gene A. Brewer and Richard M. Walker turn to the scholarly research literature to answer questions such as: does red tape undercut governmental performance? Are rule-bound public organizations lower performers than those with more flexibility and latitude? What strategies can public managers employ to counteract the harmful effects of red tape? The authors find that research on red tape has focused on three important areas. First, scholars have sought to improve how they define and operationalize the term by examining global measures of red tape and management subsystem measures, differences between objective and perceptual measures of the concept, internal and external forms, and organizational and stakeholder red tape. Second, scholars have sought to document public/private differences in levels of red tape and have shown that public organizations are more red-tape bound than their private sector counterparts. Third, and most important, scholars have recently begun investigating the impact of red tape on governmental performance, and they have sought to identify ways that policy-makers and public managers can effectively combat these ill effects. This research has shown that red tape does indeed exert powerful, negative effects on performance, but these effects are not as consistent and uniform as the red-tape myth suggests. Studies investigating strategies to alleviate red tape have also produced some interesting findings. Such studies have found that forward-leaning, proactive management strategies and developmental organizational cultures can offset some harmful effects of red tape, but inert, defensive and reactive strategies tend to make it worse. The chapter reviews these developments in more detail, with particular attention to the impact of red tape on organizational performance, promising avenues for future research and ways that policy-makers and public managers can effectively combat red tape.

External organization

Networking

Kenneth J. Meier and Laurence J. O'Toole Jr. explore networks and networking – subjects of increasing importance in research and practice of public management, the growth of which has been extensive since the four studies that were published prior to 2002. Efforts to deliver outputs and outcomes often take place in contexts in which the work of public organizations is enmeshed in settings of structural and behavioural interdependence with a variety of other organizations and actors. Structural, technical and/or political forces may drive the interdependence, and it may occur through increasingly complex transactions between these actors and organizations. Managers are called upon to help coordinate co-production, encourage inter-organizational cooperation and exploit opportunities presented by and from the networked environment of the focal organization, as well as to work externally to buffer production in the core organization from environmental disruptions. Even policy implementation schemes designed as single hierarchies require public managers to create networks in the organization's environment and to manage these networks to achieve greater levels of performance.

While the research literature on networks and networking is large and growing, systematic empirical work linking these subjects to performance has been generated only in recent years. Chapter 6 reviews what is now known about the relationship between the networking conducted by public managers and the performance of their organizations and networks. In particular, the chapter offers evidence that managerial networking can boost performance; that the performance improvements may be unevenly distributed across clientele or stakeholders; and that the performance effects of networking are subject to diminishing returns. This evidence is found when studies primarily focus upon networking (Goerdel 2005; Hicklin *et al.* 2008) and alongside a range of other variables (see Meier *et al.* 2007). The chapter concludes by sketching an agenda for future research on networks, networking and public management, with an emphasis on understanding the performance impacts of what public managers do.

Management

Four chapters examine questions of management. Human resource management questions associated with public service motivation (PSM) and diversity are examined alongside those of performance management and strategy. While Boyne was able to identify a small number of studies on some of these topics in 2003, there is now a much wider literature. For example, strategy figures as an important topic (Andrews *et al.* 2006; Meier *et al.* 2007) while new work has emerged on diversity (e.g. Pitts 2007) and PSM (for an earlier summary of the evidence, see Brewer 2008). By contrast, relatively little empirical research has sought to understand the impact of leadership and culture on organizational performance in the public sector – for exceptions see Avellaneda (2008) who reports that the education level and experience of politicians works to enhance performance, or Carmeli (2006) who shows how high levels of managerial skills in senior managers are associated with better performance, and Fernandez (2005) on the benefits of integrative leadership.

Human resource management

In the seventh chapter Gene A. Brewer investigates the relationships between PSM and individual and organizational performance. A compelling argument about PSM is that it is associated with high performance. Patrick François (2000), reflecting on the power of the PSM–performance argument, went so far as to entitle an article, 'Public service motivation as an argument for government provision'. Yet early empirical research produced somewhat mixed findings about the relationships between PSM and individual and organizational performance. At the individual level, empirical studies offer equivocal evidence, though they draw upon different sample populations and measures, making it hard to reach clear conclusions. At the organizational level, studies produced tantalizing evidence that PSM may be more strongly related to organizational performance, which is ironic because it had been originally conceptualized as an individual trait, but these studies suffer methodological weaknesses that cast doubt on their validity and generalizability. Most importantly, researchers aggregated individual-level measures of PSM to study its effects on organizational performance – arguably an ecological fallacy (but not necessarily, as Brewer contends) – but again no clear conclusions emerge from these studies. More recently, however, the pattern of findings gives clarity to these relationships and the chapter explores these studies in some detail. The story is one of exemplary social science where researchers set forth hypotheses and follow up with a series of empirical studies that incrementally help us understand the relationships that exist, which are not always as straightforward or powerful as the hypotheses might suggest. To further advance research on PSM, Brewer argues that researchers need to be more consistent when measuring PSM at the individual level, and they need to pioneer some new, sounder measures of PSM at the organizational level so that the robustness of the relationship can be plumbed. Moreover, PSM needs to be included in frameworks and empirical models that seek to explain performance so that the PSM variable can compete alongside the several other performance-related variables discussed in this book. This is important both to avoid model specification error and to see if PSM might subsume some of the variation presently being explained by other management variables, such as strategy making and content, and managerial networking (or the opposite – that these variables might subsume some of the effects that have been attributed to PSM). The chapter investigates the PSM–performance relationship conceptually and empirically and offers advice on how researchers can progress this important topic.

Public organizations in developed countries are becoming increasingly diverse, particularly along racial, ethnic and gender lines. Globalization, technology and shifting cultural norms have contributed to increased percentages of women and people of different ethnicities and colour in the workforce. This surge in workforce diversity has created challenges for public managers who are used to managing in a homogeneous environment. Diversity provides both opportunities and struggles for organizations with shifting demographic profiles, or those serving populations that are dynamic and changing. But research on managing diversity is still in its infancy. This important topic of diversity and its relationship with organizational performance is examined by David W. Pitts in Chapter 8.

Diversity-oriented research in public organizations frequently consists of arguments made on normative grounds, but since NPM and market-based reforms have hit the public sector, organizations are increasingly tasked to make diversity a strategic, performance-oriented issue. Many believe that workforce diversity makes organizations more competitive – if an organization is diverse, then it is in the best position to respond to the needs of various target populations and formulate creative solutions to complex problems. In short, diversity is thought to increase organizational capacity. Ignored in these arguments, however, is the increased likelihood that these organizations will suffer from communication, collaboration and conflict problems stemming from diversity. In other words, diversification may take a heavy toll on efficiency and effectiveness – especially if the latter term is conceived narrowly. Just as it creates the potential for innovation and creativity, diversity often leads to decision-making delays, communication struggles and heightened conflict between employees.

The purpose of Chapter 8 is to reflect upon the state of research on diversity in public organizations. The chapter evaluates research on how different types of diversity, such as race, ethnicity and gender, affect performance. This is explored through the theoretical lenses with which diversity is approached in the academic literature, such as similarity-attraction theory, social categorization theory, and decision-making/information theory. In addition to reviewing the empirical research on diversity in organizations, grounding the theory in evidence that either supports or refutes it, Pitts also assesses the extent to which the field may be confident in its findings, identifying questions that warrant further inquiry. The chapter concludes by issuing recommendations and propositions to advance this area of public management research.

Performance management

The idea that performance can be 'managed' is one of the central mantras associated with NPM. Performance management is generally seen as including: setting objectives and quantified targets for future achievements, the selection of indicators to measure progress, gathering data against these indicators, formally evaluating whether progress is being made, and taking corrective action where required. This model of performance management strongly resonates with previous public service reforms, such as the waves of rational planning in the 1960s and 1970s.

In Chapter 9 George A. Boyne tackles this question by examining the theoretical bases of the various elements of performance management, and the internal consistency of the whole package. For example, why should quantified targets lead to better performance, and what is the theoretical rationale for the 'top-down' corrective action implied in the cycle of measurement and management? What behavioural effects is performance management likely to have on service providers, and will these effects lead to better public services? The chapter reviews the international evidence on the effects of performance management, including studies of national governments, public hospitals and local governments. The chapter concludes with suggestions for the theoretical and methodological developments that are required to build more comprehensive and solid evidence on the impact of performance management on public services.

Strategy content

Richard M. Walker explores the strategy–performance hypothesis in Chapter 10. Strategy content has come to occupy a central position in the minds of governments when looking to make improvements to public organizations. This reflects arguments in the academic literature on public and private management suggesting that strategy is one of the primary means through which organizational performance can be enhanced. Strategic management is conceived in two ways; strategy formulation is the way in which strategy is formed, while the substance of those decisions is strategy content: the broad way in which organizations seek to maintain or improve their performance, and the focus of this chapter is upon the latter.

In recent years attention has been focused on applying strategy content frameworks to public organizations. This work is found predominantly in the USA and examines typologies related to fiscal stress, strategic action and varying environmental contexts. The range of proposed models and frameworks are reviewed. Yet, like much of the knowledge and evidence that has been accumulated on public management, remarkably few of these approaches have been related to organizational performance. More recently Miles and Snow's (1978) framework that identifies the strategic categories of prospector, defender, analyser and reactor has been subject to extensive application in public agencies in the UK and USA.

The main bulk of Chapter 10 is dedicated to reviewing the literature on strategy content and performance. It identifies and isolates the strategic content approaches more frequently associated with higher levels of organizational performance, and those not so. It examines how strategy content may moderate other management practices and the relationship between strategy content and environmental context. As with much of the literature reviewed in this book, work on strategy content is in its infancy in public management circles. The chapter, therefore, examines the big questions that need to be posed on this topic in the coming years, including questions about strategy-content configurations and considerations about what public managers might need to do to adopt strategy-content frameworks that will result in higher levels of performance.

Methods for investigating the management–performance hypotheses

The preceding chapters identified the many ways in which the study of public management and performance has grown, both in scope and complexity. Our ability to test these new theories depends, in part, on our ability to employ methodologies that can appropriately account for the multifaceted relationships that we have identified as important in linking public management to organizational performance. In Chapter 11 Alisa Hicklin reviews the more common methodologies used in quantitative studies of management, discusses some of the obstacles faced in studying management and performance, and outlines a number of methodologies that may prove useful in future work. This chapter builds upon and complements prior work published by Peter Smith and others (Martin and Smith 2005; Smith 2006; Heinrich and Lynn 2001).

Recent work has shown that the effect of public management on performance is often a function of many diverse influences. As such, empirical tests often seek to measure very different concepts (structural, environmental, behavioural and cultural), often at multiple levels (individual/organization, superior/subordinate), that are linked by complex hypothesized relationships (reciprocal, non-linear and interactive) that require different methods of estimation. Most of the recent quantitative work relies on some version of ordinary least squares (OLS) analysis, but OLS has its limits. Additionally, as scholars begin to incorporate various methodologies into this body of work, new theoretical questions may emerge, especially as relationships are explored that have been hypothesized but not previously tested.

Some of these analytical techniques are only small additions to OLS regression, aimed at controlling for influences that cannot be formally incorporated into our models. A number of scholars have regularly included *fixed effects* in their regression models, to control for fluctuations attributed to time (often yearly fluctuations) or differences across jurisdictions (whether organizational or political) that cannot be measured appropriately for inclusion as independent variables. Additionally, some of our theories concerning management and performance speculate that managers can affect performance, but that the organization's previous performance may also affect how managers will behave. The empirical models used to explore these types of reciprocal relationships often used *three-stage least squares analysis* (among other methods) to explore the direction of these relationships.

Chapter 11 explores statistical methods that are relatively foreign to the study of public management. Developments in HLM (*hierarchical linear modelling*), and *experimental methods* offer incredible promise for giving the management community new ways to answer interesting and important research questions. As our methodological capacities increase, the scholarly community should advance in a way that will generate more accurate and useful knowledge about the ways in which public management affects organizational performance.

In conclusion, the editors draw together some themes and strands from the forgoing analysis and note the need for continued research to improve management practice and increase public service performance.

REFERENCES

Andersen, Lotte Bøgh, and Marianne Blegvad. 2006. 'Does ownership matter for the delivery of professionalized public services? Cost-efficiency and effectiveness in private and public dental care for children in Denmark', *Public Administration*, 84, 1, 147–64.

Andrews, Rhys, and George A. Boyne. 2008. 'Organizational environments and public-service failure: an empirical analysis', *Environment and Planning C: Government and Policy*, 26, 4, 788–807.

Andrews, Rhys, George A. Boyne, Jennifer Law, and Richard M. Walker. 2005. 'External constraints on local service standards: the case of comprehensive performance assessment in English local government', *Public Administration*, 83, 3, 639–56.

2008. 'Organizational strategy, external regulation and public service performance', *Public Administration*, 86, 1, 185–203.

2009. 'Centralization, organizational strategy and public service performance', *Journal of Public Administration Research and Theory*, 19, 1, 57–80.

Andrews, Rhys, George A. Boyne, M. Jae Moon, and Richard M. Walker. 2010. 'Assessing organizational performance: explaining differences between internal and external measures', to appear in *International Public Management Journal*.

Andrews, Rhys, George A. Boyne, and Richard M. Walker. 2006. 'Strategy content and organizational performance: an empirical analysis', *Public Administration Review*, 66, 1, 52–63.

2006. 'Subjective and objective measures of organizational performance: an empirical exploration', in George A. Boyne, Kenneth J. Meier, Laurence J. O'Toole, Jr., and Richard M. Walker (eds.) *Public Services Performance: Perspectives on Measurement and Management*. Cambridge University Press.

Audit Commission. 2002. *Comprehensive Performance Assessment*. London: Audit Commission.

Avellaneda, Claudia N. 2008. 'Municipal performance: does mayoral quality matter?', *Journal of Public Administration Research and Theory*, 19, 2, 285–312.

Bohte, John, and Kenneth J. Meier. 2000. 'Goal displacement: assessing the motivation for organizational cheating', *Public Administration Review*, 60, 1, 173–82.

Bommer, William. H., Jonathan L. Johnson, Gregory A. Rich, Philip M. Podsakoff, and Scott B. MacKenzie. 1995. 'On the interchangeability of objective and subjective measures of employee performance: a meta-analysis', *Personnel Psychology*, 48, 3, 587–605.

Boyne, George A. 2002. 'Concepts and indicators of local authority performance: an evaluation of the statutory framework in England and Wales', *Public Money and Management*, 22, 2, 17–24.

2003. 'Sources of public service improvement: a critical review and research agenda', *Journal of Public Administration Research and Theory*, 13, 3, 367–94.

Boyne, George A., and Richard M. Walker. 2005. 'Determinants of performance in public organizations symposium', *Journal of Public Administration Research and Theory*, 15, 4, 483–639.

Boyne, George A., Catherine Farrell, Jennifer Law, Martin Powell, and Richard M. Walker. 2003. *Evaluating Public Management Reform*. Buckingham: Open University Press.

Boyne, George A., and Kenneth J. Meier. 2009. 'Environmental turbulence, organizational stability, and public service performance', *Administration & Society*, 40, 8, 799–824.

Boyne, George. A., Kenneth. J. Meier, Laurence J. O'Toole, Jr., and Richard M. Walker (eds.). 2006. *Public Services Performance: Perspectives on Measurement and Management*. Cambridge University Press.

Brewer, Gene A. 2008. 'Employee and organizational performance', in James L. Perry and Annie Hondeghem (eds.) *Motivation in Public Management: The Call of Public Service*. Oxford University Press, pp. 136–56.

Brewer, Gene A., and Sally Coleman Selden. 2000. 'Why elephants gallop: assessing and predicting organizational performance in federal agencies', *Journal of Public Administration Research and Theory*, 10, 4, 685–711.

Brewer, Gene A., and Richard M. Walker. 2009. 'The impact of red tape on governmental performance: an empirical analysis', *Journal of Public Administration Research and Theory*, published online: doi:10.1093/jopart/mun040, February.

Carmeli, Abraham. 2006. 'The managerial skills of the top management team and the performance of municipal organisations', *Local Government Studies*, 32, 2, 153–76.

Chun, Young Han, and Hal G. Rainey. 2005. 'Goal ambiguity and organizational performance in US federal agencies', *Journal of Public Administration Research and Theory*, 15, 4, 529–57.

Eckardt, Sebastian. 2008. 'Political accountability, fiscal conditions and local government performance – Cross-sectional evidence from Indonesia', *Public Administration and Development*, 28, 1, 1–17.

Fernandez, Sergio. 2005. 'Developing and testing an integrative framework of public sector leadership: evidence from the public education arena', *Journal of Public Administration Research and Theory*, 15, 2, 197–217.

Francois, Patrick. 2000. 'Public service motivation as an argument for government provision', *Journal of Public Economics*, 78, 3, 275–99.

Goerdel, Holly T. 2005. 'Taking initiative: proactive management and organizational performance in networked environments', *Journal of Public Administration Research and Theory*, 16, 3, 599–611.

Golden, Brian R. 1992. 'Is the past the past – or is it? The use of retrospective accounts as indicators of past strategies', *Academy of Management Journal*, 35, 5, 848–60.

Government Executive. 2004. Daily briefing, January 29th, 2004. Retrieved 19 May 2004 from www.GovExec.com.

Heinrich, Carolyn J., and Youseok Choi. 2007. 'Performance-based contracting in social welfare programs', *The American Review of Public Administration*, 37, 4, 409–35.

Heinrich, Carolyn J., and Laurence E. Lynn, Jr. (eds.). 2000. *Governance and Performance: New Perspectives*. Washington, DC: Georgetown University Press.

2001. 'Means and ends: a comparative study of empirical methods for investigating governance and performance', *Journal of Public Administration Research and Theory*, 11, 1, 109–38.

Hicklin, Alisa, Laurence J. O'Toole, Jr., and Kenneth J. Meier. 2008. 'Serpents in the sand: managerial networking and nonlinear influences on organizational performance', *Journal of Public Administration Research and Theory*, 18, 2, 253–73.

Jackson, Peter. 1982. *The Political Economy of Bureaucracy*. Oxford: Phillip Allen.

Ingraham, Patricia W., Phillip G. Joyce, and Amy Kneedler Donahue. 2003. *Government Performance: Why Management Matters*. Baltimore, MD: Johns Hopkins University Press.

de Lancer Julnes, Patria and Marc Holzer. 2001. 'Promoting the utilization of performance measures in public organizations: an empirical study of factors affecting adoption and implementation', *Public Administration Review*, 61, 6, 693–708.

Lukemeyer, Anna, and Richard C. McCorkle. 2006. 'Privatization of prisons: impact on prison conditions', *American Review of Public Administration*, 36, 2, 189–206.

Lynn, Laurence E., Jr., Carolyn J. Heinrich, and Carolyn J. Hill. 2001. *Improving Governance: a New Logic for Empirical Research*. Washington DC: Georgetown University Press.

Martin, Stephen, and Peter Smith. 2005. 'Multiple public service performance indicators: towards an integrated statistical approach', *Journal of Public Administration Research and Theory*, 15, 3, 599–613.

Meier, Kenneth J., and Laurence J. O'Toole, Jr. 2002. 'Public management and organizational performance: the effect of managerial quality', *Journal of Policy Analysis and Management*, 21, 4, 629–43.

2003. 'Plus ça change: public management, personal stability, and organizational performance', *Journal of Public Administration Research and Theory*, 13,1, 43–64.

2009. 'The dog that didn't bark: how public managers handle environmental shocks', *Public Administration*, 87, 3, 485–502.

Meier, Kenneth J., Laurence J. O'Toole, Jr., George A. Boyne, and Richard M. Walker. 2007. 'Strategic management and the performance of public organizations: testing venerable ideas against recent theories', *Journal of Public Administration Research and Theory*, 17, 3, 357–77.

Meier, Kenneth J., Laurence J. O'Toole, Jr., and Sean Nicholson–Crotty. 2004. 'Multilevel governance and organizational performance: investigating the political bureaucratic labyrinth', *Journal of Policy Analysis and Management*, 23, 1, 31–47.

Miles, Raymond E., and Charles C. Snow. 1978. *Organizational Strategy, Structure and Process*. New York: McGraw-Hill.

Mitchell, Ronald K., Bradley R. Agle, and Donna J. Wood. 1997. 'Towards a theory of stakeholder identification and salience: defining the principle of who and what really counts', *Academy of Management Review*, 22, 4, 853–86.

Moynihan, Donald P., and Sanjay K. Pandey. 2005. 'Testing how management matters in an era of government by performance management', *Journal of Public Administration Research and Theory*, 15, 3, 421–39.

Office of the Deputy Prime Minister. 2000. *Best Value Performance Indicators for 2000/2001*. London: Office of the Deputy Prime Minister.

Organisation for Economic Co-operation and Development (OECD). 2005. *Modernising Government: The Way Forward*. Paris: OECD.

O'Toole, Laurence J., Jr., and Kenneth J. Meier. 1999. 'Modelling the impact of public management: the implications of structural context', *Journal of Public Administration Research and Theory*, 9, 3, 505–26.

2004. 'Parkinson's Law and the new public management? Contracting determinants and service-quality consequences in public education', *Public Administration Review*, 64, 3, 342–52.

Pandey, Sanjay K., and Donald P. Moynihan. 2006. 'Bureaucratic red tape and organizational performance: testing the moderating role of culture and political support', in George A. Boyne, Kenneth J. Meier, Laurence J. O'Toole, Jr. and Richard M. Walker (eds.) *Public Service Performance: Perspectives on Measurement and Management*. Cambridge University Press.

Pitts, David W. 2007. 'Representative bureaucracy, ethnicity, and public schools: examining the link between representation and performance', *Administration & Society*, 39, 4, 497–526.

Rainey, Hal G., and Paula Steinbauer. 1999. 'Galloping elephants: developing elements of a theory of effective government organizations', *Journal of Public Administration Research and Theory*, 9, 1, 1–32.

van Ryzin, Gregg G. 2005. 'Testing the expectancy disconfirmation model of citizen satisfaction with local government', *Journal of Public Administration Research and Theory*, 16, 4, 599–611.

Smith, Peter. 2006. 'Quantitative approaches towards assessing organizational performance', in George. A. Boyne, Kenneth. J. Meier, Laurence J. O'Toole, Jr. and Richard M. Walker (eds.) *Public Services Performance: Perspectives on Measurement and Management*. Cambridge University Press.

Symon, Peter, and Richard M. Walker. 1995. 'A consumer perspective of performance indictors: the Report to Tenants Regime in England and Wales', *Environment and Planning C: Government and Policy*, 13, 2, 195–216.

United Nations Development Programme (UNDP). 2004. *Governance Indicators: A User's Guide*. Oslo: UNDP.

Walker, Richard M., and George A. Boyne. 2009. 'Determinants of performance in public organizations symposium II', *Public Administration*, 87, 3, 433–518.

Walker, Richard M., and Gene A. Brewer. 2009. 'Can management strategy minimize the impact of red tape on organizational performance?', *Administration & Society*, 41, 4, 423–48.

Wall, Toby B., Jonathan Michie, Malcolm Patterson, Stephen J. Wood, Maura Sheehan, Chris W. Clegg, and Michael West. 2004. 'On the validity of subjective measures of company performance', *Personnel Psychology*, 57, 1, 95–118.

Witte, John, David Weimer, Arnold Shober, and Paul Schlomer. 2007. 'The performance of Charter Schools in Wisconsin', *Journal of Policy Analysis and Management*, 26, 3, 557–73.

Williamson, Oliver E. 1975. *Markets and Hierarchies: Analysis and Antitrust Implications*. New York: Free Press.

Yamamoto, Kiyoshi. 2006. 'Performance of semi-autonomous public bodies: linkage between autonomy and performance in Japanese agencies', *Public Administration and Development*, 26, 1, 35–44.

Yang, Kaifeng, Jun Yi Hsieh, and Tzung Shiun Li. 2009. 'Contracting capacity and perceived contracting performance: nonlinear effects and the role of time', *Public Administration Review*, 69, 4, 681–96.

2 Extending goal ambiguity research in government: from organizational goal ambiguity to programme goal ambiguity

Hal G. Rainey and Chan Su Jung

This chapter describes recent research on goal ambiguity (or goal clarity) in government organizations. Almost unanimously, scholars and experts say that public organizations have goals that are more multiple, conflicting and vague than the goals of business firms. (e.g. Allison 1983; Dahl and Lindblom 1953; Downs 1967; Drucker 1980; Frederickson and Frederickson 2006: 174; Heinrich 1999; Lowi 1979; Lynn 1981; Moynihan 2008: 142–5; Wildavsky 1979; Wilson 1989). These authors usually relate these characteristics of government organizations' goals to other important organizational characteristics, such as greater difficulty in measuring performance and hence in achieving high performance; in maintaining organizational control; in avoiding 'red tape'; and in motivating employees, as compared to business firms. To the extent that there are theories of government organizations, these observations play a central role in them. Many governmental reform initiatives include directives that government organizations state goals, clarify them and measure the extent to which they are achieved (Frederickson and Frederickson 2006; Gilmour 2006; Moynihan 2008: 28–31). In spite of the ubiquity of such observations about public organizations' goals, researchers have reported few analyses of the goal characteristics of government organizations, or of organizations of any kind.

This chapter will review important examples of the assertions cited above about the goals of government organizations and the influences on the ambiguity of those goals. Then it will review recent research on the goals of public organizations. Next, the discussion will focus on recent studies that have analysed the level of goal ambiguity of large samples of government organizations and programmes (smaller organizational entities that are components of government agencies). These recent studies have developed measures of the level of goal ambiguity of such organizations and programmes, and have related those levels to other characteristics of the organizations and the programmes. The chapter then discusses the remaining challenges, and makes some propositions about the relations between goal ambiguity and clarity and the performance of public organizations.

Observations about the goals of public organizations

The claims that public agencies have particularly vague, hard-to-measure, multiple, and conflicting goals are nearly universal among scholars and experienced practitioners (see Rainey 1993). They often refer to the lack of sales and profit indicators and incentives for public agencies, complications due to political oversight and interventions by multiple authorities and interest groups, value-laden and sharply conflicting mandates (as in, for example, simultaneous demands for efficiency and equity, or for conservation and development). Over three decades ago, a review of the literature on the differences between public and private organizations cited a dozen authors who asserted that public organizations have goals that are more vague, multiple, and mutually conflicting than the goals of most private organizations (Rainey, Backoff and Levine 1976). The authors included two of the major political scientists of that era, Robert Dahl and Charles Lindblom (1953: 459ff). They asserted that 'agencies (government agencies) are distinct from "enterprises" (private firms) in the greater multiplicity and diversity of the agencies' objectives'. Later, Lowi (1979), in a book that, according to one survey of political scientists, was the most important book in political science over that half century, expressed a similar perspective. He argued that vague legislative statutes, born of the need for compromise among conflicting interests, disseminated vague goals throughout government and contributed to major problems in achieving effective governance, including the governance of public organizations.

That same year, one of the major political scientists of the twentieth century, Aaron Wildavsky (1979: 215), wrote about the difficulties involved in evaluating the effects of public policies. Goals, he wrote, posed one of the most difficult challenges for evaluators: 'We know that objectives invariably may be distinguished by three outstanding qualities: they are multiple, conflicting, and vague.' In one of the most widely-cited books on government bureaucracy, Wilson (1989: 33) stated flatly that most government agencies have unclear goals (although he gives more attention than many other authors to the variations in goal clarity among government agencies). Other authors (Pitt and Smith 1981; Rainey 2003; Warwick 1975) point out that oversight agencies impose a variety of requirements that amount to goals, such as civil service rules and purchasing and procurement rules.

While authors in political science and public administration tend to emphasize political and governmental influences on organizational goals, economists emphasize the roles of markets and aspects of markets such as prices and products, or the absence of them. They point out that most public organizations address market failures (by regulating monopolies or externalities, for example), and provide public or quasi-public goods that markets do not provide (Downs 1967: 32–5; Lindblom 1977: 78–84).

Effects of goal ambiguity on organizations

Researchers and practitioners attribute important influences to public organizations' goal ambiguity, and these are usually negative. Buchanan (1974, 1975) reported that a sample of federal government managers showed lower levels of organizational commitment, job involvement and work satisfaction than did a sample of business managers. The federal managers also reported a weaker sense of their own impact on their organizations, and a weaker sense of challenge in their jobs. He concluded that vagueness in the public organizations' goals made it harder to design challenging jobs for the managers and harder for them to perceive their own impact on the organization's performance. This, in turn, weakened commitment and satisfaction. Boyatzis (1982) studied the competencies of a large sample of managers and found that public managers displayed weaker 'goal and action' competencies – those concerned with formulating and emphasizing means and ends. He concluded that in the public sector the absence of clear goals and performance measures such as profits reduces public managers' opportunities to develop such competencies, as compared to the opportunities in business.

Others have observed that goal ambiguity weakens the administrative authority of executives in government (e.g. Allison 1983; Blumenthal 1983). Still others say that goal ambiguity contributes to centralization of authority (ironically, in relation to the observations just mentioned about the weakening of authority). Goal ambiguity also allegedly leads to proliferation of rules and procedural requirements, resulting in more elaborate bureaucracy because ambiguous organizational goals create problems in devising clear performance measures. This makes it harder to assess the performance of individuals and units of the organization on the basis of performance results and outcomes. Performance evaluation then focuses on assessing performance as adherence to rules and required procedures, and on the basis of inputs and processes, rather than results (e.g. Barton 1980; Dahl and Lindblom 1953; Lynn 1981: 35; Meyer 1979; Warwick 1975: 123). Higher-level administrators have more difficulty assessing performance so they delegate less, and impose more requirements for rule adherence, and for approvals and clearances. This leads to a pattern of 'inevitable bureaucracy' (Lynn 1981) and a tendency for public administrators to avoid decentralizing authority in the way business executives do when they establish such entities as profit centres or their equivalents (Meyer 1979). Still other authors suggest that public organizations' goal ambiguity complicates decision making and strategic planning (March and Olsen 1976: 12; Hickson *et al.* 1986; Schwenk 1990) and distorts hierarchical communication (Downs 1967: 116; Tullock 1965: 137).

The authors mentioned above usually advance more elaborate and subtle observations than depicted here. Their observations include other factors besides goal ambiguity that contribute to the characteristics of public organizations. In general, however, they converge on a consensus that public organizations have higher levels of goal ambiguity than business firms, and that goal ambiguity contributes to undesirable organizational characteristics or at least poses serious challenges. Ultimately, with some variations, the literature tends to state that the goal ambiguity of public organizations diminishes their performance.

Research on goal ambiguity in government organizations

Because goal ambiguity figures so importantly in so many observations about the nature of public organizations, and in so many proposals for reforming such organizations, some researchers began to seek empirical evidence about goal ambiguity. Early efforts involved surveys of managers in government and business that included questions about whether they regarded their organization's goals as clear or ambiguous. The questions asked for agreement or disagreement with statements such as these (Lan and Rainey 1992; Rainey, Pandey and Bozeman 1995):

The goals of my organization are clearly defined.

It is easy to measure the degree to which this organization achieves its goals.

This organization's mission is clear to almost everyone who works here.

It is easy to give a precise explanation of the goals of this organization.

Several surveys, with respondents from all levels of government, many types of government agencies and business firms, different areas of the United

States, and spanning about fifteen years, used these questions to ask government and business managers about the clarity and measurability of their organizations' goals (e.g. Rainey 1983; Lan and Rainey 1992; Rainey, Pandey and Bozeman 1995). The authors had hypothesized that the government managers would say that their organizations' goals were vague. Instead, however, the government managers gave high ratings of the clarity of the goals of their organizations, and differed little from the private sector managers on these ratings. This presented the anomaly that prominent scholars and experienced executives agree that public managers face more ambiguous goals than do managers in business firms, but the public managers themselves did not agree. These anomalous findings raised questions. How do we analyse these characteristics of goals better and gather evidence of the actual influences of such goal characteristics on other variables? How do public agencies, private firms and other organizations vary among themselves on such dimensions?

Analysing organizational goal ambiguity

Such questions indicate that scholars need to develop much better and more objective measures of organizational goal ambiguity than survey questions alone can provide. The US Government Performance and Results Act (GPRA) of 1993 still requires federal agencies to develop strategic plans that include statements of the agencies' goals, with measures of performance in relation to those goals. Could one develop measures of the ambiguity or clarity of the agencies' goal statements and analyse the variations among the agencies in goal ambiguity? Could one then relate those variations to other variables that should influence goal ambiguity and be influenced by it, as hypothesized or claimed in so much of the literature? Analysing these goal statements required some debatable assumptions, such as that goal statements are actually reasonably valid as representations of an agency's goals. At the outset, too, this research posed a risk of failure. Few researchers had measured organizational goal ambiguity, other than those using surveys described earlier. Would analysing organizational goal ambiguity prove fruitless?

In spite of such concerns, Chun and Rainey (2005a, based on Chun 2003) developed measures of goal ambiguity from the agencies' strategic plans and other archival sources. They referred to organizational goal ambiguity as 'the extent to which an organizational goal or set of goals allows leeway for interpretation, when the organizational goal represents the desired future state of the organization' (Chun and Rainey 2005a: 2). They then proposed four dimensions of goal ambiguity: mission comprehensive ambiguity, directive goal ambiguity, evaluative goal ambiguity and priority goal ambiguity. First, *mission comprehensive ambiguity* refers to 'the level of interpretive leeway that an organizational mission allows in comprehending, explaining, and communicating the organizational mission' (Chun and Rainey 2005a: 3; as cited from Daft 2007; Miller and Dess 1993; Thompson 1997). This goal ambiguity was measured by the Gunning-Fog Index evaluating the degree of fog in a mission (Chun and Rainey 2005a). The second dimension was *directive goal ambiguity*, which is defined as 'the amount of interpretive leeway available in translating an organization's mission or general goals into directives and guidelines for specific actions to be taken to accomplish the mission' (Chun and Rainey 2005a: 3; as cited from Moore 1995; Scott 2003). They used the measure of organizational power developed by Meier (1980: 364), which was 'the ratio of the number of pages of rules that the bureau issues to the number of pages of substantive legislation that applies to the agency', as the measure of this goal ambiguity. Third, *evaluative goal ambiguity* refers to 'the level of interpretive leeway that an organizational mission allows in evaluating the progress toward the achievement of the mission' (Chun and Rainey 2005a: 4). For this dimension, they developed a new measure, 'the percentage of subjective or workload-oriented performance indicators, as opposed to objective and results-oriented performance indicators, for each agency' (Chun and Rainey 2005a: 13). Fourth, *priority goal ambiguity* refers to 'the level of interpretive leeway in deciding on priorities among multiple goals' (Chun and Rainey 2005a: 4). The average of the Z-scores of the number of long-term goals and annual goals is used as the measure of this goal ambiguity (Chun and Rainey 2005a). This dimension was based on the hierarchy of organizational goals.

With the measures of different types of goal ambiguity developed, the next step analysed antecedents that should influence or relate to the level of organizational goal ambiguity. (The term 'antecedents' avoids the more assertive term 'causes', because the causal directions and linkages are complex and the antecedents may not serve as direct, immediate causes.) They demonstrated that, except for mission comprehensive ambiguity, different dimensions of organizational goal ambiguity are differently related to different antecedents. The antecedents included financial publicness, competing demands from constituencies, type of policy responsibility (regulatory, non-regulatory, or hybrid), complexity of the policy problem, organizational age, organizational size and institutional location.

While the results of the first analysis proved encouraging, their very success prompted the next question. Can one relate the goal ambiguity measures to important consequences, such as organizational performance? Performance measures that apply in common to government agencies are scarce, however. For performance measures, this phase of the analysis drew on the responses of nearly 26,000 federal employees who responded to the 2000 US Federal Employee Survey. The survey had questions that reflected respondents' perceptions about their organization's performance that Chun and Rainey (2005b) employed as measures of performance: managerial effectiveness, customer service orientation, productivity and work quality. They also determined that different dimensions of organizational goal ambiguity are differently related to the four different dimensions of perceived organizational performance. Except for mission ambiguity, the other dimensions are significantly and negatively related to different performance dimensions. The analyses included control variables for the respondent's length of service as a federal employee, pay grade, job category (professional, administrative, technician, clerical or other) and managerial level. In addition, the variables used as independent variables in the previous study (size, age, policy problem complexity, financial publicness and others) were included as control variables.

All of the dependent variables described above as indicators of perceived performance showed statistically significant and negative relations with directive goal ambiguity and evaluative goal ambiguity. Priority goal ambiguity related significantly and negatively only to managerial effectiveness. One might consider these results remarkable, in that employees' survey responses about organizational performance show relations to independently and 'objectively' developed measures of the ambiguity of their organization's goals. Finding relations between variables from very different and independent data sources is usually much more convincing and interesting than, for example, finding relations between variables drawn from responses to questions on the same survey about employee perceptions of organizational goals and organizational performance. On the other hand, while the results were highly 'statistically significant', the measures of the effect size or strength of the relationship (R-squared) were low. In this case, the evidence does not support the existence of a strong relationship between the goal ambiguity measures and the survey measures of perceptions about organizational performance. Perhaps this is as it should be, since simple claims that clear goals improve performance and ambiguous goals impede performance are usually just that – simple. We know that premature or excessive clarification of goals may be dysfunctional under various circumstances. Perhaps we should be finding, at this stage in the development of this line of research, a negative but limited relationship between goal ambiguity and organizational performance.

Advancing analysis of the political environment, work characteristics and goals

Another frequent observation about public sector organizations refers to their operation in a 'political' environment. Public organizations become more subject than business firms to external influences by the institutions of government (e.g. legislative bodies, chief executives) and the political processes of government (such as lobbying by interest groups). Research on how external political and governmental institutions and actors influence organizations is limited, however (e.g. Carpenter 2001; Huber and Shipan 2002; Whitford 2002, 2005; Wood and Waterman 1994). Organization theorists have produced an elaborate literature on organizational environments, but it has usually paid little attention to political and governmental factors (with exceptions, such as Frumkin and Galaskiewicz 2003; Tolbert 1985; Tolbert and Zucker 1983). Could further analysis show evidence of the effects of external 'political' influences?

An additional study provided such evidence. Lee (2006; Lee, Rainey and Chun, forthcoming) found that a federal agency's 'political salience' to the president, Congress, and the media related to increased agency goal ambiguity. This analysis assumed that when an agency has high salience for major political officials and actors, such that they focus attention on that agency, they do so as part of an attempt to influence its goals and priorities. Political officials will try to influence agency officials' decisions about where to devote their own attention (May *et al.* 2008). Thus, the analysis treats 'salience' as an indication of attempts to influence. Actually, the salience measures described below include direct influence attempts such as legislation and presidential directives that give instructions to an agency.

How, then, can one assess the degree of salience an agency has for major political officials? Lee (2006; Lee, Rainey and Chun 2009) measured an agency's salience to the president, or 'presidential salience' by counting references to the agency in two archival sources: (1) the *Weekly Compilation of Presidential Documents* and (2) the *United States Government Policy and Supporting Positions*. The agency's 'congressional salience' was measured by counting references in two archival sources: (1) the *Congressional Record* and (2) Government Accountability Office (GAO) reports. The media salience measure drew on two prominent news outlets: the *New York Times* and the *Washington Post*. The procedure involved counting the number of articles in these two newspapers during 1997 that contained the agency's name (Winter and Eyal 1981: 379; Kiousis 2004; Worsham and Gatrell 2005). The six different indicators in these three salience measures were also combined into an 'overall salience' measure. The study analysed the relations between the three salience indicators and the overall salience indicator and the goal ambiguity measures. The analysis included most of the other control variables described above and some newly developed ones.

The analysis led to strikingly consistent results. Each of the three salience measures, for presidential, Congressional and media salience, as well as the overall salience measure, showed very strong relations to evaluative goal ambiguity and priority goal ambiguity. These results took into account and 'controlled' for the numerous other variables described earlier, such as agency age, size, policy type and complexity, and financial publicness. The findings thus provided evidence supporting assertions and claims often voiced in the literature, but seldom directly tested with empirical procedures. Agencies that had greater salience to the three political entities and hence were subject to more influence attempts from them had higher evaluative goal ambiguity. That is, their goal statements and performance measures were more oriented to subjective measures and input indicators than to objective measures and indicators of actual results. Higher levels of political salience also related to higher levels of priority goal ambiguity – higher numbers of unprioritized goals and performance indicators. The results advance analysis of the goal characteristics of government agencies and variations among the agencies on those characteristics.

Extending this series of studies on organizational goal ambiguity, Lee, Rainey and Chun (forthcoming) also argued that the type of work that the people in an agency do – the tasks they perform and the technologies they apply – should have important relations to goal ambiguity. Therefore, they analysed how organizational technology (Scott 2003: 230–61) or, more specifically, the routineness and complexity of the work people do, relates to goal ambiguity in public organizations. They measured work complexity and routineness from the same archival source, the Central Personnel Data File (CPDF) of the US Office of Personnel Management (OPM). First, for the work complexity measure, the researchers calculated the percentage of full-time 'professional' employees in an agency in the year 1997. Second, the percentage of full-time clerical or wage-grade (i.e. blue-collar) workers was used as a proxy measure for routineness (Ford 1997). According to the results, complexity related positively to one dimension of goal ambiguity, 'directive goal ambiguity'. Routineness of tasks related negatively to 'evaluative goal ambiguity', while complexity related positively to it. These results further show the value of the measures of goal ambiguity and their potential contribution to analysis of variations among government agencies, and to such issues as the applicability of various managerial reforms to different agencies.

Analysing goal ambiguity in public programmes

The most recent research extends the scope of goal ambiguity research from government agency level to public programme level, besides using objective measures rather than relying perceptual measures. These studies analysed variations in goal ambiguity among US federal programmes. These studies responded to an opportunity. A major topic in public administration for many decades, evaluating the performance of governmental activities has received increased attention in recent years. As part of this trend, the US Office of Management and Budget (OMB) created the Program Assessment Rating Tool (PART) in 2003 to assess the performance of federal programmes. The PART assesses programme purpose and design, strategic planning, programme management, programme results (performance on strategic goals) and an overall performance rating that combines these four categories of indicators. (Figure 2.1 provides examples of questions in the PART). Critics have attacked the PART's alleged weaknesses, but researchers have mounted strong defences of its use for research purposes (see Lewis 2008; Moynihan, 2008, for discussions of the controversy). Researchers have reported analyses of PART results in relation to such variables as budget decisions in OMB and whether the programme head is a careerist or political appointee (e.g. Lewis 2008; Gilmour and Lewis 2006). Common performance measures for disparate government programmes are rare, especially in the USA at the federal level, and PART scores provide comparable performance indicators. All federal programmes prepared the data for the PART under OMB guidelines. In addition, OMB made it clear that federal programmes should describe their goals based on statutory mandates (OMB 2006). This links goal statements to statutes more closely than in studies where researchers have had to try to identify goals indirectly from formal mandates (e.g. Perry *et al.* 1999; Meyers *et al.* 2001). Therefore, the availability of PART results for a very large number of federal programmes (767 programmes, for these analyses) provides an opportunity for analysis of an important performance assessment initiative, and analysis of antecedents related to performance indicators for federal programmes. Jung and Rainey (2008) developed

Program Purpose and Design

- Does the program address a specific and existing problem, interest, or need?
- Is the program designed so that it is not redundant or duplicative of any other Federal, State, local or private effort?
- Is the program design free of major flaws that would limit the program's effectiveness or efficiency?

Strategic Planning

- Does the program have a limited number of specific long-term performance measures that focus on outcomes and meaningfully reflect the purpose of the program?
- Do all partners (including grantees, sub-grantees, contractors, cost-sharing partners, and other government partners) commit to and work toward the annual and/or long-term goals of the program?
- Has the program taken meaningful steps to correct its strategic planning deficiencies?

Program Management

- Does the agency regularly collect timely and credible performance information, including information from key program partners, and use it to manage the program and improve performance?
- Are funds (Federal and partners') obligated in a timely manner, spent for the intended purpose, and accurately reported?
- Does the program collaborate and coordinate effectively with related programs?
- Does the program use strong financial management practices?

Program Results/Accountability

- Does the program (including program partners) achieve its annual performance goals?
- Does the program demonstrate improved efficiencies or cost effectiveness in achieving program goals each year?
- Does the performance of this program compare favorably to other programs, including government, private, etc., with similar purpose and goals?
- Do independent evaluations of sufficient scope and quality indicate that the program is effective and achieving results?

Figure 2.1:   Examples of Specific Questions in the Program Assessment Rating Tool (PART)

objective measures of programme goal ambiguity from the PART and found that different dimensions of programme goal ambiguity negatively related to different dimensions of PART performance scores, that is, programme design, planning, management, results and overall assessment rating. Another study (Jung 2009) demonstrated that different dimensions of programme goal ambiguity are associated with different antecedents such as management capacity, planning capacity, programme type, assessment year, programme size, budget increase, political party initiative and agency type. As in the research on organizational goal ambiguity, the findings further supported the viability of this approach to conceiving and measuring programme goal ambiguity.

Defining programme goal ambiguity

Jung and Rainey (2008) defined *programme goal ambiguity* as the degree to which a group of goals of federal programmes allow room for interpretation, by extending Chun and Rainey's (2005a) goal ambiguity research scope from federal agencies to federal programmes. Programme or policy can be defined as 'the programmatic activities formulated in response to an authoritative decision' (Matland 1995: 154). In addition, Grizzle (1982: 134) defined goals as 'broad, general statements of desired conditions external to programs'. According to Feldman (1989: 5), ambiguity means 'the state of having many ways of thinking about the same circumstances or phenomena'. Therefore, when programme goals invite room for different interpretations, they are regarded as ambiguous (Chun 2003; Chun and Rainey 2005a).

Jung (2009) pursued the contention that the unclearness in interpretation of programme goals can vary along three dimensions (target, time span and the possibility of evaluation), based on the goal system of the PART. According to OMB (2006: 81), target refers to the 'quantifiable or otherwise measureable characteristic that tells how well a program must accomplish a performance measure'. In the PART, all the federal programmes should provide performance goals or measures. In terms of target, while some performance goals report concrete targets, others do not. Next, time span refers to whether a programme performance goal is a long-term goal or an annual goal. Like organizations, federal programmes can vary in the degree to which they can use objective performance indicators in identifying the possibility of accomplishing the performance target (Chun 2003; Smith 1999; Gable 1998). The PART includes four kinds of performance indicators in relation to performance evaluation: outcome indicators, output indicators, outcome-oriented efficiency indicators, and output-oriented efficiency indicators .

Target-specification goal ambiguity refers to the lack of clarity in deciding on the quantity and/or quality of work toward the achievement of a programme's performance goals. This study measures this construct as the percentage of a programme's stated goals for which the PART report does not state concrete performance targets. (For some of the goals reported in the PART reports, such target information is stated. For other goals, it is not.) Heinrich (2003) argued that public organizations' choices of performance goals are critical for the complex job of deciding quantitative measures of performance because ambiguous objectives make it more challenging to specify precise and informative measures. Furthermore, some motivation theorists posit that more specific goals lead to higher motivation and performance (Bandura 1989; Lee *et al.* 1989). Some public management scholars contend that explicit performance measures are critical motivators for public managers (Heinrich 2003; Khademian 1995). Researchers analysing the specification of goals use the concept of *goal specificity* to refer to 'the degree of quantitative precision required by the goal' (Lee *et al.* 1989: 299). A new concept, target-specification goal ambiguity, needed to be developed as a more objective and more comprehensive measure of goal ambiguity related to target-specification for individual public programmes with multiple objectives.

Time-specification goal ambiguity refers to the lack of clarity in deciding on the distinction between annual goals and long-term goals in each programme. Federal programmes in the PART data can be classified into three types of performance objectives in relation to time specification: annual performance objectives, long-term performance objectives and duplicate objectives. In this study, duplicate performance goals are newly defined as the goals stated as both annual and long term at the same time without any explanations or any progressive steps to attain final targets. According to the report of the GAO (1997), executives in public agencies argued that it is quite difficult to predict the result level for long-term goals that might be accomplished over a shorter term and to translate the long-term goals into annual performance goals (Heinrich 2003). Thus, we can expect that there will be significant variations of time-specification goal ambiguity among federal public programmes.

In terms of time span, the absence of a clear hierarchy of objectives can lead to goal conflict in public programmes with multiple objectives (Pandey and Garnett 2006). Therefore, goal ambiguity, lack of goal clarity, is characterized by the vagueness of hierarchy and by conflict among goals (Rainey 1993; Pandey and Garnett 2006). According to goal-setting theory (Bandura 1989), proximate goals, such as annual goals, are more helpful in activating self-influences than distant goals, such as long-term goals, thus the former heighten performance more than the latter. Yet distant goals, such as long-term goals, provide less effective incentives to facilitate current motivation and performance. However, Bandura (1989) argued that when long-range goals are employed as the comparative standard, and where there is clarity about the steps of progress for complete achievement, present achievements can mobilize intrinsic interest and long-range goals can be helpful to increase performance. Based on goal-setting theory, we can expect that annual performance objectives will have effects different from longer-term performance objectives on the achievements of goals and higher performance. Unlike annual performance objectives, long-term performance objectives need to offer progressive steps to attain final targets for higher performance in public programme management. When long-term and annual goals are clearly distinct and show necessary progressive steps, public programmes can have lower goal ambiguity and improved performance.

For *programme evaluation goal ambiguity*, this study followed Chun and Rainey's (2005a: 4) definition of evaluative goal ambiguity, referring to the level of interpretive leeway that a programme goal allows in evaluating progress toward the achievement of the goal, although the measuring methods of the two empirical studies are different. However, the logic for the two kinds of evaluation goal ambiguity is the same for both federal agencies and federal programmes. According to Grizzle (2002, 1982), programme managers should transform programme goals into performance indicators and targets for performance evaluation. From the standpoint of a rational model of decision making, identifying the goals on which comparisons of performance are to be based would be the first stage for the development of a performance measurement system (Heinrich 2007). Therefore, programme goals can become performance yardsticks to make judgements of the programme results. Some federal programmes have more outcome-oriented objectives, while others have more output-oriented objectives. That is, some federal programmes can express performance goals in an objective and measurable way, while other programmes often describe performance goals in a subjective manner, which brings about unclearness for interpretation of whether or not the performance goals are achieved (Rainey forthcoming). In addition, some scholars (Grizzle 2002; Bohte and Meier 2000) have argued that the lack of objective outcome performance measures might lead to avoiding results or outcome measures and using workload or output indicators.

Analysing antecedents of federal programme goal ambiguity

With the three new measures of different types of programme goal ambiguity developed, the next step analysed antecedents that should influence or relate to the level of programme goal ambiguity. This analysis examined the relationship of the following variables to the programme goal ambiguity measures:

Programme Management Capacity. Goal ambiguity can be lowered by management activities (Ingraham *et al.* 2003). Management capacity is the ability of government to develop, direct and control its necessary resources to support the fulfilment of its policy and programme responsibilities (Ingraham and Donahue 2003). It includes capacity for management activities such as financial management, structuring relationships with various partners related to the programmes and performance management (OMB 2006).

Programme Planning Capacity. Planning capacity is defined as the ability of the organization or the programme to plan and assign work across programme members and the methods used to integrate their actions. Planning capacity includes making the purpose clear and establishing valid short-term and long-term goals for programmes (OMB 2006). Better planning capacity should contribute to decreasing goal ambiguity. In the public policy field, for a long time many scholars have mentioned the significance of planning for clear goal-setting and the success of a policy (e.g. Baum 1976; Berman and McLaughlin 1976; Berman 1978; Hambleton 1983).

Federal Programme Type (Third-Party or Direct). The type of programme that federal agencies implement can predict goal ambiguity. Following the assumption that 'policies determine politics' (Lowi 1972), one should expect that different types of federal programmes will face different political conditions, which will in turn bring about different results in the policy processes (Meier 2000; Ripley and Franklin, 1982; Lowi 1972). Therefore, different types of public programmes can have different levels of goal ambiguity.

The analysis of programme types followed Frederickson and Frederickson's (2006) classifying procedure. Their categories of programme types included direct (direct federal, credit, regulatory, and capital assets and service acquisition) and third-party programmes (block and formula grant, competitive grant, and research and development) from the classifying system of OMB. Third-party programmes are grant- and contract-based (Frederickson and Frederickson, 2006). In relation to this classification, Salamon (2002) divided public 'tools' into direct and indirect tools. Direct tools with medium coerciveness, high directness and high visibility include direct government, government corporations, economic regulation, public information and direct loans. Indirect tools have medium coerciveness, low or medium directness and low or medium visibility. They include contracting, loan guarantees, grant, tax expenditures, fees and charges, insurance, tort law, vouchers, and government-sponsored enterprises.

In the analysis of programme goals, the researchers predicted that direct programmes would be affected or intervened less by multiple constituencies than third-party ones in the policy process and thus have lower goal ambiguity (Behn 2001; Lowi 1979; Wilson 1980). Direct programmes show higher overall PART scores and management scores than the indirect ones (Frederickson and Frederickson 2006). On the basis of these results, Frederickson and Frederickson (2006: 182) claim that 'quality of management and the nature of accountability in hollowed-out third-party-operated federal programs are very different from the management and accountability of directly operated federal programs'. Third-party programmes have more competing demands from multiple constituencies and such conditions will lead to more goal ambiguity with the need for political compromise (Chun and Rainey 2005a).

Assessment Year. Assessment year should be negatively related to goal ambiguity. The Bush administration emphasized strategic planning and 'managing for results'. Programme goals may become more specific, detailed and refined over time as policy-makers improve their ability to follow the OMB guidelines (Chun and Rainey 2005a; Matland 1995).

Programme Size. Like the results of organizational goal ambiguity in federal agencies (Chun and Rainey 2005a), programme size should also have a positive impact on goal ambiguity in federal programmes. Larger federal programmes often have more functions and performance goals. More goals can increase goal conflict (Bandura 1989) and ultimately lead to higher goal ambiguity (Chun 2003).

Political Party Initiative (Democratic or Republican-Oriented). Gilmour and Lewis (2006) classified programmes into two categories, Republican and Democratic Party programmes, according to the party with more influence and interest in the department where a programme is housed. They contended that the department that houses a programme serves as 'a reasonable proxy for the political content of the program', since 'some departments do work that is more central to the agenda of the Democratic Party than other departments' (Gilmour and Lewis 2006: 177). It is important to take this factor into account because OMB officials in the Bush administration designed the PART process, which provided the evidence for the programme goal analysis. Critics complained that Bush administration officials would be biased against programmes supported by Democrats. Gilmour and Lewis (2006) provide evidence against this conclusion, but this matter needs to be clarified in any analysis.

Agency Type (Regulatory or Non-Regulatory). Chun and Rainey (2005a) divided agency types according to whether the agency has a regulatory or non-regulatory mission, on the basis of its policy responsibility. 'The existence of clear winners and losers in regulatory politics makes it difficult for political leaders to develop specific policy goals or directives since they often must avoid details to reach an agreement between the winners and losers' (Chun and Rainey 2005a: 8). Goals or statutes of regulatory programmes should have higher levels of vagueness (Noll 1971).

Encouraging results

Given that no scholar had conducted empirical research into variations in US federal programme goal ambiguity using objective measures, there was some concern that the analysis would not produce any significant findings.

However, the results were encouraging. They suggested that the independent variables described above did have statistically significant relations to the programme goal ambiguity measures in ways hypothesized and that seemed reasonable and logical. This provided evidence that the variables were viable and meaningful. Some of the main findings were as follows:

- Target-specification goal ambiguity was negatively related to management capacity and planning capacity. When a programme has lower management and planning capacity, it has more performance objectives without concrete targets.
- Democratic Party-oriented programmes showed significantly higher levels of target-specification goal ambiguity than programmes with a Republican Party orientation.
- Third-party programmes had significantly higher levels of target-specification goal ambiguity and time-specification goal ambiguity than direct programmes.
- Time-specification goal ambiguity was also strongly and negatively related to management capacity. That is, better management capacity led to a reduction in the number of goals stated as both long-term and annual goals and hence ambiguous in time specification. In addition, this dimension of goal ambiguity was lower for non-regulatory agencies. Public programmes located in non-regulatory agencies had significantly lower levels of time-specification goal ambiguity than programmes in regulatory agencies. This makes sense in that public managers or political leaders related to regulatory agencies avoid developing specific programme goals since it is difficult to reach an agreement between the winners and loser in regulatory politics (Chun and Rainey 2005a).

Programme evaluation goal ambiguity also had a strong and negative relationship with planning capacity, as expected. Thus, the results from this first large sample analysis of programme goal ambiguity appeared promising and encouraging. The measures of programme goal ambiguity were significantly and meaningfully related to other variables in ways that public policy scholars, political scientists and public administration scholars would predict and find reasonable.

The next step: relating programme goal ambiguity to programme performance

While the results of the first analysis of programme goal ambiguity proved encouraging, their very success prompted the next challenge. Can one relate the new programme goal ambiguity measures to important consequences, such as programme or organizational performance? For programme performance measures, this phase of the analysis used PART scores (Jung and Rainey 2008; Jung 2009). The availability of performance assessment results for 767 federal programmes provides an opportunity for analysis of the relationships between the new programme goal ambiguity measures and the five performance indicators for federal programmes. The PART's four sections have different weights for the calculation of the overall programme assessment rating. Each PART questionnaire includes approximately twenty-five questions, divided into the four sections (see examples in Figure 2.1). OMB (2006) explains the four sections as follows:

- The first section of questions (design) asks whether a programme's purpose is clear and whether it is well designed to achieve its objectives.
- The second section (planning) involves strategic planning, and weighs whether the agency establishes valid annual and long-term goals for its programmes.
- The third section (management) rates the management of an agency's programme, including financial oversight and programme improvement efforts.
- The fourth section (results/accountability) focuses on results that programmes can report with accuracy and consistency.

The scores of all four sections are presented as percentages. For the fifth dimension of programme performance assessment, OMB provided the overall assessment rating score which is the total weighted score for the programme by using the weights of the four assessment sections: programme purpose and design (20%), planning (10%), management (20%), and results and accountability (50%) (OMB 2006).

More encouraging results: relationships between programme goal ambiguity and performance

Regression analyses examined the relations between the new programme goal ambiguity measures and the PART scores described above. The programmes' PART scores related significantly and negatively to most of the measures of goal ambiguity, as hypothesized. Specifically, target-specification goal ambiguity very strongly and negatively related to all five PART scores and higher levels of time-specification goal ambiguity related to lower levels of PART design, management and overall rating scores. Programme evaluation goal ambiguity also showed a significant and negative relationship with all the five PART performance scores, although the relationship was not stronger than target-specification goal ambiguity. These relations held when the analysis took into account other antecedents that could represent alternative, biasing influences on the PART scores, other than programme performance itself. These included programme type, whether the programme budget had increased, the year of assessment (that can indicate whether there is a learning factor over time that helps programme leaders simply make better reports, as opposed to actually improving performance), programme size, and the political party orientation of a programme (which could cause a bias against more Democratic-oriented programmes in a process designed and implemented by a Republican administration).

These additional variables support the conclusion that the goal ambiguity measures relate strongly and negatively to the PART scores, even taking into account alternative influences on those scores. These results further support the observations, repeated again and again by prominent scholars and experts, that public organizations tend to have vague goals, and that goal vagueness impedes their performance.

Conclusion

These challenges and many others loom, but the progress reported here suggests the value of confronting them. By no means does this research aim at advancing a simplistic nostrum that claims that clear goals are good. As mentioned at the outset, premature or excessive specification of goals can be dysfunctional. The analysis has sought to clarify and examine statements about public organizations' and programmes' goal clarity and ambiguity that have been echoed in the literature. A first objective involved developing concepts and measures to see if analysis of organizational and programme goal characteristics was even feasible, and the research has established at least a preliminary positive answer to that question. Another objective aimed at understanding what factors influence the level of ambiguity and clarity. Examples of advances along these lines from the studies described earlier include the following: as often claimed but seldom tested with large samples and empirical measures, regulatory agencies have higher levels of goal ambiguity. Where more politically active groups seek to influence the agency's priorities, all the forms of goal ambiguity are higher. Where agencies have higher 'salience' to the president, Congress and the media, they will show tendencies to state goals in terms of workload measures rather than results, and to state higher numbers of unprioritized goals. The research also shows evidence that goal ambiguity relates negatively to organizational performance, but the relationship is not strong. This suggests that the relationship is complex and subtle.

The few previous studies of the goal characteristics of government agencies have concentrated on the overall agency level. The most recent ones add measures and evidence for the programme level. The results showed that different programme goal ambiguity measures have different antecedents. These findings confirm hypotheses drawn from the literature and can increasingly be woven together for more detailed and systematic explanations of when and why agencies and programmes vary on goal ambiguity and performance assessments.

Practical and policy decisions can take into consideration variations among agencies that can influence their performance scores, and consider whether those variations can be taken into account in programme design. The findings support the conclusion that appropriate efforts to clarify goals can benefit performance (Latham *et al.* 2008; Wright 2004). More importantly, the evidence here extends the stream of research seeking to clarify the concept of goal ambiguity (or clarity), find ways of measuring it and deepening our understanding of it. In these and other ways, the research described in this chapter advances knowledge about a topic central to theory and practice for government organizations and programmes.

These conclusions support propositions about relations between public agencies' and public programmes' goal ambiguity and the performance of the agencies and programmes, including the following:

Proposition 1: Government agencies that state clear goals and performance objectives in appropriate, valid ways achieve higher levels of performance than those that do not.

The evidence indicates that clarifying goal and performance objectives does contribute to improved performance. A simple exhortation to clarify goals, however, ignores the alternative threat of premature or inappropriate goal specification that can lead to dysfunctions. The evidence reported earlier in this chapter about the relations between goal ambiguity and performance was limited due to low R^2s and reliance on subjective performance measures. This is consistent with the interpretation that the relationship between goal clarification and performance is complex, with the strength of that linkage depending on such factors as the validity and appropriateness of the stated goals and their levels of specificity, as well as the implementation and use of the goal statements in evaluation processes.

Proposition 2: Government agencies will face greater challenges in goal specification when they are subject to political salience (as defined earlier), and when they perform complex tasks and implement complex policies.

Higher levels of political attention and influence on the agency, technically complex tasks involving highly professionalized workforces, and complex policy objectives (as often observed in regulatory policies) will make goal specification more challenging.

Proposition 3: Government programmes that state clear goals and performance measures in appropriate and valid ways will achieve higher levels of performance than those that do not.

The evidence, described earlier in this chapter, of a linkage between clear goals and performance targets in government programmes is stronger than the evidence of such a linkage in government agencies. The evidence does rely on the PART evaluations of programme performance, which are controversial and limited in ways described earlier. Still, where programme representatives are able to state clearer performance objectives and targets, the programmes received higher performance ratings. Again, however, a simple prescription to clarify goals and specify targets is not justified, since conditions such as programme type (e.g. regulatory versus non-regulatory and direct versus third party), programme size, and programme management and planning capacity can influence the ability of programme representatives to specify goals clearly. Even taking such conditions into account, however, the evidence suggests that investment in specifying programme goals in appropriate and valid ways contributes to higher levels of programme performance.

REFERENCES

Allison, Graham T. 1983. 'Public and private management: are they fundamentally alike in all unimportant respects?', in James L. Perry and Kenneth L. Kraemer (eds.) *Public Management*. Palo Alto: Mayfield.

Barton, Allen H. 1980. 'A diagnosis of bureaucratic maladies', in Carol H. Weiss and Allen H. Barton (eds.) *Making Bureaucracies Work*. Thousand Oaks, CA: Sage.

Bandura, Albert. 1989. 'Self-regulation of motivation and action through internal standards and goal systems', in Lawrence A. Pervin (ed.) *Goal Concepts in Personality and Social Psychology*. Hillsdale, NJ: Lawrence Erlbaum, pp. 19–85.

Baum, Lawrence. 1976. 'Implementation of judicial decisions: an organizational analysis', *American Politics Quarterly*, 4, 1, 86–114.

Behn, Robert D. 2001. *Rethinking Democratic Accountability*. Washington, DC: Brookings Institution.

Berman, Paul. 1978. 'The study of macro- and micro-implementation', *Public Policy*, 26, 2, 157–84.

Berman, Paul, and Milbrey McLaughlin. 1976. 'Implementation of educational innovation', *Educational Forum*, 40, 3, 347–70.

Blumenthal, Michael. 1983. 'Candid reflections of a businessman in Washington', in James L. Perry and Kenneth L. Kraemer (eds.) *Public Management*. Palo Alto: Mayfield.

Bohte, John, and Kenneth J. Meier. 2000. 'Goal displacement: assessing the motivation for organizational cheating', *Public Administration Review*, 60, 2, 173–82.

Boyatzis, Richard E. 1982. *The Competent Manager*. New York: Wiley.

Buchanan, Bruce. 1974. 'Government managers, business executives, and organizational commitment', *Public Administration Review*, 34, 4, 339–47.

1975. 'Some unexpected differences between public and private managers', *Administration & Society*, 6, 4, 423–44.

Carpenter, Daniel P. 2001. *The Forging of Bureaucratic Autonomy*. Princeton, NJ: Princeton University Press.

Chun, Young Han. 2003. 'Goal ambiguity in public organizations: dimensions, antecedents, and consequences', Ph.D. dissertation, University of Georgia.

Chun, Young Han, and Hal G. Rainey. 2005a. 'Goal ambiguity in US federal agencies', *Journal of Public Administration Research and Theory*, 15, 1, 1–30.

2005b. 'Goal ambiguity and organizational performance in US federal agencies', *Journal of Public Administration Research and Theory*, 15, 4, 529–57.

Daft, Richard L. 2007. *Organization Theory and Design*, 9th edn. Mason, OH: Thomson/ South-Western.

Dahl, Robert A., and Charles E. Lindblom. 1953. *Politics, Economics, and Welfare*. New York: Harper.

Downs, Anthony. 1967. *Inside Bureaucracy*. Boston: Little, Brown.

Drucker, Peter F. 1980. 'The deadly sins in public administration', *Public Administration Review*, 40, 2, 103–6.

Feldman, Martha S. 1989. *Order Without Design: Information Production and Policy Making*. Stanford University Press.

Ford, James 1997. 'Earnings by level of work: results from pilot studies of the national compensation survey program', *Compensation and Working Conditions*, Summer, 24–31.

Frederickson, David G., and George H. Frederickson. 2006. *Measuring the Performance of the Hollow State*. Washington, DC: Georgetown University Press.

Frumkin, Peter, and Joseph Galaskiewicz. 2003. 'Institutional isomorphism of the public sector', *Journal of Public Administration Research and Theory*, 14, 3, 283–307.

Gable, Cate. 1998. *Strategic Action Planning Now! A Guide for Setting and Meeting your Goals*. Boca Raton, FL: St. Lucie Press.

General Accounting Office (GAO). 1997. *Managing for Results: Prospects for Effective Implementation of the Government Performance Results Act*. GAO/AIMD-97-113.

Gilmour, John B. 2006. *Implementing OMB's Program Assessment Rating Tool (PART)*. Washington, DC: IBM Center for the Business of Government.

Gilmour, John B., and David E. Lewis. 2006. 'Assessing performance budgeting at OMB: the influence of politics, performance, and program size', *Journal of Public Administration Research and Theory*, 16, 2, 169–86.

Grizzle, Gloria A. 1982. 'Measuring state and local government performance: issues to resolve before implementing a performance measurement system', *State and Local Government Review*, 14, 3, 132–6.

2002. 'Performance measurement and dysfunction: the dark side of quantifying work', *Public Performance and Management Review*, 25, 4, 363–69.

Hambleton, Robin. 1983. 'Planning systems and policy implementation', *Journal of Public Policy*, 3, 4, 397–418.

Heinrich, Carolyn J. 1999. 'Do government bureaucrats make effective use of performance management information?', *Journal of Public Administration Research and Theory*, 9, 3, 363–93.

2003. 'Measuring public sector performance and effectiveness', in Guy B. Peters and Jon Pierre (eds.) *Handbook of Public Administration*. London: Saga Publications, pp. 25–37.

2007. 'False or fitting recognition? The use of high performance bonuses in motivating organizational achievements', *Journal of Policy Analysis and Management*, 26, 2, 281–304.

Hickson, David J., R. J. Butler, D. Cray, G. R. Mallory, and David C. Wilson. 1986. *Top Decisions: Strategic Decision Making in Organizations*. San Francisco: Jossey-Bass.

Huber, John D., and Charles R. Shipan. 2002. *Deliberate Discretion: The Institutional Foundations of Bureaucratic Autonomy*. New York: Cambridge University Press.

Ingraham Patricia W., and Amy K. Donahue. 2003. 'Dissecting the black box revisited: characterizing government management capacity', in Laurence E. Lynn (ed.) *Models and Methods for the Empirical Study of Governance*. Washington, DC: Georgetown University Press.

Ingraham, Patricia. W., Philip G. Joyce, and Amy Kneedler Donahue. 2003. *Government Performance: Why Management Matters*. Baltimore, MD: Johns Hopkins University Press.

Jung, Chan Su. 2009. 'Goals, ambiguity, and performance in US federal programs and agencies', Ph.D. dissertation, University of Georgia.

Jung, Chan Su, and Hal G. Rainey. 2008. 'Developing the concept of program goal ambiguity and explaining federal program performance', Best Conference Papers, *Academy of Management Proceedings of the Annual Meeting of the Academy of Management*, Anaheim, California, August 8–13.

Khademian, Anne M. 1995. 'Reinventing a government corporation: professional priorities and a clear bottom line', *Public Administration Review*, 55, 1, 17–28.

Kiousis, Spiro. 2004. 'Explicating media salience: a factor analysis of New York Times issue coverage during the 2000 US Presidential election', *Journal of Communication*, 54, 1, 71–87.

Lan, Zhiyong, and Hal G. Rainey. 1992. 'Goals, rules, and effectiveness in public, private, and hybrid organizations: more evidence on frequent assertions about differences', *Journal of Public Administration Research and Theory*, 2, 1, 5–28.

Latham, Gary P., Laura Borgogni, and Laura Petitta. 2008. 'Goal setting and performance management in the public sector', *International Public Management Journal*, 11, 4, 385–403.

Lee, Jung Wook. 2006. 'The political environment of public organizations: political salience, structural insulation, and goal ambiguity in US federal agencies', Ph.D. dissertation, University of Georgia.

Lee, Jung Wook, Hal G. Rainey, and Young Han Chun. 2009. 'Of politics and purpose: political salience and goal ambiguity of US federal agencies', *Public Administration*, 87, 3, 457–84.

Forthcoming. 'Goal ambiguity, work complexity and work routineness in federal agencies', *American Review of Public Administration*. (Online: 2009 DOI:10.1177/0275074009337620.)

Lee, Thomas W., Edwin A. Locke, and Gary P. Latham. 1989. 'Goal setting theory and job performance', in Lawrence A. Pervin (ed.) *Goal Concepts in Personality and Social Psychology*. Hillsdale, NJ: Lawrence Erlbaum.

Lewis, David E. 2008. *The Politics of Presidential Appointments: Political Control and Bureaucratic Performance*. Princeton, NJ: Princeton University Press.

Lindblom, Charles E. 1959. 'The science of "muddling through"', *Public Administration Review*, 19, 2, 79–88.

1977. *Politics and Markets*. New York: Basic Books.

Lowi, Theodore J. 1972. 'Four systems of policy, politics, and choice', *Public Administration Review*, 32, 4, 298–310.

1979. *The End of Liberalism*. New York: Norton.

Lynn, Laurence E. 1981. *Managing the Public's Business*. New York: Basic Books.

March, James G., Johan P. Olsen *et al.* 1976. *Ambiguity and Choice in Organizations*. Bergen: Universitetsforlaget.

Matland, Richard E. 1995. 'Synthesizing the implementation literature: the ambiguity-conflict model of policy implementation', *Journal of Public Administration Research and Theory*, 5, 2, 145–74.

May, Peter J. Samuel Workman, and Bryan D. Jones. 2008. 'Organizing attention: responses of the bureaucracy to agenda disruption', *Journal of Public Administration Research and Theory*, 18, 4, 517–41.

Meier, Kenneth J. 1980. 'Measuring organizational power: resources and autonomy of government agencies', *Administration & Society*, 12, 3, 357–75.

2000. *Politics and the Bureaucracy*. Fort Worth, TX: Harcourt College Publishing Company.

Meyer, Marshall W. 1979. *Change in Public Bureaucracies*. Cambridge University Press.

Meyers, Marcia K., Norma M. Riccucci, and Irene Lurie. 2001. 'Achieving goal congruence in complex environments: the case of welfare reform', *Journal of Public Administration Research and Theory*, 11, 2, 165–201.

Miller, Alex, and Gregory G. Dess. 1993. *Strategic Management*. New York: McGraw-Hill.

Moore, Mark H. 1995. *Creating Public Value: Strategic Management in Government*. Cambridge, MA: Harvard University Press.

Moynihan, Donald P. 2008. *The Dynamics of Performance Management: Constructing Information and Reform*. Washington, DC: Georgetown University Press.

Noll, Roger G. 1971. *Reforming Regulation*. Washington, DC: Brookings Institution.

Office of Management and Budget (OMB). 2006. *Guidance for Completing 2006 PARTs*. Available at www.whitehouse.gov/omb/part/index.html.

Pandey, Sanjay K., and James L. Garnett. 2006. 'Exploring public sector communication performance: testing a model and drawing implications', *Public Administration Review*, 66, 1, 37–51.

Perry, James L., Ann M. Thompson, Mary Tschirhart, Debra Mesch, and Geunjoo Lee. 1999. 'Inside a Swiss army knife: an assessment of AmeriCorps', *Journal of Public Administration Research and Theory*, 9, 2, 225–50.

Pitt, Douglas C., and Brian C. Smith. 1981. *Government Departments: An Organizational Perspective*. London: Routledge & Kegan Paul.

Rainey, Hal G. 1983. 'Public agencies and private firms: incentive structures, goals, and individual roles', *Administration & Society*, 15, 2, 207–42.

1993. 'Toward a theory of goal ambiguity in public organizations', in James L. Perry (ed.) *Research in Public Administration*. Greenwich, CT: JAI Press.

2003. 'Work motivation', in Jack Rabin (ed.) *Encyclopedia of Public Administration and Public Policy*. New York: Marcel Dekker.

Forthcoming. 'Analyzing the goals of government agencies: research on organizational goal ambiguity', in Robert F. Durant (ed.) *The Oxford Handbook of American Bureaucracy*. Oxford University Press.

Rainey, Hal G., Robert W. Backoff, and Charles H. Levine. 1976. 'Comparing public and private organizations', *Public Administration Review*, 36, 2, 233–44.

Rainey, Hal G., Sanjay K. Pandey, and Barry Bozeman. 1995. 'Public and private managers' perceptions of red tape', *Public Administration Review*, 55, 6, 567–74.

Ripley, Randall B., and Grace A. Franklin. 1982. *Bureaucracy and Policy Implementation*. Homewood, IL: Dorsey Press.

Salamon, Lester M. 2002. 'The new governance and the tools of public action: an introduction', in Lester M. Salamon (ed.) *The Tools of Government: A Guide to the New Governance*. New York: Oxford University Press, 1–47.

Schwenk, Charles R. 1990. 'Conflict in organizational decision making: an exploratory study of its effects in for-profit and not-for-profit organizations', *Management Science*, 36, 4, 436–48.

Scott, W. Richard. 2003. *Organizations: Rational, Natural, and Open Systems*. Englewood Cliffs, NJ: Prentice-Hall.

Smith, Douglas K. 1999. *Make Success Measurable!* New York: John Wiley & Sons.

Thompson, John L. 1997. *Strategic Management: Awareness and Change*. Boston: International Thomson Business Press.

Tolbert, Pamela S. 1985. 'Resource dependence and institutional environments: sources of administrative structure in institutions of higher education', *Administrative Science Quarterly*, 30, 1, 1–13.

Tolbert, Pamela S., and Lynn G. Zucker. 1983. 'Institutional sources of change in the formal structure of organizations: the diffusion of civil service reform, 1880–1935', *Administrative Science Quarterly*, 28, 1, 22–39.

Tullock, Gordon. 1965. *The Politics of Bureaucracy*. Washington, DC: Public Affairs Press.

Warwick, Donald P. 1975. *A Theory of Public Bureaucracy.* Cambridge, MA: Harvard University Press.

Whitford, Andrew B. 2002. 'Decentralization and political control of the bureaucracy', *Journal of Theoretical Politics*, 14, 2,167–93

2005. 'The pursuit of political control by multiple principals', *Journal of Politics*, 67, 29–49.

Wildavsky, Aaron. 1979. *Speaking Truth to Power.* New York: Little, Brown.

Wilson, James Q. 1980. *The Politics of Regulation.* New York: Basic Books.

1989. *Bureaucracy.* New York: Basic Books.

Winter, James P., and Chaim H. Eyal. 1981. 'Agenda setting for the civil rights issue', *Public Opinion Quarterly*, 45, 376–83.

Wood, B. Dan, and Richard W. Waterman. 1994. *Bureaucratic Dynamics: The Role of Bureaucracy in a Democracy.* Boulder, CO: Westview Press.

Worsham, Jeff, and Jay Gatrell. 2005. 'Multiple principals, multiple signals: a signaling approach to principal-agent relations', *Policy Studies Journal*, 33, 3, 363–76.

Wright, Bradley E. 2004. 'The role of work context in work motivation: a public sector application of goal and social cognition theories', *Journal of Public Administration Research and Theory*, 14, 1, 59–78.

3 Budgets and financial management

Donald P. Moynihan and Matthew Andrews

Introduction

Money is the lifeblood of public service provision. It is where 'everything of importance comes together', because '[n]early everything we want government to do requires money' (Kettl 1992: 1). Financial decisions invite conflict, because as White notes, 'perhaps deciding the budget is not the most significant choice in any political system, but it is clearly the most important and controversial decision that is made again and again' (White 1994: 113).

Given the central importance of money, the search for better government performance inevitably interacts with public financial management (PFM) systems. PFM systems represent a series of institutional routines that offer a powerful means to direct bureaucratic behaviour (Campos and Pradhan 1996). Most contemporary reforms that promise improved performance implicitly recognize this, advocating in various ways the reform of resource allocation and financial incentives. Ultimately, reform efforts that fail to align with financial processes represent the folly of rewarding A while expecting B (Kerr 1993).

Despite the centrality of PFM to reform and even the emphasis on resource allocation issues in most reforms, PFM has not always featured prominently in the nascent empirical public administration literature on public service performance. For this reason, this chapter takes a wide-ranging perspective on the relationship between PFM and performance. In addition, the chapter examines efforts to improve the performance of PFM systems. Such reforms are based on doctrinal claims, and scholarship remains split on the most basic questions: What is PFM performance? Why should PFM affect performance outcomes?

One characteristic that differentiates this chapter from others in this volume is the paucity of clear empirical links between the independent variable PFM, and the dependent variable performance. In part this has to do with how we define performance, and in part because of the difficulty of making such links. Relative to the importance of the topic, and to the wealth of prescriptive suggestions, the lack of empirical evidence is surprising. The chapter is also different because it takes a more broadly comparative view than other chapters in this text, covering both developed and developing countries. The comparative analysis illustrates both differences and similarities, in challenges, contextual constraints and potential opportunities. Overall, the chapter illustrates that we know quite a bit about this topic, but also have some very real and important gaps to think further about. Research propositions emerging out of both sets of observations are identified as perspectives on where the literature has reached and a guide for where it still needs to go.

Defining PFM: issues for modelling

PFM systems are complicated sets of routines, involving players in multiple interrelated but often separated processes focused on some aspect of the flow of money into, through and out of government. Figure 3.1 shows a stylized version of this system, ranging from planning through budgeting, resource management (cash, procurement and debt, for example), internal control and audit, accounting and reporting, external audit and legislative oversight mechanisms. The different subcomponents essentially connect planning functions to execution functions and produce information on the connection between the two, allowing verification by oversight bodies. The budgeting processes and reforms tend to enjoy disproportionate attention in scholarship on PFM, but these components are followed by internal resource management processes in which money is actually collected and distributed via cash, procurement and human resource management routines. These routines are influenced by the internal control, monitoring and accounting systems in place that provide information about actual resource movement as well as risks emerging in the execution process. These routines then facilitate reporting to broader audiences, and oversight by bodies like external auditors and legislatures, who can ensure legality and efficiency of the spending activity. Over time, all of these routines tend to become more formalized and elaborate, with specific rules and documents identifying how specific actors are to produce information and decisions.

The model of PFM outlined in Figure 3.1 represents contemporary thinking on how such processes should be arranged, incorporating strategic planning, and performance measurement. Increasingly governments are urged to redesign PFM systems to gain a sense of the result of financial transactions. The

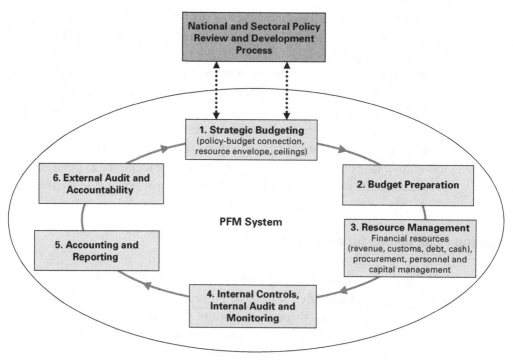

Figure 3.1:   Basic elements in a national PFM system
Source: Andrews (2007).

literature of performance in PFM and actual design of reform efforts define a PFM performance-orientation as occurring when information on non-financial performance (what budgetary entities have done or expect to do with the money flowing in, through and out of the system) is presented in any PFM process area, from planning through to legislative review. Entities seek evidence of performance in the PFM downstream (particularly boxes 4, 5 and 6 in Figure 3.1). This could be an external audit office or legislature asking for evidence of results (in box 6) or central agencies making the demand (via annual reports in box 5) or even managers within agencies holding internal agents accountable for performance (via adjusted internal audit and monitoring mechanisms in box 4).

Different governments may prioritize use of information at different stages of the PFM system. There is evidence of performance information use in areas such as contracting (Behn and Kant 1999; Kelman 2005), debt management (Wheeler 2003), accounting and reporting practices (Guthrie 1998); internal auditing (Diamond 2002); financial reporting (Kloot and Martin 2000; Van Landingham *et al.* 2005), and external performance audits (Barzelay 1997; Pollitt 2003; Andrews 2001; Roberts 2003).

The nature of PFM systems has some implications for how we model its relationship with performance. Collectively, these modelling challenges help to explain why the empirical literature on PFM is not as comprehensive as it might be. Relative to other aspects of public sector management, PFM is often considered a series of technical formal exercises. Such a perspective understates the political aspects of PFM. While the individual processes captured by PFM may be minute and specific, collectively PFM is involved in almost all aspects of governance, from resource allocation, to implementation and accountability. It is, therefore, inextricably tied to political decisions. If politics is about 'who gets what, when, where and how' (Laswell 1990), PFM provides the formal framework in which political disputes are resolved. The implications of this political context in terms of how we consider PFM performance and the factors that shape this performance are discussed below.

An additional problem in cross-sectional studies of PFM systems is whether the variables being considered are actually comparable. Financial practices or reforms that carry the same name are often quite distinct from one another. This reflects the ambiguity of administrative practices (Moynihan 2006). For example, there is a good deal of variation between practices that are collectively described as performance budgeting. Two countries might both have a performance budget, but rely on very different types of performance information. One might utilize cost performance or efficiency information (as in 1950s performance budgeting in the United States and also in more recent activity-based costing reforms worldwide), while another might rely on programme-budget output and outcome performance (manifest, for example, in different forms in New Zealand and Australian reforms dating to the early 1990s). This factor makes comparisons difficult, even before we consider contextual differences across settings.

A related complication is that, to a greater extent than in other treatments of governmental behaviour, research on PFM tends to focus on formal designs. Empirical studies of organizational behaviour do not stop with a description of the organizational chart. But in budgeting description of formal systems or reforms is done often and without reference to actual practice. The gap between formal systems and actual practice is both larger and more consequential for developing countries, which may have sophisticated formal rules that are unrelated to actual practice.

Another aspect of PFM that affects our capacity to model its relationship with performance is its synecdochic qualities, i.e. parts of the PFM systems are often portrayed as representative of the whole, and vice versa. Those seeking to model PFM may seek to model the entire system or significant portions of it. Those who model the entire system run the risk of over-aggregation, over-looking the fact that specific subsystems have their own dynamics, and offering overly broad findings. Researchers who tackle one specific aspect of PFM, and tie it to a relatively narrow measure of performance have the advantage of providing clearer and more plausible causal links, but also offer narrower findings. An example is research on revenue forecasting accuracy (Krause *et al.* 2006). This variable has real importance because an inability to accurately predict revenues undermines fiscal discipline and leads to emergency spending cuts. It is also relatively easy to measure, and has led to interesting findings. For example, Bretschneider and Gorr (1989) and Bretschneider *et al.* (1989) find that partisan and institutional competition results in better forecasts, while Krause *et al.* (2006) find that forecasting offices with a mix of political appointees and career employees tend to do better than governments that are dominated by one or the other.

A pertinent question for researchers, therefore, is what the appropriate level of aggregation is for studying PFM. The studies where the strongest empirical links between PFM and performance emerge also tend to offer the narrowest contributions. In this chapter we present claims and evidence from many different levels of analysis.

What is PFM performance?

Performance is generally understood in the context of efficiency and effectiveness. For PFM, performance is considered more broadly to incorporate three primary goals (Schick 1998a; World Bank 1998): fiscal discipline, allocative quality, and technical or cost efficiency. Each is described below:

- Fiscal discipline is the capacity of a government to live within a predetermined spending target. Fiscal discipline is supported by accurate forecasting, hard budget constraints, and centralized control on spending.
- Allocative quality or efficiency is 'the capacity of government to distribute resources on the basis of the effectiveness of public programs in meeting strategic objectives' (Schick 1998a: 89). It represents better decisions in allocating resources, and therefore applies particularly to budgeters and elected officials. It is supported by information on programme effectiveness, and competition between policies for funding.
- Technical efficiency is also known as cost or operational efficiency, and is the ratio of resources spent relative to outputs generated by the government.

It is aided by providing managers with information on programme efficiency, and the flexibility to act on that information.

Identifying the three goals of PFM is important for three main reasons. First, it makes clear that in PFM the concept of effectiveness is broadly understood to go beyond any narrow conception of performance improvement, a point which researchers and reformers may sometimes miss. Second, the relative importance of the three goals has evolved over time in particular settings, as have the systems to foster these goals, and may be reflected in different ways across countries today. Third, as with any system designed to achieve multiple goals, there may be trade-offs between the goals: rules that ensure fiscal constraint may also limit the capacity for technical efficiency, for example. The interplay of these factors is discussed in greater detail below.

In one crucial respect, the three outcomes identified above are incomplete. They represent a view of PFM consistent with administrative traditions and the scholarship of public finance. Ultimately, it is elected officials who are responsible for the design of such systems, and they are often concerned with maximizing political values, such as transparency, political dialogue, or democratic control. Whether one would describe such values as indicators of performance or not is a matter of debate (for different perspectives see the exchange between Rosenbloom (2007), and Ammons and Stenberg (2007)), but they are clearly goals that PFM systems, to varying degrees, are intended to achieve. In some cases they may have little to do with the three goals noted above, and in some cases such goals may actively conflict with them. But a full conception of PFM and performance cannot ignore these values.

For example, the Programming Planning Budgeting System (PPBS) implemented by US Defense Secretary Robert McNamara in the 1960s represents one of the most influential efforts to reorganize PFM processes, and is usually considered in terms of its efforts to maximize all three of the goals outlined above. But this is only part of the story of PPBS. McNamara also used it as a tool to seek to reassert civilian control over the military, especially as the Vietnam War escalated (Chwastiak 2001). Indeed, many reforms to PFM systems are popular because they are hoped to provide greater transparency and political control over bureaucrats (Moynihan 2008).

The key point that emerges is that PFM performance is not simple and uni-dimensional. Even if we were to agree that only the three goals listed above are appropriate measures of performance, these goals tend to be vague, overlapping and sometimes contradictory. Other democratic values are also fused into PFM systems. Politics therefore shapes the performance of PFM systems, and political values can be considered alternative measures of PFM performance, observations which drive the proposition that:

> *Proposition 1*: PFM performance is difficult to measure, involving vague, overlapping and sometimes contradictory goals that are ultimately shaped by political values.

The evolution of PFM performance

To understand contemporary thinking on the relationship between PFM and performance we must take a short detour through the evolution of PFM, which frames our second proposition:

> *Proposition 2*: PFM performance is contextually dependent, with focal points changing as governments develop and face new challenges.

Historically, the pursuit of fiscal discipline control emerges from the desire to limit corruption, assert political control and maintain fiscal probity. Mikesell points out that the early versions of PFM systems 'emerged in a period where concern was, purely and simply, prevention of theft' (Mikesell 1995: 165). But such systems were also used as a means to ensure that statutory intent was followed. In the United States, for example, colonial assemblies used to specify items where it was permissible for the government to spend money in an effort to control governors appointed by the British monarchy. As government has grown, this desire for control has been accompanied by a need to ensure that spending does not exceed the means of the economy. To do so, central budget offices enforce controls on agencies, ensuring that they spend money on the specific items authorized. This effectively limits the discretion of agency officials in allocating resources. This is a useful *ex ante* protection in cases where managers are irresponsible or corrupt. But it also prevents managers from reallocating resources to pursue allocative or technical efficiency.

In recent decades, reforms have sought to better focus PFM systems toward allocative and technical efficiency. 'Reform is the Holy Grail of budget people, their unending quest for a better way to parcel out money and plan the work of government' (Schick 2002a: 8). Schick makes the case that the focus on performance represented a Copernican turn in the evolution of PFM, representing a significant challenge to received wisdoms about how formal systems, incentives and flexibilities should interact and what they are expected to produce.

Among reformers, traditional budget systems were portrayed as too rule-bound, without incentives or information that would allow actors to use money wisely. Changes to PFM systems, often proposed in the context of the New Public Management, were portrayed as a form of modernization, consistent with a belief that traditional budget systems were designed for simpler times, when government was smaller and took on less complex responsibilities.

Scholarship on financial management reflects the preoccupation with reform, though generally focuses more on prescribing and describing reforms rather than testing whether reforms have actually improved performance. Nevertheless, the logic of reform provides the basis for some broad hypotheses which researchers can examine. In the sections below, we summarize the basic logic behind these hypotheses, and then review relevant empirical evidence. A consistent pattern is that the empirical evidence suggests that the link between the independent variable and performance is more fragmented, contingent and uncertain than reformers tend to acknowledge.

Incentives

Traditional budgeting systems were criticized as providing incentives that were obstructive to performance, resulting in larger government, continued investment in failed public policies and little regard for efficiency. These arguments were made most forcefully by public choice economists, who argued that excessive public spending and inattention to outcomes were the logical outcome of incentive failures (Niskanen 1971; Kraan 1996). The central logic of these criticisms, sometimes explicit, sometimes not, was an institutional one. Institutional theory was applied to argue that the rules and norms represented by PFM systems could have a significant influence on incentives, behaviour and outcomes (Poterba and Von Hagen 1998; Campos and Pradhan 1996; World Bank 1998). Performance-oriented adjustments to rules and information content could change incentives and improve performance (Ingraham *et al.* 2008). This logic could be captured in the following proposition.

> *Proposition 3A*: Traditional budgeting norms and institutions do not align self-interest with positive outcomes, and therefore reduce PFM performance.

The stability of traditional PFM systems offered some benefits. Predictability of roles and rules reduces uncertainty and the potential for conflict (Wildavsky and Caiden 2003). But reformers saw stubborn, outdated systems that limited innovation and the capacity to improve performance. In particular, they targeted incrementalism, the acceptance of previous spending as a base upon which to establish current spending. The great virtue of incrementalism is that it makes the budget process easier – by accepting agreements from previous years, the potential for conflict in the current year is minimized. But to achieve this accord previously established policies are protected from serious evaluation or competition with new policy alternatives, allowing budgets to grow over time. PFM systems that accepted incrementalism as an institutional norm might pay close attention to the rate and probity of spending patterns, but not to whether spending itself is effective. Of course, much depends on the effectiveness of initial investments. Where existing budgets are generating better performance, incrementalism fosters policy stability, which in turn results in better policy outcomes. Andersen and Mortensen (2010) report such a finding in their study of Danish School performance. This gives rise to a more positive view of incrementalism.

Proposition 3B: Incremental resource allocation patterns foster policy stability and higher performance.

Public choice scholars argued that budget growth was not just a function of incremental inattention to past allocations, but a direct result of bureaucratic self-interest, as increased budgets give bureaucrats greater access to salary, people and power (Niskanen 1971). While very influential, Niskanen's arguments have been criticized on a number of grounds. First, bureaucrats have little direct capacity to personally benefit from larger budgets, since salaries are fixed and large items of spending must be approved by central budget agencies (Siegelman 1996). Second, larger budgets are associated with more responsibilities, which rational bureau chiefs will often seek to minimize (Dunleavy 1991). Third, bureaucrats do not dominate elected officials, who generally have a stronger self-interest in maximizing budgets (re-election) than bureaucrats do (Forrester 2001).

It is possible that while Niskanen was wrong in his assumptions of bureaucratic motivations, his contention that bureaucrats try to maximize budgets could be defended on the basis of more altruistic motives. For example, bureaucrats might seek to maximize budgets because they sincerely believe in the benefit of their programmes (Siegelman 1996). However, a cross-time survey of bureau chiefs in US states revealed marked heterogeneity in budgetary preferences, undermining claims of consistent budget maximization (Bowling *et al.* 2004). The survey also suggested that the budgetary aspirations of bureau chiefs have declined over time. Other research finds that US federal managers prefer less spending than the public, even on issues that fall within their own departments' jurisdictions (Dolan 2002). These findings suggest that bureau chiefs have accommodated their preferences to fit an era where more conservative politics and tax limitations have slowed the growth of government, and made scarcity and cutbacks a new norm (see also Bartle 2001; Hou and Moynihan 2008). The finding also suggests that bureau chiefs are operating in an environment where they must be increasingly aware of the efficiency of their limited allocations, which undercuts another standard criticism of traditional budget systems.

Given the apparent heterogeneity in incentives and motivations of agents involved in PFM, it becomes simplistic to assert that efforts to improve performance can rely on any particular set of incentives or behaviour. An alternative to proposition 3A is as follows:

> *Proposition 3C*: As public officials moderate demands to fit institutional norms and resources, incentive-based reforms will have varying effects on performance.

Performance information

Another critique of traditional PFM systems was a preoccupation with inputs without consideration of results. Proposals to make PFM systems more performance oriented usually take the form of adding the collection and dissemination of performance data to existing routines, and linking that data to decision venues (Moynihan 2008). The logic of such reforms is that performance information will cause budgeters and elected officials to become less concerned with inputs, and more focused on providing allocations according to strategic goals, observing whether these goals are achieved and holding managers accountable for results. In addition, more performance information is expected to improve technical efficiency by adding transparency to the production function, making shirking more difficult, and increasing the potential for learning and process re-engineering. In short:

> *Proposition 4A*: More and better-quality performance information will lead to higher PFM performance.

The possible link between performance information and fiscal discipline is less clear. Reforms promise to improve this goal only indirectly, on the assumption that cost savings and better allocation of resources will mean less expenditure overall. One possible and relatively underutilized measure of perceived fiscal discipline are market perceptions of government default risks. There should be a positive relationship between these perceptions and performance indicators, given that bond-rating agencies pushed for governments to adopt performance reporting practices. Plummer *et al.* (2007) find weak evidence of the link between measures of financial performance and actual perceptions of creditworthiness, but Denison, *et al.* (2007) suggest that management performance indicators, as reflected in school district data, are positively associated with the bond ratings of these districts.

The area where the use of performance information has garnered greatest attention is in resource allocation (Schick 2002b; Bourdeaux 2006). The United States interest in performance budgeting, for example, began in the 1950s (following the Hoover Commission) largely because growth in government in the 1930s and 1940s led to increased demand for non-financial performance information to be used in both allocating money and holding government accountable. This demand also motivated the introduction of PPBS in the 1960s and the passage of the Government Performance and Results Act in 1993. Among New Public Management adopters such as New Zealand and Australia, the adoption of accrual accounting was presented as appropriate largely because it was the approach that modern private organizations had adopted as they moved away from traditional forms of cash accounting that governments still favoured.

Traditional cash-based accounting methods failed to fully allocate overhead or depreciation costs for services, or identify the per unit cost of a service. Creating per unit costs was hoped to enable decisions based on efficiency, for example, whether it was worthwhile maintaining or contracting out a service. The variants of such accounting changes include activity-based costing and accrual accounting. Moving to cost information was based on the belief that the format of information in PFM matters. Give people line item budgets, and they will care about line items. Give them performance budgets and cost information and they will focus on results (Grizzle 1986; Lynch and Lynch 1997).

But there is significant disagreement about how tight the link should be between the information and decisions. Advocates of rigid performance-based budgets call for 'a budget that explicitly links each increment in resources to an increment in outputs or other results' (Schick 2003: 101).

This view of performance-driven budgeting would utilize the PFM to introduce quasi-market conditions in budgeting where results constitute a bottom line – if an agency produces results, it gets more money and thrives, if not it gets less and dies. Others have criticized such a tight link between performance and resources. For example, Posner suggests that 'performance budgeting is not about a mechanical link between performance trends and budget decisions' (Moynihan 2008: 7). A pure performance budget robs budgeters of the discretion to incorporate other relevant information in decisions. It is generally resisted in funding core government agencies, though sometimes is reflected in contracts with third-party providers. So instead of a mechanistic performance-based budgeting, we are more likely to see what Joyce (2003) refers to as performance-informed budgeting, where information is available but not determinative as to the resource allocation outcome. This informs our proposition that:

> *Proposition 4B*: Performance information can influence, but does not determine, specific budget decisions, or the degree to which governments meet fiscal discipline and efficiency goals.

Evidence on performance information and allocative efficiency

So, have the benefits of performance budgeting come to pass? There is not a strong evidentiary base that they have. In part, this is because it is not clear what success means. For example, the concept of allocative efficiency makes sense, but trying to operationalize it in practice is inherently subjective. There may be examples where cost–benefit analyses can demonstrate the superiority of one programme over another, but definitions of what is important are driven by political values that lack a common basis for comparison. For example, the perceived relative benefits of education versus defence expenditures are driven by an individual's predisposition toward one function or the other.

A relatively modest intermediate measure of whether performance information affects performance is a behavioural measure of whether individuals are actually using performance data to make decisions. Some survey data has begun to identify the factors associated with performance-informed budgeting. Collectively, this research suggests that the relationship between performance information and its use to actually improve performance is contingent on a variety of alternative organizational factors. The nature of the task will shape ease of measurement, which in turn is likely to shape use (Askim *et al.* 2008; Dull 2009; Radin 2006). There is evidence that the quality and availability of the data fosters use (de Lancer Julnes and Holzer 2001; Bourdeaux and Chikoto 2008; Moynihan and Ingraham 2004). Supportive leadership has also been associated with the use of performance data (Askim, Johnsen and Christophersen 2008; Andrews 2006; Dull 2009; Melkers and Willoughby 2005; Moynihan and Ingraham 2004). Organizational culture also matters, with more goal-oriented cultures associated with use (de Lancer Julnes and Holzer 2001).

Andrews and Hill's (2003) review of the literature on the impact of performance information on budgeting leads them to conclude that there is little evidence of systematic use; governments that have performance budgeting systems are not likely to spend less (indeed Klase and Dougherty [2002] find the opposite); there has been less research than one would expect; and that such research struggles with methodological problems.

Even as research is beginning to identify factors associated with performance information use, it does not appear that the level of use indicates the dramatic changes in decision making that would be required to suggest a new focus on allocative efficiency. Comparative analyses of budgeting practices among the OECD suggest that performance data is not strongly influencing either allocation or management decisions in wealthier countries: 'In most cases, they have not completely transformed or shifted systems away from inputs' (Curristine 2005: 124).

A detailed example comes from the USA, where the George W. Bush administration pushed the integration of performance data with the budget process by creating formal routines of programme analysis, and connecting these evaluations to the budget. The Program Assessment Rating Tool (PART) was a set of standard questions that US Office of Management and Budget (OMB) examiners, in consultation with agency representatives, used to assess federal programmes. It collated information from existing performance indicators and programme evaluations. The OMB 'PARTed' 1,016 programmes (approximately 98 per cent of the federal budget) over a five-year period. By requiring budget examiners to undertake the performance evaluation, the OMB hoped that their employees would take the connection between budgeting and performance more seriously. PART assessments did seem to have some influence within the White House. They were discussed in OMB budget meetings (Moynihan 2008) and were correlated with changes in programme allocations in the President's budget proposal (Gilmour and Lewis 2006). But the US Congress, the institution where the budget is actually made, largely ignored PART. Significant funding changes or programme reorganizations based on PART analyses were explicitly rejected.

Efforts to make budget formats more performance oriented can raise the ire of legislators, who may prefer objects of expenditure that serve as a source of power and accountability. For example, the Bush administration asked agencies to organize their budget by fully costed outputs. This has not always been easy, as agencies varied in how they treated overhead costs. A more serious problem was that legislators objected to the process, saying that the new budget formats had removed valuable information, and the performance budgets had limited utility. In some cases legislators used statutory language to force agencies to continue to use the traditional budget format (Moynihan 2008).

The limited evidence on poorer countries again does not suggest significant changes in allocative efficiency. A Tanzanian study suggests that 'the allocative process shows little responsiveness to performance of spending units' (World Bank, 2003: vi). Research on potential reform impacts in Ghana and Bolivia do not disentangle reform effects from other influences (Oduro 2002; Montes and Andrews 2005). Reforms with a performance orientation have less than anticipated effects in these and other developing country settings, given factors discussed above. The evidence on allocative efficiency therefore provides further support for proposition 4B, with additional insight on the importance of political and organizational processes, discussed further below.

Evidence on performance information and technical efficiency

In the area of technical efficiency, the evidence is more promising. There are certainly cases where the provision of targets appears to have improved objective (Boyne and Chen 2007; Kelman and Friedman 2009) or subjective (Brewer 2005) performance measures.

The use of activity-based costing to create competition between public and private contractors in the City of Indianapolis became a model that other governments attempted to emulate (Andrews and Moynihan 2002). But other research questions how widely and how deeply such techniques have been adopted, and the impact they have had. In Australia, one of the pioneers of the accrual accounting method, Carlin and Guthrie (2003) find a gap between rhetoric and reality. The outputs used to derive per unit costs underwent dramatic change from year to year, making it difficult to sustain cost comparisons. They also noted that the managerial culture did not incorporate the new costing methods: 'Where an internal management shift does not take place, there is no reason to expect, simply because the format and content of external budget documents changes, measurably improved organizational economy, efficiency or effectiveness' (Carlin and Guthrie 2003: 156).

The Bush administration pursued competitive sourcing, and promised to use activity-based costing for services being bid for competition. Federal workers have won the vast majority of competitions – 83 per cent of total jobs competed between 2003 and 2007 (OMB 2007). In part, this is because of real cost cutting. Agencies developed detailed plans to limit costs, and the OMB (2007) has claimed billions in savings. But there are other reasons. Many of the programmes bid out were small, and generated little private sector interest. Public sector unions were successful in lobbying the US Congress to make outsourcing more difficult, by limiting bids to cost comparisons while excluding considerations of possible performance improvements, by banning efforts to require a certain percentage of jobs to be competed, by excluding the typically more generous government benefits from cost comparisons, and by allowing employees to protest sourcing awards. As a result, the process often features limited actual competition, and a streamlined approach to cost accounting. But the results seem consistent with the observations of Andrews and Moynihan (2002), who found that governments did not necessarily have to actually implement full managed competition to benefit from the process of taking a hard look at their costs. Instead, cost savings were prompted by the provision of new information and top-down pressure to perform.

There are some difficulties in interpreting the relationship between performance data and actual technical efficiency. One is that the pursuit of improvement is driven by organizational factors described in the previous section, such as leadership, culture and task. It is difficult to control for the influence of such factors when considering the performance impacts of budget reforms, but it is clear that without these factors, performance data is not enough. While results-based reforms can force managers to create and share performance data, other factors shape whether this information is actually used in positive ways.

Even if performance information does foster performance improvement efforts in some instances, it is difficult to know its sum effect because other important factors are rarely accounted for, including the transaction costs involved in actually creating and applying data, or potential gaming responses that weaken technical efficiency (see Boyne, Chapter 9, in this volume for more detail). If important aspects of performance are unmeasured, it also becomes difficult to speculate about trade-offs between goals. In sum, then, while there are certainly examples of how performance information has fostered performance-oriented behaviour, the evidence is far from overwhelming, but we can propose a relationship:

> *Proposition 4C*: Performance information can improve the technical efficiency of spending, but is contingent upon adjustments in organizational factors (like leadership, culture and task).

The role of politics

The lack of clear evidence on the link between performance information and performance partially reflects the influence of politics and political structures on the relationship. It is tempting to view performance data as a means to cut through the clutter of ideological disagreements and generate consensus on what really matters. But performance information is almost always incomplete, ambiguous and up for debate. For most programmes and goals there will be multiple ways of measuring performance, and actors can choose to emphasize the ones that suit their interests. For example, the failure of the Bush administration to implement performance budgeting does not mean that the US Congress is not interested in performance data. Legislators are very adept at requesting specific performance information in statute (Moynihan 2008). But, thus far, they have not shown a great deal of interest in organizing the budget around performance indicators.

Performance data is also ambiguous. It tells us that something happened, but not whether that performance was good or bad, or how it was achieved. It does not tell us whether to provide more or less resources to a programme (i.e. should we reward high performers or assume that lower performing programmes need the money more?). This has certain implications for efforts to pursue performance. Within homogeneous groups there is likely to be greater agreement about goals than within heterogeneous groups, suggesting that we are more likely to see consensus within public organizations than in cross-institutional debate (Moynihan 2008).

Important structural factors include the respective roles of the legislature and the executive in the budget process; the use of federalist or unitary structures; the degree of centralization of the public administration system; and the relative power of the Ministry of Finance and the wider institutional structure. For example, it seems likely that political systems with a dominant authority can define performance and force others to go along with it. Perhaps because of this Pollitt (2005) argues that majoritarian, single-party governments institute performance-based changes more readily than others. The UK provides an example of where a centralized system aggressively uses performance information, with the national government willing to impose specific performance standards on both national agencies and local government (Bevan and Hood 2006; Boyne and Chen 2007). Such an approach also characterizes contracting relationships (Dias and Maynard Moody 2007; Heinrich and Choi 2007). This approach does focus attention on measured performance, but has also been associated with gaming of measures, and displacement of unmeasured aspects of performance.

In settings where political power is more widely distributed, or where central authorities choose not to define performance, the prospect that performance data will actually foster consensus around budget decisions is significantly lessened, and it becomes more likely that performance data is characterized by subjectivity, advocacy and disagreement (Moynihan 2008). Different actors will look at the same data and interpret it differently, or select different data to make their point. Roles exacerbate advocacy, as actors will be informed by their institutional interests in using data. The US system, characterized by diffuse power, easy access for advocacy groups, and a tradition of giving agencies great discretion in selecting their measures, exemplifies the conditions under which performance data will be used for advocacy purposes. In such a situation, we should expect performance data not to simplify the budget process, but according to Richard Nathan (2005), to 'complexify' it. This might appear to be a performance free-for-all that undercuts the benefits of performance budgeting. After all, it is more difficult to focus on performance when we disagree on what performance means. But a silver lining of this looser, more advocacy-friendly environment is that because actors have discretion in data selection, they have less incentive to engage in the type of moral hazard that is encouraged when agents are forced to use targets of another's choosing.

Overall then, the role of politics makes the theoretical link between performance information and performance more complex, but it does imply some specific theoretical relationships.

> *Proposition 5A*: Performance information will be selected, disseminated and interpreted consistent with the political or institutional purposes of the actors involved.

Proposition 5B: Performance information is more likely to be used to make decisions in homogeneous, centralized political systems.

Flexibility

A PFM-performance orientation also requires having appropriate amounts of flexibility, especially in the resource management box (box 3 in Figure 3.1) where processes impact the way managers buy goods and services and employ people (through cash, procurement and human resource systems, for example). If managers are expected to produce results, they must be given some authority over the resources they have to do so.

For example, Thompson (1994) makes the argument that agencies in the US federal government were unable to exploit performance management reforms because conventional operational budgets required high levels of control and thus undermined flexibility. Having performance standards and incentives to improve, therefore, was not sufficient to foster greater performance. The logic of this argument is as follows:

Proposition 6A: Managers need greater PFM flexibility to make the changes necessary to achieve PFM performance.

There are a number of rationales for this proposition. If agencies fail to spend allocated resources by the end of the budget cycle, they typically are required to return these resources to the central budget office, and may be perceived as needing a lower budget in future years (Klay 1987). There is, therefore, an incentive to spend down any remaining resources at the end of the fiscal year. Similarly, by not allowing agencies to switch money between programmes, or even between fairly specific objects of expenditures, managers lack the ability to find more efficient or effective use of resources to meet changing needs.

It is difficult to find clear evidence that financial flexibility has in fact improved performance. One problem is the relatively limited provision of true flexibility in practice. Many governments have been cautious in providing agencies with new authority, reflecting a continuing desire to maintain control over spending items. At the same time, such governments are often happy to demand the creation of new performance data and standards, since such changes generally increase rather than threaten political control (Moynihan 2008).

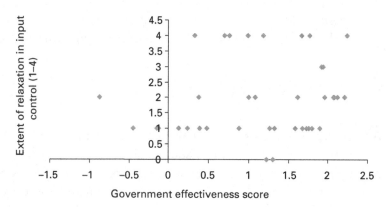

Figure 3.2:   Input control relaxation and government effectiveness scores

Comparative evidence suggests that there is a good deal of variation in the extent to which countries have pursued flexibility in their PFM system, but that this variation does not seem to be significantly associated with effectiveness. Figure 3.2 shows the major differences that exist between thirty-eight governments completing the 2007 OECD Budget Practices and Procedures Database, when asked about how much flexibility exists in the PFM system. Countries that retained rigid *ex ante* controls on agency spending scored lower, while countries where agencies had significant discretion in spending scored higher. Figure 3.2 shows these scores on the vertical axis, and the World Bank's World Governance Index (WGI) measure for government effectiveness measure (ranging from 2.5 to −1 in the figure) on the horizontal axis (See Andrews 2010 for a full discussion).

The figure shows that many governments no longer have traditional input controls, but there is significant variation between countries. Further, basic tests of differences in means for countries above and below 1 on the government effectiveness score do not yield significant results. Countries deemed more effective are not significantly more likely to have adopted flexibility. This is perhaps one of the reasons why it is difficult to connect flexibility to performance, and so we supplement the above proposition:

> *Proposition 6B*: Government provision of managerial flexibility lags efforts to measure performance.

The enduring role of controls

The arguments for flexibility may understate the value of formal controls. But such controls remain important for a variety of reasons. First, such controls have proved valuable in the development of PFM systems (Mikesell 1995). Schick (1998b) argues that the development of external controls over spending is not just a historical accident, but a necessary precursor to the development of more flexible PFM systems. External controls foster a culture of responsible and accountable spending, making them the first step in a logical sequence of budgeting reforms. The first job of budget systems is to control spending, and only then should they look to create rules and norms that facilitate allocative and technical efficiency.

Second, there are many contemporary settings where flexibility could be abused. For example, among developed countries, the US continues to rely on a relatively high number of political appointees. Perhaps because of the risks that flexibility could become a partisan tool in such a setting, the loosening of financial controls systems has moved relatively slowly. In contrast, other countries that did not have the same tradition of politicized administration were more willing to provide managers with significantly greater control over personnel and other assets. Schick (1998b) argues that among poorer countries, norms of honest behaviour have not been well established in the public sector, and providing flexibility could be disastrous (see also Wescott 2008). This logic has led Schick to argue that poorer countries cannot 'leapfrog' the slow evolution of budgeting systems to adopt some of the reforms they see in more developed countries. By this logic, external controls can foster greater performance in settings where norms of responsible and accountable spending have not been internalized.

A less extreme way of applying Schick's proposition is that there are different kinds of PFM systems, in which governments have different kinds of rules that generally foster certain outcomes better than others. If a government lacks basic capacities in some process areas but has advanced capacities in others, it is highly likely to have a deficient system in all. This is unfortunately the situation in many developing countries that have advanced performance-oriented planning processes but weak accounting and reporting, for instance. Governments like this fail to achieve discipline, allocations quality or cost efficiency.

Another reason to continue to pay attention to formal rules is that they are the primary means by which reform occur. Joyce (2003) lists the various PFM reforms of the twentieth century in terms of formal laws. For example, the addition of performance information to the budget system resulted in new rules and procedures on when and how to collect, disseminate and verify this data. In some settings, these new obligations have been offset by greater flexibility, but in cases such as the United States, budget officials seem to face a greater rule burden now than they did in the pre-reform era.

Finally, there is also empirical evidence on the continued relevance of formal rules to PFM performance in specific areas. For example, Marlowe and Matkin (2009) find that internal control deficiencies are associated with more costly bond sales processes for local governments in the United States. In the area of fiscal reserves, Hou *et al.* (2003) identify how formal financial constraints, such as strict balanced budget requirements, allow governments to build up countercyclical fiscal resources to be used in economic downturns, while Hou and Smith (2009) shows how informal interpretations of those rules influence their implementation. Hou and Moynihan (2008) in turn show that such funds mitigate the need for emergency spending cuts or tax hikes.

While research on fiscal reserves therefore points to the benefits of balanced budget constraints on one aspect of PFM performance, such strict balanced budget requirements can also bring negative effects to other parts of PFM systems. Krause *et al.* (2006) find that strict balanced budget requirements encourage states to produce less accurate revenue forecast in order to provide a revenue cushion. Together, these findings suggest that general claims about the influence between flexibility/constraints and PFM performance depends upon the specific nature of the flexibility/constraint and the specific aspect of PFM being examined. The context of a PFM system also shapes the relationship with performance, which we explore in the next section.

Contextual factors

The design and reform of PFM systems, and ultimately PFM performance, are shaped by a mix of static and dynamic contextual factors. For example, Pollitt (2005) argues that more individualistic and risk-accepting cultures best accommodate the use of devices like performance-related pay and transparent public reporting of targets and achievements. Consensualist countries are likely to accept performance measurement as a legitimate modern technique but use performance information in a less direct, more negotiated manner.

If context matters, it is perhaps not surprising that in practice PFM systems vary quite a bit. Among rich countries that offer advice to other countries on PFM systems, there is no single model of PFM, even if we restrict analysis to only those deemed most effective by the World Bank. Table 3.1 provides information on the way nine more effective governments in the sample answered questions similar to the following: do you have lump-sum appropriations

Table 3.1: Relaxed input controls and performance measures

Country	Lump sum appropriations?	Response to poor performance: A. Programmes eliminated? B. More intense monitoring? C. Budget size reduced? D. Pay and career opportunities of head official affected?	Performance against objectives routinely presented to legislature
Australia	Yes, for operating expenditures	A. Sometimes B. Almost always C. Sometimes D. Almost never	Yes, each ministry prepares performance reports accompanying the budget
Belgium	No, expenditure specified below agency level	A. Rarely B. Rarely C. Almost never D. Rarely or almost never	No
Canada	Yes, for operating expenditures, but a sub-limit on wages	A. Almost never B. Rarely C. Almost never D. Almost never	Other
Denmark	Yes, for operating expenditures, but a sub-limit on wages	A. Almost never B. Often C. Rarely D. Almost always or often	No, only on ad hoc basis
Germany	No, expenditure specified below agency level	A. Rarely B. Often C. Sometimes D. Almost never	No, only on ad hoc basis
Netherlands	Some agencies, for operating expenditure	A. Almost never B. Rarely C. Rarely D. Almost never	Yes, integrated into main budget documents
Sweden	Yes, for operating expenditures	A. Rarely B. Sometimes C. Rarely D. Almost never	Yes, each ministry prepares performance reports accompanying the budget
United Kingdom	Yes, for operating expenditures, but a sub-limit on wages	A. Almost never B. Often C. Almost never D. Almost never	Yes, each ministry prepares performance reports accompanying the budget
United States	No for Cabinet and major agencies; Yes for some small agencies	A. Almost never B. Almost always C. Almost never D. Almost never	Yes

Source: 2007 OECD Budget Practices and Procedures Database (which indicate flexibility)? Do you use performance information in various ways? Do you provide performance reports to the legislature?

This variation of experience illustrated in Table 3.1 is summarized by Curristine (2005: 124): 'There is no one model of performance budgeting; countries need to adapt their approach to the relevant political and institutional context.' As the report points out: 'Context is important.'

We do not know conclusively how different factors influence PFM performance potential, and the literature is still catching up on this issue, but the central importance of context is clear. The OECD evidence suggests that governments pursue PFM performance in different ways (Andrews 2010). The different approaches are likely to have different impacts on results as well. Where performance concerns are introduced broadly in budget preparation, resource management, reporting and external evaluation mechanisms, the chances of significant impact are higher than instances where performance concerns enter narrowly (typically only in budget preparation). In keeping with contingency theory, there is no one best way to introduce performance management, but all ways are not equal either. What appears to be the most important factor is that all the processes in the PFM system (Figure 3.1) are similarly oriented.

These observations suggest that there are appropriate contextual reasons for variation in PFM systems. Previous institutions are a central part of that context. The record of budgetary reforms suggests that institutions are not always formal and open to change, and are often deeply embedded, highly routinized and path dependent, so that even when significant changes are attempted, the past continues to influence current behaviour (Ingraham *et al.* 2008). This point is demonstrated by Curristine's discussion of performance budgeting across OECD countries: 'These reforms have been introduced into an existing institutional context and budget process' (Curristine 2005: 124). Brinkerhoff and Goldsmith call this 'institutional dualism' (Brinkerhoff and Goldsmith 2005: 199–200) which complicates further the nature of the systems in the countries observed – because there are different combinations of new and old systems likely in all domains it is very difficult to understand the true institutional qualities in place.

As a previous section identified, variance in political institutions matters to PFM systems; different political contexts result in different demand for financial accountability. Various authors argue that a strong civil society (built on social capital) creates an effective demand for results that has a vital influence on local government performance. Knack (2002) argues that social capital fosters enhanced accountability and social trust, which enables disciplined but flexible financial management systems. Knack finds that measures of social capital are associated with positive evaluations of state financial management systems in US state governments. Similarly, von Hagen and Harden (1995) find the presence of public demand (often exercised through legislatures) is highly influential on the fiscal performance of governments. In research on performance information use, there is also evidence that environmental factors also shape performance information use. Moynihan and Ingraham (2004) and Poister and Streib (1999) report that perceived citizen demand for performance-based accountability encourages performance information use among government officials. De Lancer Julnes and Holzer (2001) find that support among external interest groups (in the form of elected official/citizens) for performance management also fostered use. We combine these perspectives into a proposition about how context affects the potential performance focus of PFM systems:

> *Proposition 7*: The potential success of performance-oriented PFM reforms – and the specific manifestation of such mechanisms – is contingent on contextual factors such as culture, political structure and civic demand.

Conclusion

This chapter has focused on efforts to make budget systems more performance driven. It is difficult to verify many of the claims about public sector performance generally, because the claims are often vague, it is difficult to separate out the effects of other variables, some costs are unaccounted for, and methodologies to solve these problems either do not exist or are not applied (Pollitt 2000). Efforts to improve PFM performance were premised on the notion that traditional budget systems were not focused on results, but could have a major positive influence. Empirically, however, we have less evidence on the relationship between budgeting approaches and performance than on the link between performance and other factors discussed in other chapters in this book. One potential solution for researchers is to focus on the performance of relatively narrow aspects of the overall PFM systems. For example, this chapter has cited strong empirical findings in the areas of fiscal reserves and revenue forecasting. Of course, the major shortcoming with this approach is the limitation in generalizing to overall PFM performance.

One reason for this shortcoming in empirical knowledge is the fact that budgeting systems define performance in different ways, as fiscal discipline, allocative efficiency and technical efficiency. It is also clear that in understanding the design, reform and performance of PFM systems, context and politics matters. Efforts to reform the budget system will always have some impact, but they are contingent on many other factors at the government-wide and organizational level. Understanding the future of PFM systems requires researchers to map the relationship between these contingencies better.

REFERENCES

Ammons, David, and Carl Stenberg. 2007. 'Commentary on reinventing administrative prescriptions: the case for democratic-constitutional impact statements and scorecard', *Public Administration Review*, 67, 1, 1–8.

Andersen, Simon Calmar, and Peter B. Mortensen. 2010. 'Policy stability and organizational performance: is there a relationship?', *Journal of Public Administration Research and Theory*, 20, 1, 1–22.

Andrews, Matthew. 2001. 'Adjusting external audits to facilitate results oriented management', *The International Journal of Government Auditors*, April, 10–14.

2006. 'Beyond best practice and basics first in performance-based reforms', *Public Administration & Development*, 26, 2, 147–61.

2007. 'What would an ideal PFM system look like?', in A. Shah (ed.) *Budgeting and Budgetary Institutions*. Washington, DC: World Bank, pp. 359–83.

2010. 'Good government means different things in different countries', *Governance*, 23, 1 (January 2010), 7–35.

Andrews, Matthew, and Donald P. Moynihan. 2002. 'Why reforms don't always have to work to succeed: a tale of two managed competition initiatives', *Public Performance and Management Review*, 25, 3, 282–97.

Andrews, Matthew, and Herb Hill. 2003. 'The impact of traditional budgeting systems on the effectiveness of performance-based budgeting: a different viewpoint on recent findings', *International Journal of Public Administration*, 26, 2, 135–55.

Askim, Jostein, Åge Johnsen, and Knut-Andreas Christophersen. 2008. 'Factors behind organizational learning from benchmarking: experiences from Norwegian municipal benchmarking networks', *Journal of Public Administration Research and Theory*, 18, 2, 297–320.

Bartle, John R. 2001. 'Budgeting, policy, and administration: patterns and dynamics in the United States', *International Journal of Public Administration*, 24, 1, 21–30.

Barzelay, Michael. 1997. 'Central audit institutions and performance auditing: a comparative analysis of organizational strategies in the OECD', *Governance*, 10, 3, 235–60.

Behn, Robert D., and Peter A. Kant. 1999. 'Strategies for avoiding the pitfalls of performance contracting', *Public Productivity and Management Review*, 22, 4, 470–89.

Bevan, Gwyn, and Christopher Hood. 2006. 'What's measured is what matters: targets and framing in the English public health care system', *Public Administration*, 84, 3, 517–38.

Bourdeaux, Carolyn. 2006. 'Do legislatures matter in budgetary reform?', *Public Budgeting & Finance*, 26, 1, 126–42.

Bourdeaux, Carolyn, and Grace Chikoto. 2008. 'Legislative influences on performance management reform', *Public Administration Review*, 68, 2, 253–65.

Bowling, Cynthia, Chung-Lae Cho, and Deil S. Wright. 2004. 'Establishing a continuum from minimizing to maximizing bureaucrats: state agency head preferences for governmental expansion – a typology of administrator growth postures, 1964–98', *Public Administration Review*, 64, 4, 489–99.

Boyne, George A., and Alex A. Chen. 2007. 'Performance targets and public service improvement', *Journal of Public Administration and Research Theory*, 17, 3, 455–77.

Bretschneider, S., and Gorr, W. 1989. 'Forecasting as a science', *International Journal of Forecasting*, 5, 305–6.

Bretschneider, S., W. Gorr, G. Grizzle, and E. Klay. 1989. 'Political and organizational influences on forecast accuracy: forecasting state sales tax receipts', *International Journal of Forecasting*, 5, 307–19.

Brewer, Gene A. 2005. 'In the eye of the storm: frontline supervisors and federal agency performance.' *Journal of Public Administration Research and Theory*, 15, 4, 505–27.

Brinkerhoff, Derrick, and Arthur Goldsmith. 2005. 'Institutional dualism and international development: a revisionist interpretation of good governance', *Administration & Society*, 37, 199–224.

Carlin, Tyrone M., and James Guthrie. 2003. 'Accrual output based budgeting systems in Australia: the rhetoric-reality gap', *Public Management Review*, 5, 2, 145–62.

Campos, Ed, and Sanjay Pradhan. 1996. 'Budgetary institutions and expenditure outcomes: binding governments to fiscal performance', World Bank Policy Research Working Paper No. 1646. Washington, DC: World Bank.

Chwastiak, Michelle. 2001. 'Taming the untamable: planning, programming, and budgeting and the normalization of war', *Accounting, Organizations, and Society*, 6, 26, 501–19.

Curristine, Theresa. 2005. 'Performance information in the budget process: results of the OECD 2005 questionnaire', *OECD Journal of Budgeting*, 5, 2, 87–131.

Denison, Dwight V., Wenli Yan, and Zhirong (Jerry) Zhao. 2007. 'Is management performance a factor in municipal bond credit ratings? The case of Texas school districts', *Public Budgeting and Finance*, 27, 4, 86–98.

Diamond, Jack. 2002. 'The role of internal audit in government financial management: an international perspective', International Monetary Fund, Working Paper No. 2/94.

Dias, J. J., and S. Maynard-Moody. 2007. 'For-profit welfare: contracts, conflicts, and the performance paradox', *Journal of Public Administration Research and Theory*, 17, 189–211.

Dolan, Julie. 2002. 'The budget-minimizing bureaucrat? Empirical evidence from the senior executive service', *Public Administration Review*, 62, 1, 42–50.

Dull, Matt. 2009. 'Results-model reform leadership: questions of credible commitment', *Journal of Public Administration Research and Theory*, 19, 255–84.

Dunleavy, Patrick. 1991. *Democracy, Bureaucracy and Public Choice: Economic Explanations in Political Science*. London: Harvester Wheatsheaf.

Forrester, John P. 2001. 'Public choice theory and public budgeting: implications for the greedy bureaucrat', in John R. Bartle (ed.) *Evolving Theories of Public Budgeting*. New York: JAI Press, pp. 101–24.

Gilmour, John B., and David E. Lewis. 2006. 'Does performance budgeting work? An examination of OMB's PART scores', *Public Administration Review*, 66, 5, 742–52.

Grizzle, Gloria. 1986. 'Does budget format really govern the actions of budgetmakers?', *Public Budgeting and Finance*, 6, 1, 60–70.

Guthrie, J. 1998. 'Application of accrual accounting in the Australian information preferences', *Accounting, Accountability and Performance*, 14, 1, 1–19.

von Hagen, Jurgen, and Ian J. Harden. 1995. 'Budget processes and commitment to fiscal discipline', *European Economic Review*, 39, 3–4, 771–9.

Heinrich, Carolyn J., and Youseok Choi. 2007. 'Performance-based contracting in social welfare programs', *The American Review of Public Administration*, 37, 4, 409–35.

Hou, Yilin. 2003. 'What stabilizes state general fund spending during downturns: budget stabilization fund, general fund unreserved undesignated balance, or both?', *Public Budgeting and Finance*, 23, 3, 64–91.

Hou, Yilin, and Donald P. Moynihan. 2008. 'The case for counter cyclical fiscal capacity', *Journal of Public Administration Research and Theory*, 18, 1, 139–59.

Hou, Yilin, Donald P. Moynihan, and Patricia W. Ingraham. 2003. 'Capacity, management and performance: exploring the links', *American Review of Public Administration*, 33, 3, 295–315.

Hou, Yilin and Daniel L. Smith. 2009. 'Informal norms as a bridge between formal rules and outcomes of government financial operations: evidence from State Balanced Budget Requirements', *Journal of Public Administration Research and Theory*, doi: 10.1093/jopart/mup026

Ingraham, Patricia W., Donald P. Moynihan, and Matthew Andrews. 2008. 'Formal and informal institutions in public administration', in B. Guy Peters and Donald Savoie (eds.) *Institutional Theory in Political Science*. Manchester University Press.

Joyce, Philip J. 2003. 'Linking Performance and Budgeting: Opportunities in the Federal Budgeting Process', Washington DC: IBM Center of the Business of Government.

Kelman, Steven. 2005. *Unleashing Change: a Study of Organizational Renewal in Government*. Washington, DC: Brookings Institution.

Kelman, Steven, and John N. Friedman. 2009. 'Performance improvement and performance dysfunction: an empirical examination of distortionary impacts of the emergency room wait-time target in the English national health service', *Journal of Public Administration Research and Theory Advance Access*, 28, 1.

Kerr, S. 1993. 'An academy classic: on the folly of rewarding A, while hoping for B', *Academy of Management Executive*, 9, 1, 7–14.

Kettl, Donald. 1992. *Deficit Politics*. New York: Macmillan.

Klase, Kenneth A., and Michael John Dougherty. 2002. 'The effect of performance budgeting on state functional expenditures', a paper prepared for the 2002 meeting of the Association of Budgeting and Financial Management, Washington, DC.

Klay, W. E. 1987. 'Management through budgetary incentives', *Public Productivity and Management Review*, 41 (Spring), 59–71.

Kloot, Louise, and John Martin. 2000. 'Strategic performance management: a balanced approach to performance management issues in local government', *Management Accounting Research*, 11, 2, 1–22.

Knack, Steven. 2002. 'Social capital and the quality of government: evidence from the US states', *American Journal of Political Science*, 46, 4, 772–85.

Kraan, Dirk-Jan. 1996. *Budgetary Decisions: a Public Choice Approach*. Cambridge University Press.

Krause, George A., David E. Lewis, and James W. Douglas. 2006. 'Political appointments, civil service systems, and bureaucratic competence: organizational balancing and gubernatorial revenue forecasts in the American states', *American Journal of Political Science*, 50, 3, 770–87.

de Lancer Julnes, Patria, and Marc Holzer. 2001. 'Promoting the utilization of performance measures in public organizations: an empirical study of factors affecting adoption and implementation', *Public Administration Review*, 61, 6, 693–708.

Laswell, H. 1990. *Politics: Who Gets What When and How?* New York: Peter Smith.

Lynch, Thomas, and Cynthia Lynch. 1997. 'The road to entrepreneurial budgeting', *Journal of Public Budgeting Accounting and Financial Management*, 9, 1, 161–80.

Marlowe, Justin, and David S. T. Matkin. 2009. 'Does internal control matter to investors?' Unpublished paper.

Melkers, Julia, and Katherine Willoughby. 2005. 'Models of performance-measurement use in local governments: understanding budgeting, communication, and lasting effects', *Public Administration Review*, 65, 2, 180–90.

Mikesell, John L. 1995. *Fiscal Administration: Analysis and Applications for the Public Sector*, 4th edn. Belmont, CA: Wadsworth.

Montes, Carlos, and Matthew Andrews. 2005. 'Implementing reforms in Bolivia: too much to handle', *International Journal of Public Administration*, 28, 3–4, 273–90.

Moynihan, Donald P. 2006. 'Ambiguity in policy lessons: the agencification experience', *Public Administration*, 84, 4, 1029–50.

2008. *The Dynamics of Performance Management: Constructing Information and Reform*. Washington, DC: Georgetown University Press.

Moynihan, Donald P., and Patricia W. Ingraham. 2004. 'Integrative leadership in the public sector: a model of performance information use', *Administration & Society*, 36, 4, 427–53.

Nathan, Richard. 2005. 'Presidential address: "Complexifying" government oversight in America's government', *Journal of Policy Analysis and Management*, 4, 2, 207–15.

Niskanen, William A. 1971. *Bureaucracy and Representative Government*. Chicago: Aldine Atherton.

Oduro, Kojo N. 2002. 'Results-based oriented public expenditure system in Ghana', Overseas Development Institute Working Paper No: 208. London: Overseas Development Institute.

OECD. 2007. *Budget Practices and Procedures Database*. Paris: OECD.

Office of Management and Budget (OMB). 2007. *Competitive Sourcing*. Washington, DC: Government Printing Office.

Plummer, M. L., D. Wight, A. I. N. Obasi, J. Wamoyi, G. Mshana, J. Todd, *et al.* 2007. 'A process evaluation of a school-based adolescent sexual health intervention in rural Tanzania: the MEMA kwa Vijana programme', *Health Education Research*, 22, 4, 500–12.

Poister, Theodore H., and Gregory D. Streib. 1999. 'Strategic management in the public sector', *Public Productivity and Management*, 22, 3, 308–25.

Pollitt, Christopher. 2000. 'Is the emperor in his underwear? An analysis of the impacts of public management reform', *Public Management Review*, 2, 2, 181–99.

2003. 'Performance audit in Europe: trends and choices', *Critical Perspectives on Accounting*, 14, 1–2, 157–70.

2005. 'Performance management in practice: a comparative study of executive agencies', *Journal of Public Administration Research and Theory*, 16, 1, 25–44.9

Poterba, James M., and Jurgen Von Hagen. 1998. *Fiscal Institutions and Fiscal Performance*. University of Chicago Press.

Radin, Beryl. 2006. *Challenging the Performance Movement: Accountability, Complexity and Democratic Values*. Washington, DC: Georgetown University Press.

Roberts, J. 2003. 'Managing public expenditure for development results and poverty reduction', Overseas Development Institute. Working Paper No: 203. London: ODI.

Rosenbloom, David. 2007. 'Reinventing administrative prescriptions: the case for democratic-constitutional impact statements and scorecards', *Public Administration Review*, 67, 1, 28–39.

Schick, Allen. 1998a. *A Contemporary Approach to Public Expenditure Management*. Washington, DC: The World Bank.

1998b. 'Why most countries should not try New Zealand reforms.' *World Bank Research Observer*, 13, 1, 123–31.

2002a. 'Does budgeting have a future?', *OECD Journal of Budgeting*, 2, 2, 7–48.

2002b. 'Opportunity, strategy, and tactics in reforming public management', *OECD Journal of Budgeting*, 2, 3, 7–35.

2003. 'The performing state: reflections on an idea whose time has come, but whose implementation has not', *OECD Journal of Budgeting*, 3, 2, 71–103.

Siegelman, Lee. 1996. 'The bureaucrat as budget maximizer: an assumption examined', *Public Budgeting and Finance*, 6, 1, 50–9.

Thompson, Fred. 1994. 'Mission-driven, results-oriented budgeting: fiscal administration and the new public management', *Public Budgeting and Finance*, 14, 3, 90–105.

Van Landingham, Gary, Martha Wellman, and Matthew Andrews. 2005. 'Useful, but not a panacea: performance-based program budgeting in Florida', *International Journal of Public Administration*, 28, 3, 233–54.

Wescott, Clay G. 2008. World bank support for public financial management: conceptual roots and evidence of impact. SSRN working paper, available at: http://ssrn.com/abstract=1169783.

Wheeler, Graeme P. 2003. *Sound Practices in Public Debt Management*. Washington, DC: The World Bank.

White, Joseph. 1994. '(Almost) nothing new under the sun: why the work of budgeting remains incremental', *Public Budgeting and Finance*, Spring, 113–33.

Wildavsky, Aaron A., and Naomi Caiden. 2003. *The New Politics of the Budgetary Process*, 5th edn. New York: Longman.

The World Bank. 1998. *Public Expenditure Management Handbook*. Washington, DC: The World Bank.

The World Bank. 2003. *Tanzania Public Expenditure Review*. Washington, DC: The World Bank.

4 Organizational structure and public service performance

Rhys Andrews

Introduction

Organizational structures provide the pervasive foundation for achieving coordination and control within an organization, influencing and being influenced by a host of different inputs, outputs and outcomes. One of the key functions for public managers is therefore the creation and maintenance of activities that can provide structural support for a host of other characteristics that are central to the pursuit of organizational goals, such as values and routines (O'Toole and Meier 1999). The relationship between structure and performance is thus a timeless concern for students of public management. Indeed, some might say it constitutes the foremost object of the theory and practice of bureaucracy. Woodrow Wilson (1887) claimed that 'philosophically viewed' public administration was chiefly concerned with 'the study of the proper distribution of constitutional authority' (213). Classical organizational theorists regarded bureaucratic structure, and its relationship with decision making and behaviour, as key to understanding organizational effectiveness (e.g. Gulick and Urwick 1937; Simon 1976; Weber 1947).

Organizational structure comprises two main sets of characteristics. First, the broad 'structural' features that define the physical milieu in which organization members interact, such as the overall size of an organization and the ratio of administrators to production workers. Second, the 'structuring' activities managers undertake in order to deliberately shape the behaviour of organization members, such as the relative decentralization of decision making and the specialization of job tasks (Dalton *et al.* 1980). Although 'structural' characteristics are likely to influence organizational outcomes in the public sector, public managers have far less discretion than their private sector counterparts over these elements of organizational structure. For example, the size of public organizations often reflects statutory duties and responsibilities, and is typically only altered at the behest of overhead political authorities (see Rainey 1989). By contrast, managers are likely to have greater meaningful control over relative levels of decision participation, if not perhaps over where responsibility for the content of decisions ultimately lies. To explore the ways in which organizational structure could potentially alter the behaviour of organization members for organizational gain, this chapter focuses on theories and evidence on the impact of 'structuring' activities on public service performance.

Organization theorists suggest that there are three key 'structuring' dimensions that are susceptible to managerial control, which, in turn, may influence performance: centralization, formalization and specialization (see especially Hage and Aiken 1967). The distribution of decision-making power, the extent of procedural standardization and the degree of occupational specialization within an organization are all argued to be important determinants of its achievements. These arguments have had significant practical, as well as theoretical import. For example, the mantras of New Public Management, particularly its preference for decentralized organizational structures, and low levels of formalization and specialization, have been reflected in worldwide reforms, such as the Reinventing Government movement in the USA, and more recently the public service reform agenda pursued in the UK.

This chapter examines theories of organizational structure before exploring the potential independent effects of centralization, formalization and specialization on public service performance. The existing evidence on organizational structure and performance in public services is then critically reviewed. Studies from the USA, the UK and elsewhere will thus be used to develop a better understanding of which organizational structures are most likely to lead to better performance and in what circumstances. Some propositions for future research are provided.

Theories of structure

What is organizational structure?

The conceptualization and measurement of organizational structures is a vital issue within organizational theory. Behaviour within organizations is strongly shaped by both the physical environment in which members interact and the organizing structure set in place to enable the organization to achieve its goals. According to Hall, organizing structures have two basic functions: first, the minimization and regulation of 'the influence of individual variations on the organization', and, second, enabling power to be exercised, decisions made and 'the organization's activities to be carried out' (Hall 1982 :109). Campbell *et al.* (1974) divide the characteristics of organizing structures into those which are 'structural' and those that are 'structuring'. Structural characteristics comprise the physical attributes of an organization; its size, span of control and administrative intensity. Structuring characteristics are the policies and activities which actively shape the behaviour of organizational members; the relative centralization of decision making, formalization of rules and procedures and specialization of job tasks. The relationship between the structural characteristics of public organizations and their performance has been the subject of empirical research. For example, La Porta *et al.* (1999) provide evidence of size effects, Meier and Bohte (2000) the impact of span of control, and Boyne and Meier (2009) administrative intensity. However, it is structuring characteristics and their impact on organizational outcomes that are the focal point of the present chapter.

The physical structural characteristics of public organizations often lie beyond the purview of public managers, being typically subject to external pressures, especially the direct intervention of higher political authorities (Rainey 1989). By contrast, the relative degree of centralization, formalization and specialization are attributes that are susceptible to deliberate managerial intervention, and thereby represent key variables that managers can manipulate when seeking to deliver better public services. Structural characteristics 'define the physical milieu in which behaviour occurs', but structuring characteristics are intended to 'prescribe or restrict behaviour' (Dalton *et al.* 1980: 57). Organization theorists focus on those structuring variables that are capable of empirical verification (e.g. Hage and Aiken 1967; Pugh *et al.* 1963). This implies that it is possible to derive and measure the individual elements of an organization's structuring profile and relate these to other relevant variables, such as performance, in line with theoretically derived hypotheses. Amongst the conceptual models of organization structure proposed during the revival of studies of bureaucracy in the 1960s, Hage and Aiken's (1967) formulation has proven the most influential (see, for example, Dewar *et al.* 1980).

According to Hage and Aiken (1967) organizations are 'a collection of social positions not an aggregate of individuals' (77). Organizational structuring is therefore a 'socially created pattern of rules, roles and relationships' (Dawson 1996: 111). Thus, the key structuring dimensions of an organization are those elements that indicate 'how positions are arranged in the social structure' (Hage and Aiken 1967: 77). Based on a review of the extant literature on bureaucracy, Hage and Aiken (1967) argued that the relative levels of centralization, formalization and specialization within organizations are most relevant to the study of the social positions.

Centralization

The degree to which decision making is centralized or decentralized is a key indicator of the manner in which an organization allocates resources and determines policies and objectives. It is, moreover, an issue that has long been recognized as a critical area of research on organizational structure (see Pugh *et al.* 1968). Classical theorists of bureaucracy regarded the relative degree of centralization as integral to understanding how an organization's decision-making processes are conducive to greater organizational efficiency (Gulick and Urwick 1937; Weber 1947). Although these early theorists primarily focused on the degree of hierarchical authority within organizations, the extent of decision participation has increasingly become recognized as a critically important aspect of centralization (see Carter and Cullen 1984). Indeed, Herbert Simon (1976) stressed that an organization's anatomy was constituted both by the allocation and the distribution of decision-making functions.

For organizational theorists, the relative degree of centralization within an organization is signified by the 'hierarchy of authority' and the 'degree of participation in decision making', as these aspects of structure reflect the distribution of power across the entire organization (Carter and Cullen 1984; Hage and Aiken 1967, 1969). Hierarchy of authority refers to the extent to which the power to make decisions is exercised at the upper levels of the organizational hierarchy, while participation in decision making pertains to the degree of staff involvement in the determination of organizational policy.

A centralized organization will typically have a high degree of hierarchical authority and low levels of participation in decisions about policies and resources; while a decentralized organization will be characterized by low hierarchical authority and highly participative decision making. Thus, where only one or a few individuals make decisions, an organizational structure may be described as highly centralized. By contrast, the least centralized organizational structure possible is one in which all organization members are responsible for and involved in decision making. By providing an indication of 'how power is distributed among social positions' throughout an organization (Hage and Aiken 1967: 77), the 'hierarchy of authority' and 'participation in decision-making' can illustrate how the 'structuring' of an organization has implications for organizational effectiveness (Dalton *et al.* 1980).

Formalization

The formalization present within an organization's structure reflects the extent to which it relies on rules to achieve its goals. Typically, such rules pertain to the roles of organizational members and the procedures by which their standards of conduct are supervised. Hage and Aiken (1967) therefore distinguish between two key aspects of formalization: job codification (the degree of work standardization) and rule observation (the latitude of role behaviour tolerated). These aspects of formalization are distinct from the related concept of 'red tape', which Bozeman (2000) refers to as 'rules, regulations, and procedures that remain in force and entail a compliance burden but [do] not advance the legitimate purposes the rules were intended to serve' (12). Brewer and Walker cover the impact of potentially dysfunctional rules and regulations on public service performance in Chapter 5.

Job codification refers to the relative extent of standardization of roles and the qualifications associated with those roles. It also comprises role performance measurement systems and the titles and symbols of status associated with a role (Pugh *et al.* 1963). Weber (1947) regarded this aspect of formalization as the paradigmatic exemplar of the bureaucratic form of organization, since it establishes the principle of legal-rational authority based on the achievement of certain attributes. The degree to which rule observation is formalized is chiefly reflected in the extent to which appropriate behaviour is written down and filed. Pugh *et al.* (1963) argue that this aspect of formalization therefore comprises: statements of procedures, rules and roles; and operation of procedures dealing with decision seeking, instructions and information transfer. Dalton *et al.* (1980) suggest that job codification refers to what role holders are expected to do, while rule observation refers to how they should do it. A highly formalized organization is therefore likely to have detailed descriptions of each of the social positions occupied within the organization and a large quantity of rules prescribing the operational procedures appropriate for each of those positions. Members of such an organization will probably experience lower levels of job autonomy and greater levels of performance monitoring and supervision than their counterparts in less formalized organizations.

Specialization

The concept of specialization pertains to the division of labour amongst organizational members. The relative degree of specialization within the structure of an organization therefore reflects the complexity of the various social positions at its heart. Hage and Aiken (1967) distinguish between the occupational complexity (number of occupational specialities) and the professionalization (professional activity and training) within those specialities. Occupational complexity can be gauged by examining either the professional specialities of staff (e.g. teacher, psychiatrist, logistician) or the broad areas of responsibility associated with different social positions, such as external stakeholder relations, resource management, innovation and so on (see Pugh *et al.* 1963). The degree of professionalization within the occupational specialities is reflected in professional networking activity carried out by organizational members and the training that they have received and are able to access in order to extend their expertise within their individual areas of specialism.

Specialization is the core structural characteristic Mintzberg (1979) associates with the archetypal professional bureaucracy. Such organizations are likely to have a large number of diverse professional groupings, which engage in extensive professional activity and have comprehensive training programmes. Examples of professional bureaucracies abound within the public sector. For example, hospitals and multipurpose local governments all comprise numerous professional groups, each of which engages in practices that often further entrench and develop their professional power, prestige and knowledge (see Kirkpatrick *et al.* 2005).

Hypothetical effects of structure on performance

Centralization

Organizational structures are assumed to provide a pervasive foundation for achieving coordination and control within an organization. They simultaneously constrain and prescribe the behaviour of organization members (Hall 1982), and perform a symbolic function indicating that someone is 'in charge' (Pfeffer and Salancik 1978). As a result, it may reasonably be expected that the degree of centralization will have a significant effect on organizational outcomes. Some researchers contend that even modest improvements in the structuring of organizations can generate large gains for customers, employees and managers (see Starbuck and Nystrom 1981). However, contrasting views on the benefits of centralization suggest that the degree of hierarchical authority and participation in decision making within an organization may have mixed effects on performance.

On the one hand, it has been argued that centralized decision making is integral to the effective and efficient functioning of any large bureaucracy (e.g. Goodsell 1985; Ouchi 1980). For example, Taylor (1911) famously argued that the 'scientific' management of organizations was only possible where decision making was restricted to a small cadre of planners. On the other hand, centralization is associated with many of the dysfunctions of bureaucracy, especially rigidity, red tape and abuses of monopoly power (e.g. Downs 1967; Niskanen 1971; Tullock 1965). For instance, Lipsky (1980) highlighted that bureaucratic controls may lead front-line staff to devote disproportionate time to finding ways to bypass established decision-making procedures, thereby damaging internal and external accountability. Broadly speaking, then, the substance of this divergence about the structuring of internal decision making is summarized in two rival positions. Proponents of centralized decision making suggest that it leads to better performance by facilitating greater decision speed, providing firm direction and goals, and establishing clear lines of hierarchical authority thereby circumventing the potential for damaging internal conflict. By contrast, supporters of more participative decision making suggest that centralization harms performance by preventing middle managers and street-level bureaucrats from making independent decisions, enshrining inflexible rules and procedures, and undermining responsiveness to changing environmental circumstances. The plausibility of both views thus implies that centralization may have inconsistent, contradictory or even no meaningful effects on performance.

Formalization

Divergent perspectives exist amongst researchers on the relative merits or otherwise of formalization for organizational performance. One interesting way in which the relationship between job codification and rule observation and organizational outcomes may be viewed is through the lens of principal-agent theory. Principal-agent models suggest that the information asymmetries that exist between senior managers and subordinates can be overcome by tightly specifying the roles of subordinates and imposing strict guidelines for carrying out operational procedures (see, for example, Jensen and Meckling 1976). This, in turn, enables the principal to monitor and control output carefully, harnessing the benefits of such control by reducing the opportunities for self-interested agents to pursue goals that may be less conducive to an organization's advantage (Wood and Waterman 1994). However, it is also possible that the transaction costs associated with imposing formal structures on able, motivated and potentially resentful employees may outweigh those that can be gained from giving them greater freedom to shape organizational responses to changing operational demands (see Miller 1992). Thus, the impact of formalization on performance is likely to have complex and possibly contradictory effects for several reasons.

Management theory suggests that high levels of formalization can reduce the harmful effects of role ambiguity amongst middle managers and front-line staff. Studies in the private sector have indicated that uncertainty about the responsibilities associated with their role can damage employees' motivation and organizational commitment (see, for example, Rizzo *et al.* 1970). However, it is also conceivable that job codification and rule observation limit the potential for organization members to act on their own initiative. This, in turn, may lead to a host of undesirable consequences associated with job dissatisfaction, such as absenteeism, turnover and lower productivity (Hackman and Lawler 1971). Job autonomy can enhance employees' motivation to master new tasks and look for innovative solutions to operational problems (Parker 1998). Critically, it can also enable 'experienced responsibility of the outcomes of the work' to emerge (Hackman and Oldham 1976). Broad-banding initiatives, such as those implemented in the US civil service, have drawn on the notion that broad job descriptions enhance the prospect of employee self-actualization. Similarly, flexible rules and procedures can enable such positive attitudes to flourish (Kelly 1992).

Despite an emerging consensus on the negative impact of formalization on organizational outcomes amongst management scholars (for a public sector example, see Kuvaas 2008), there remains a strong suspicion that without appropriate controls employees naturally gravitate towards utility maximization on their own terms, especially within the public sector. The potential for formalization to have such diverse contradictory effects on performance leads Dalton *et al.* (1980) to suggest that the relationship may be non-linear, with the positive effects of formalization turning negative at a certain optimal level. Unfortunately, to date no empirical studies have systematically examined this hypothesis in the public sector, but it remains an interesting point.

Specialization

Specialization may bring benefits to organizations by enhancing the impact of the motivation and skill professionals are able to bring to bear on complex organizational problems. High levels of occupational specialization arguably present managers and workgroups with more scope for reaping the benefits of their expertise (Burt 2004). If role holders have few peers able to carry out their duties, they are better placed to define the terms of their role, increasing their chances of subsequently exploiting wider opportunities for unlocking and transferring new knowledge and ideas (Burt 2004). This suggests that enhancing specialization is one way in which senior managers can seek to resolve principal-agent dilemmas. However, other scholars claim that specialization is harmful for performance, and that ensuring employees are equipped to carry out multiple tasks is necessary to overcome the negative externalities associated with excessive reliance on professional expertise.

Organizations can actively seek to reduce the level of specialization within their structure in several ways. For instance, they may standardize the job descriptions of all organizational members, or create a split between professional and administrative officers, wherein employees have primary specializations and a range of secondary specializations, or expand the use of multi-skilled project teams. Such 'non-specialist working' can build flexibility and responsiveness because organizational members are expected to be able to handle a range of problems, rather than the single issue for which they were initially trained. Burns *et al.* (1994) stress that 'the advantages to be gained from the development of more flexible working practices will inevitably be undermined if the management structure of the organisation is built on rigid departmental and professional boundaries' (99). Breaking down 'silos' may therefore be a critical means for organizational principals to exert greater control over agents in order to pursue organizational goals. This may be especially important in the public sector.

According to Mintzberg (1979), professional bureaucracies suffer from risk aversion amongst the different occupation groupings that are likely to rely on established solutions to problems or the incremental development of new ideas based on past experience. This can be especially damaging if an organization is confronted by rapid environmental shift and requires transformatory change in order to survive. Thus, it is highly conceivable that specialization, like formalization, will exhibit a non-linear relationship with performance, with its benefits turning negative once a threshold of organized professional power is reached.

Empirical evidence on organizational structure and performance

Empirical studies and their characteristics

There is a growing literature on street-level bureaucracy in the public sector, pertaining to those individuals responsible for directly providing public services, such as teachers, police officers and social workers (e.g. Lipsky 1980;

Maynard-Moody and Musheno 2003; Riccucci 2005). However, there is still comparatively little research systematically investigating the effects of centralization, formalization and specialization within public organizations on performance, rather than at the industry level.

A wide array of studies assess the effects of the structure of the organizational population: (de)centralization on local (e.g. Boyne, 1992) and regional governments (e.g. Andrews and Martin, 2010); formalization on schools (e.g. Fuchs and Wossmann 2007), hospitals (e.g. Hoque *et al.* 2004) and public utilities (e.g. Braadbaart *et al.* 2007); and specialization on healthcare programmes (e.g. Mancini *et al.* 2003) and hospitals (e.g. Lee *et al.* 2008). However, rather less is known about the impact of intra-organizational structure on public service performance. Moreover, few studies utilize a comprehensive theoretical model of the structuring of organizations. Rather than adopt the kind of conceptual framework proposed by Hage and Aiken (1967), they focus on specific structural variables, such as hierarchy of authority (e.g. Schmid 2002) and autonomy (e.g. Verhoest 2005). As a result, a thorough review of the available evidence requires the adaptation of additional search terms for relative centralization (e.g. hierarchy, participation), formalization (e.g. rule-following, autonomy) and specialization (e.g. occupational complexity, division of labour), in conjunction with those for performance (e.g. achievement, effectiveness). Despite the appropriateness of the studies identified below, their content is nevertheless problematic in at least two ways.

First, public sector studies have so far focused on the independent impact of different structuring dimensions on performance (e.g. centralization in Andrews *et al.* 2009). Only two studies have examined the effects of centralization, formalization and specialization simultaneously (Schmid 2002; Whetten 1978). To develop and fully test theoretical models of organizational structures, it is necessary to investigate the influence of all three structuring dimensions on organizational outcomes.

Second, many of the quantitative empirical studies utilize subjective perceptual measures of effectiveness that may not be as robust and reliable as objective archival indicators of performance. Indeed, Dalton *et al.* (1980) identify this as a weakness of research on structure and performance more generally. To build confidence in the findings on organizational structure and public service performance, it will therefore be essential for future quantitative studies to draw on objective measures that reduce the prospect for common-source bias to contaminate the findings.

Notwithstanding their limitations, the studies examined below provide a strong platform for developing an understanding of the relationship between organizational structure and performance. The evidence covers a wide range of public services ranging from single-purpose organizations, such as schools, to multipurpose organizations, such as local governments. Each of the studies typically draws on a large sample of organizations and utilizes different dependent variables, including measures of efficiency and effectiveness, thereby increasing the generalizability of the findings. Most use formal tests of statistical significance, and implement multivariate techniques to control for the potential effects of other relevant contextual variables.

Measuring structure

Centralization, formalization and specialization are operationalized in several ways within the existing studies identified here. A number of researchers (Andrews *et al.* 2009; Glisson and Martin 1980; Martin and Segal 1977; Moynihan and Pandey 2005; Richardson *et al.* 2002; Schmid 2002; Whetten 1978) draw directly on or adapt one or more of the survey indices utilized in Hage and Aiken's (1967) study of the structural properties of sixteen social welfare and health agencies. Others either use or develop alternative indices or rely on some form of interview data to measure organization structure (see below).

Hage and Aiken (1967) developed a measure of participation in decision making based on four questionnaire items asking how frequently organization members participated in hiring and promotion decisions, and policy and programme adoption decisions. A measure of hierarchy of authority was constructed from five items gauging the extent to which organization members required the approval of superiors in order to make decisions. Job codification was measured with five questions assessing the degree of autonomy organization members experienced when carrying out work tasks, while rule observation was evaluated with two items enquiring about the extent of oversight to which members were subject. Finally, Hage and Aiken measure occupational complexity by classifying organization members according to their specialism, and professionalization by asking three questions about participation in professional organizations and another assessing the level of professional training of job occupants.

Anderson (1995) measures hierarchy of authority in state-owned pharmacies on the basis of semi-structured interviews. In his meta-analysis of studies of bureaucratic effectiveness in cabinet agencies, Wolf (1993) codes the extent of hierarchy of authority and professionalization observed in each study on a five-point scale. Ashmos *et al.* (1998) develop their own measure of participation in decision making in hospitals based on questionnaire items evaluating the composition of decision-making groups, the timing of entrants' induction into the decision process, the breadth of their participation, the number of decision activities in which they were involved and number of decision mechanisms. Maynard-Moody *et al.* (1990) derive a measure of decision participation based on several questions assessing the extent of influence different occupation groupings have in making policy in community correction facilities. Holland (1973) relies on single questions to gauge hierarchy of authority and decision participation in a large mental health institution, Fiedler and Gillo (1974) use a single questionnaire item asking respondents how much control or influence they have over major policy decisions.

Molnar and Rogers (1976) use interview data to gauge rule observation in public agencies. Kuvaas (2008) draws on Morgeson and Humphrey's (2006) previously validated nine-item scale tapping the extent to which local government managers make their own decisions about their work schedule. Cheung and Cheng (2002) gauge the extent of job codification in three primary schools through interviews. Verhoest (2005) assesses managerial autonomy in public agencies using documentary analysis and structured interviews. Boreham *et al.* (2000) measure professionalization through a combination of interviews and participant observation.

Evidence from the studies

Centralization

Studies of performance in the public sector have so far uncovered contrasting effects of centralization. Andrews *et al.* (2009) find that variations in the performance of Welsh local government service departments are unrelated to hierarchy of authority and the degree of participation in decision making. Similarly, Schmid's (2002) study of therapeutic boarding schools in Israel failed to uncover statistically significant relationships between hierarchy of authority and performance. Nevertheless, other researchers do find such relationships.

Glisson and Martin's (1980) study of human service organizations in the USA reveals that an index of centralization measuring hierarchy of authority and participation in decision making has a large statistically significant positive effect on productivity, even when controlling for other aspects of organizational 'structuring' such as formalization. Glisson and Martin (1980) also found a small positive effect on efficiency. However, although this study implies that centralization may play an important role in determining the quantity of organizational output, its effect may be related in a different manner to alternative measures of service performance. For instance, Whetten (1978) finds that participation in decision making has a negative effect on the output of US manpower agencies, but a positive one on staff perceptions of effectiveness. This study suggests that centralization facilitates production-orientated goals because it reduces environmental uncertainty and provides a clear indication of the service mission to middle managers and front-line staff. Nevertheless, increased levels of decision participation can maximize the points of contact between service managers and users, leading to more responsive service development.

Anderson (1995) indicates that decentralization of authority was associated with high performance in the National Corporation of Swedish Pharmacies between 1971 and 1990. Evidence from the mental healthcare sector also suggests decentralizing decision making enables managers to provide clients with more individual attention, leading to better clinical outcomes (Holland 1973). Maynard-Moody et al.'s (1990) analysis of street-level bureaucracy highlights that programme implementation in two contrasting US community correctional organizations was best where there was 'greater street-level influence in policy processes' (845). Indeed, other researchers have furnished evidence suggesting that excluding professional staff from decision making is likely to result in poor quality public services (Ashmos et al. 1998; Martin and Segal 1977).

Research which has drawn exclusively on subjective ratings of organizational effectiveness has found little or no relationship between centralization and performance. While Moynihan and Pandey (2005) uncover a negative relationship between centralization and perceptions of effectiveness in eighty-three US human and health services, Wolf's exhaustive (1993) case survey of bureaucratic effectiveness found no significant relationship between centralization and performance in a range of US federal agencies. Similarly, in an earlier investigation, Fiedler and Gillo (1974) show that decentralizing decision making has little effect on the comparative perceived achievements of different faculties within community colleges.

Formalization

Although researchers have paid considerable attention to the relationship between centralization and organizational performance in the public sector, to date, fewer studies have examined the impact of rule observation and job codification on public service performance. Glisson and Martin (1980) find that an index of formalization has a small statistically significant negative effect on the productivity and efficiency of human service organizations in the USA. Whetten's (1978) study of US manpower agencies finds that an index of formalization has a positive effect on output, but a negative one on community leaders' perceptions of effectiveness. By contrast, in his study of nationalized pharmacies in Sweden, Anderson (1995) associates an 'exceptionally high' degree of formalization of management systems and procedures with improvements on multiple dimensions of performance. Similarly, Molnar and Rogers' (1976) analysis of public agencies in Iowa suggests that those that are more formalized are more productive than their less formalized counterparts.

Schmid (2002) finds that formal rules and procedures have a positive impact on service responsiveness and client and staff satisfaction in a sample of fifty-one therapeutic boarding schools in Israel. However, this analysis also revealed negative effects of job codification, suggesting that it is important to disaggregate the different aspects of formalization in order to assess its overall influence on performance. While few researchers examine the separate effects of both aspects of formalization in the same study, there is growing evidence on the impact of job codification on organizational performance in the public sector.

Kuvaas's (2008) analysis of the attitudes of 779 employees in 3 Norwegian municipalities indicates that job autonomy is a statistically significant predictor of perceived work performance, even when controlling for other relevant variables, such as intrinsic motivation. Verhoest (2005) explores the relative degree of managerial autonomy within the job brokerage and vocational training divisions of the Flemish Employment Service. On the basis of interviews with key actors, he finds that autonomy concerning financial management has a strong positive association with objective measures of divisional objectives. However, autonomy concerning human resource management is much less likely to have a positive impact on performance.

Cheung and Chen's (2002) case study of three Hong Kong primary schools indicates that greater scope for self-management can have beneficial effects for performance across multiple levels of an organization. Indeed, they suggest that the positive benefits of job autonomy for student achievement cascades upwards from teachers through their respective workgroups to the efforts of senior managers to maintain organizational legitimacy. This study highlights that it is only by considering the impact of organizational structuring across the entire organization that researchers can fully appreciate its pervasive influence.

Specialization

The empirical evidence on the impact of specialization on organizational performance in the public sector is extremely sparse. The literature review presented here identified only four studies that met the search criteria. Schmid's (2002) study of therapeutic boarding schools in Israel found no relationships between occupational complexity and performance. According to Anderson (1995), the success of public pharmacies in Sweden was attributable to the low level of occupational specialization amongst employees. Whetten (1978) presents evidence suggesting that occupational complexity may have mixed effects on the performance of US manpower agencies. Although it is positively correlated with output, such specialization is negatively correlated with employees' perceptions of effectiveness.

Boreham *et al.*'s (2000) investigation of twenty-five failures within the emergency departments of two UK hospitals provides an indication of the complex effects of professionalization on performance. Based on extensive direct observation of emergency staff using the critical incident technique, they find that many serious failures could have been averted if decisions about appropriate responses were not so tightly linked to professional authority. Boreham *et al.* (2000) suggest that risk can be greatly reduced where the 'sapiential' authority of more experienced though less qualified staff is recognized. However, they also offer the cautionary note that this too carries substantial risk if systems for developing collective competences amongst teams are absent.

Future research directions

The empirical studies reviewed above illustrate that variations in the performance of public organizations are not consistently influenced by measures of the degree of organizational centralization, formalization and specialization. The balance of evidence tends to suggest that decentralized organizations and those with low levels of specialization may perform best. Nonetheless, the studies indicate that each of the 'structuring' dimensions identified by Dalton *et al.* (1980) appears likely to have distinct contradictory independent impacts on the prospects of service improvement. This illustrates that it is essential for researchers, policy-makers and practitioners to acknowledge that the impact of structures on organizational outcomes is highly complex and is likely to be contingent on other relevant internal and external organizational characteristics. In this section, directions and propositions for future research are identified.

The impact of organizational structures on outcomes rarely occurs in isolation from other relevant internal organizational characteristics. In particular, each of the three 'structuring' dimensions is likely to have important combined as well as separate effects on organizational outcomes. Organization theorists suggest that the impact of centralization, formalization and specialization is likely to be mutually reinforcing. For example, Mintzberg's (1979) theory of structural configurations suggests that large centralized organizations are likely to require high levels of formalization and specialization to be successful. By contrast, decentralized organizations are likely to benefit from low formalization and specialization. However, so far little research has sought to explore these more complex interactive influences of the different structuring dimensions on public service performance. Glisson and Martin (1980) find, in line with studies in the private sector, that formalization strengthens the positive influence of centralization on the productivity and efficiency of human service organizations. Thus, while to date there are no comprehensive empirical studies of this critical issue, the extant theory and evidence leads to the proposition that:

> *Proposition 1*: The combined effects of centralization, formalization and specialization on organizational outcomes will be greater than the independent effects.

Configurational and contingency theorists highlight that organizational strategy is likely to constitute an important boundary condition of the structure–performance relationship (Miles and Snow 1978; Mintzberg 1979). Richardson *et al.* (2002) show that organizational growth strengthens the relationship between participation in decision making and profitability in healthcare treatment centres in the USA. Andrews *et al.* (2009) find that the impact of hierarchy of authority and the degree of participation in decision making on the performance of Welsh local government service departments is moderated by organizational strategy. Centralized defending organizations that focus on their core activities, in particular, perform better, but innovative prospecting organizations with high decision participation are also likely to do well. These studies therefore imply that:

> *Proposition 2*: Centralization, formalization and specialization constrain the positive impact of expansion and innovation on performance.

Principal-agent theories suggest that organizational structures have far-reaching implications for the attitudes of organization members. For instance, decentralized decision making may enable senior managers to reap the benefits of more trusting relationships with subordinates (Miller 1992). A number of other empirical studies identify the moderating effect of structure on those positive employee attributes that are arguably critical to achieving better organizational outcomes. For example, McMahon (1976), Richter and Tjosvold (1980) and Tannenbaum (1962) all find that extending participation in decision making can increase organizational effectiveness by enhancing mutual influence, motivation and satisfaction. All of which suggests structuring activities are particularly likely to have a major impact on the commitment that is regarded as critical to achieving organizational goals (Benkhoff 1997). The third and final proposition advanced in this review of the evidence, is therefore:

Proposition 3: Centralization, formalization and specialization constrain the positive impact of organizational commitment on performance.

Conclusions

This chapter has explored organizational structure and public service improvement. The evidence surveyed here suffers from a number of limitations that should be addressed in future studies. In particular, the reported findings may simply be a product of where and when the empirical studies were conducted. The evidence base thus far is largely restricted to anglophone countries. Are the organizational structures in these countries comparable with those faced by public organizations in other developed countries with contrasting managerial philosophies? To what extent, and in what ways, do organizational structures differ in developing countries? In addition, the use of cross-sectional data in the articles reviewed here also raises the issue of causality. It is possible that causation leads in the reverse direction to that hypothesized: levels of performance in certain contexts determine the adoption of particular organizational structures (Khandwalla 1977). Future studies could pool data over a longer time period to study the lagged effect of structure in greater depth. Moreover, the existing evidence base tells us little about the ways in which public managers at different organizational levels seek to adapt and change the structures with which they operate and the resulting effects on performance. Multilevel modelling of structure, organization, management and performance like that advocated by Hicklin in Chapter 11 may therefore represent the most appropriate means for addressing the major unresolved research issues in this area. In meeting these challenges public management researchers would make an important contribution to this venerable debate in the theory and practice of public administration.

REFERENCES

Anderson, Stuart. 1995. 'Organizational status and performance: the case of the Swedish pharmacies', *Public Administration*, 73, 2, 287–301.

Andrews, Rhys, George A. Boyne, Jennifer Law, and Richard M. Walker. 2009. 'Centralization, organizational strategy and public service performance', *Journal of Public Administration Research and Theory*, 19, 1, 57–80.

Andrews, Rhys, and Steve Martin. 2010. 'Regional variations in public service outcomes: the impact of policy divergence in England, Scotland and Wales', to appear in *Regional Studies* (DOI: 10.1080/00343400903401592).

Ashmos, Donde P., Dennis Duchon, and Reuben R. McDaniel Jr. 1998. 'Participation in strategic decision-making: the role of organizational predisposition and issue interpretation', *Decision Sciences*, 29, 1, 25–51.

Benkhoff, B. 1997. 'Ignoring commitment is costly: new approaches establishing the missing link between commitment and performance', *Human Relations*, 50, 701–26.

Boreham, N. C., C. E. Shea, and K. Macway-Jones. 2000. 'Clinical risk and collective competence in the hospital emergency department in the UK', *Social Science & Medicine*, 51, 1, 83–91.

Boyne, George A. 1992. 'Local government structure and performance: lessons from America', *Public Administration*, 70, 3, 333–57.

Boyne, George A., and Kenneth J. Meier. (2009) 'Burdened by bureaucracy? Determinants of administrative intensity in public service organizations', unpublished manuscript, available from authors.

Bozeman, Barry M. 2000. *Bureaucracy and Red Tape*. Upper Saddle River, NJ: Prentice Hall.

Braadbaart, Okke, Neils van Eybergen, and Jan Hoffer. 2007 'Managerial autonomy: does it matter for the performance of water utilities?', *Public Administration and Development*, 27, 2, 111–21.

Burns, Danny, Robin Hambleton, and Paul Hoggett. 1994. *The Politics of Decentralisation*. Houndmills: Macmillan.

Burt, Ronald S. 2004. 'Structural holes and good ideas', *American Journal of Sociology*, 110, 2, 349–99.

Campbell, John P., David A. Bownas, Norman G. Peterson, and Marvin D. Dunnette. 1974. 'The measurement of organizational effectiveness: a review of the relevant research and opinion', Report Tr-71-1 (Final Technical Report). San Diego: Navy Personnel Research and Development Center.

Carter, Nancy M., and John B. Cullen. 1984. 'A comparison of centralization/decentralization of decision making concepts and measures', *Journal of Management*, 10, 2, 259–68.

Cheung, Francis W. M., and Yin C. Cheng. 2002 'An outlier study of multilevel self-management and school performance', *School Effectiveness and School Improvement*, 13, 3, 253–90.

Dalton, Dan R., William D. Todor, Michael J. Spendolini, Gordon J. Fielding, and Lyman Porter. 1980. 'Organizational structure and performance: a critical review', *Academy of Management Review*, 5, 1, 49–64.

Dawson, Sandra. 1996. *Analysing Organisations*. Basingstoke: Macmillan.

Dewar, Robert D., David A. Whetten, and David Boje. 1980. 'An examination of the reliability and validity of the Aiken and Hage scales of centralization, formalization, and task routineness', *Administrative Science Quarterly*, 25, 1, 120–8.

Downs, Anthony. 1967. *Inside Bureaucracy*. Boston: Little, Brown and Company.

Fiedler, Fred E., and Martin W. Gillo. 1974. 'Correlates of performance in community colleges', *Journal of Higher Education*, 45, 9, 672–81.

Fuchs, Thomas, and Ludger Wossman. 2007. 'What accounts for international differences in student performance? A re-examination using PISA data', *Empirical Economics*, 32, 433–46.

Glisson, Charles A., and Patricia Y. Martin. 1980. 'Productivity and efficiency in human service organizations as related to structure, size and age', *Academy of Management Journal*, 23, 1, 21–37.

Goodsell, Charles T. 1985. *The Case for Bureaucracy: A Public Administration Polemic*, 2nd edn. Chatham, NJ: Chatham House Publishers.

Gulick, Luther, and Lindall Urwick (eds.). 1937. *Papers on the Science of Administration*. New York: Columbia University.

Hackman, J. Richard, and Edward E. Lawler. 1971. 'Employee reactions to job characteristics', *Journal of Applied Psychology*, 55, 3, 259–86.

Hackman, J. Richard, and Greg Oldham. 1976. 'Motivation through the design of work: test of a theory', *Organizational Behavior and Human Performance*, 16, 250–79.

Hage, Jerald, and Michael Aiken. 1967. 'Relationship of centralization to other structural properties', *Administrative Science Quarterly*, 12, 1, 72–93.

1969. 'Routine technology, social structure, and organizational goals', *Administrative Science Quarterly*, 14, 3, 366–76.

Hall, R. H. 1982. *Organizations: Structure and Process*, 3rd edn. Englewood Cliffs, NJ; London: Prentice-Hall.

Holland, Thomas P. 1973. 'Organizational structure and institutional care', *Journal of Health and Social Behavior*, 14, 3, 241–51.

Hoque, Kim, Simon Davis, and Michael Humphreys, M. 2004. 'Freedom to do what you are told: senior management team autonomy in an NHS trust', *Public Administration*, 82, 2, 355–75.

Jensen, Michael C., and William H. Meckling. 1976. 'Theory of the firm: managerial behaviour, agency costs and ownership structure', *Journal of Financial Economics*, 3, 4, 305–60.

Kelly, John E. 1992. 'Does job re-design theory explain job re-design outcomes?', *Human Relations*, 45, 8, 753–74.

Khandwalla, P. N. 1977. *The Design of Organizations*. New York: Harcourt Press.

Kirkpatrick, Ian, Stephen Ackroyd, and Richard M. Walker. 2005. *The New Managerialism and Public Service Professions: Change in Health, Social Services and Housing*. Houndmills: Palgrave.

Kuvaas, Bard. 2008. 'A test of hypotheses derived from self-determination theory among public sector employees', *Employee Relations*, 31, 1, 39–56.

La Porta, Rafael, Florencio Lopez De-Silanes, Andrei Shleifer, and Robert Vishny. 1999. 'The quality of government', *Journal of Law Economics and Organization*, 15, 1, 222–79.

Lee, Kwang-soo, Kee-hong Chun, and Jung-Soo Lee. 2008. 'Reforming the hospital service structure to improve efficiency: urban hospital specialization', *Health Policy*, 87, 1, 41–9.

Lipsky, Michael. 1980. *Street-level Bureaucracy: Dilemmas of the Individual in Public Services*. New York: Russell Sage Foundation.

Mancini, Dominic J., Guy Secklov, and John F. Stewart. 2003. 'The effects of structural characteristics on family planning performance in Cote d'Ivoire and Nigeria', *Social Science & Medicine*, 56, 10, 2123–37.

Martin, Patricia Y., and Brian Segal. 1977. 'Bureaucracy, size and staff expectations for client independence in halfway houses', *Journal of Health and Social Behavior*, 18, 4, 376–90.

Maynard-Moody, Stephen, Michael Musheno, and Dennis Palumbo. 1990. 'Street-wise social policy: resolving the dilemma of street-level influence and successful implementation', *Western Political Quarterly*, 43, 4, 833–48.

Maynard-Moody, Stephen, and Michael Musheno. 2003. *Cops, Teachers and Counsellors: Stories from the Front Lines of Public Service*. University of Michigan Press.

McMahon, J. Timothy. 1976. 'Participative and power-equalized organizational systems', *Human Relations*, 29, 3, 203–14.

Meier, Kenneth J., and John Bohte. 2000. 'Ode to Luther Gulick: span of control and organizational performance', *Administration and Society*, 32, 2, 115–37.

Miles, Raymond E., and Charles C. Snow. 1978. *Organizational Strategy, Structure and Process*. New York: McGraw-Hill.

Miller, Gary. 1992. *Managerial Dilemmas: The Political Economy of Hierarchy*. New York: Cambridge University Press.

Mintzberg, Henry. 1979. *The Structuring of Organizations*. Englewood Cliffs, NJ: Prentice-Hall.

Molnar, Joseph J., and David L. Rogers. 1976. 'Organizational effectiveness: an empirical comparison of the goal and system resource approaches', *Sociological Quarterly*, 17, 4, 401–13.

Morgeson, F. P., and S. E. Humphrey . 2006. 'The work design questionnaire (WDQ): developing and validating a comprehensive measure for assessing job design and the nature of work', *Journal of Applied Psychology*, 91, 6, 1321–39.

Moynihan, Donald P., and Sanjay K. Pandey. 2005. 'Testing how management matters in an era of government by performance management', *Journal of Public Administration Research and Theory*, 15, 3, 421–39.

Niskanen, William A. 1971. *Bureaucracy and Representative Government*. Chicago: Aldin.

O'Toole, Laurence J., Jr., and Kenneth J. Meier. 1999. 'Modelling the impact of public management: implications of structural context', *Journal of Public Administration Research and Theory*, 9, 4, 505–26.

Ouchi, William G. 1980. 'Markets, bureaucracies and clans', *Administrative Science Quarterly*, 25, 1, 129–41.

Parker, S. K. 1998. 'Enhancing role breadth self-efficacy: the role of job enrichment and other organizational interventions', *Journal of Applied Psychology*, 83, 6, 835–52.

Pfeffer, Jeffrey, and Gerrard Salancik. 1978. *The External Control of Organizations: A Resource Dependence Perspective*. New York: Harper & Row.

Pugh, D. S., D. J. Hickson, C. R. Hinings, K. M. MacDonald, C. Turner, and T. Lupton. 1963. 'A conceptual scheme for organizational analysis', *Administrative Science Quarterly*, 8, 2, 289–315.

Pugh, D. S., D. J. Hickson, C. R. Hinings, and C. Turner. 1968. 'Dimensions of organization structure', *Administrative Science Quarterly*, 13, 1, 65–105.

Rainey, Hal G. 1989. 'Public management – recent research on the political context and managerial roles, structures and behaviors', *Journal of Management*, 15, 2, 229–50.

Riccucci, Norma M. 2005. *How Management Matters: Street-level Bureaucrats and Welfare Reform*. Washington, DC: Georgetown University Press.

Richardson, Hettie A., Robert J. Vanderberg, Terry C. Blum, and Paul M. Roman. 2002. 'Does decentralization make a difference for the organization? An examination of the boundary conditions circumscribing decentralized decision-making and organizational financial performance', *Journal of Management*, 28, 2, 217–44.

Richter, F. D., and Dean Tjosvold. 1980. 'Effects of student participation in classroom decision-making on attitudes, peer interaction, motivation, and learning', *Journal of Applied Psychology*, 65, 1, 74–80.

Rizzo, John R., Robert J. House, and Sidney I. Lirtzman. 1970. 'Role conflict and ambiguity in complex organization', *Administrative Science Quarterly*, 15, 2, 150–63.

Schmid, Hillel. 2002. 'Relationships between organizational properties and organizational effectiveness in three types of nonprofit human service organizations', *Public Personnel Management*, 31, 377–95.

Simon, Herbert A. 1976. *Administrative Behavior: a Study of Decision-making Processes in Administrative Organization*, 3rd edn. London: Macmillan.

Starbuck, William H., and P. C. Nystrom (eds.). 1981. *Handbook of Organizational Design: Volume 1: Adapting Organizations to their Environments*. Oxford University Press.

Tannenbaum, Arnold S. 1962. 'Control in organizations: individual adjustment and organizational performance', *Administrative Science Quarterly*, 7, 2, 236–57.

Taylor, Frederick W. 1911. *The Principles of Scientific Management*. New York: Harper & Bros.

Tullock, Gordon. 1965. *The Politics of Bureaucracy*. Washington, DC: Public Affairs Press.

Verhoest, Koen. 2005. 'Effects of autonomy, performance contracting, and competition on the performance of a public agency: a case study', *Policy Studies Journal*, 33, 2, 235–58.

Weber, Max. 1947. *The Theory of Social and Economic Organizations*. Glencoe, IL: The Free Press.

Whetten, David A. 1978. 'Coping with incompatible expectations: an integrated view of role conflict', *Administrative Science Quarterly*, 23, 2, 254–71.

Wilson, Woodrow. 1887. 'The study of administration', *Political Science Quarterly*, 2, 197–222.

Wolf, Patrick J. 1993. 'A case survey of bureaucratic effectiveness in US cabinet agencies: preliminary results', *Journal of Public Administration Research and Theory*, 3, 2, 161–81.

Wood, B. Dan, and Richard W. Waterman. 1994. *Bureaucratic Dynamics: The Role of Bureaucracy in Democracy*. Boulder, CO: Westview Press.

5   Red tape: the bane of public organizations?

Gene A. Brewer and Richard M. Walker

Introduction

The term 'red tape' has its origins in sixteenth-century English local government, and as such, it is one of the native concepts of public management. As Bozeman (2000: 12) explains, red tape is 'rules, regulations, and procedures that remain in force and entail a compliance burden but [do] not advance the legitimate purposes the rules were intended to serve'. While a number of bureaucratic maladies have attained mythical stature over the years (such as goal ambiguity and structural inflexibility, topics covered in Chapters 2 and 4 respectively), red tape is perhaps the most pervasive and damaging overall. This is, in part, because critics claim that red tape makes life hard for public employees and citizens alike, and takes a heavy toll on the performance of public organizations. This is attested to by the widespread international literature on red tape and regulation by key policy organizations such as the Organisation for Economic Co-operation and Development, the World Bank and the International Monetary Fund.

Research on red tape has focused on three important areas. First, scholars have sought to improve how they define and operationalize the term by examining global measures of red tape and management subsystem measures, differences between objective and perceptual measures of the concept, internal and external forms, and organizational and stakeholder red tape. Second, scholars have sought to document public–private differences in levels of red tape and determine whether public organizations are more red-tape bound than their private sector counterparts. Third and most important, scholars have recently begun investigating the impact of red tape on governmental performance, and they have sought to identify ways that policy-makers and public managers can effectively combat these ill effects. This research has shown that red tape does indeed exert powerful, negative effects on performance, but these effects are not as consistent and uniform as the red-tape myth suggests. Studies investigating strategies to alleviate red tape have also produced some interesting findings. Such studies have found that forward-leaning, proactive management strategies (such as those discussed in Chapter 10) can offset some of the harmful effects of red tape; but that inert, defensive and reactive strategies tend to make it worse.

In summary, this chapter will review these developments in more detail, with particular attention on the impact of red tape on organizational performance, promising avenues for future research, and concluding with some key propositions on the red tape–performance hypothesis.

Red tape

Definitions, dimensions and measures

Red tape is important to the study and practice of public management because it is concerned with rules – that is, norms, regulations, procedures and expectations. Rules regulate individual behaviour and interactions between individuals in organizations (March *et al.* 2000). They exist to ensure accountability, equity and ethical behaviour. Rules provide some of the basic building blocks of public administration (see Crozier 1964; Merton 1957; Weber 1988). Rules also provide us with knowledge about behaviour, organization, and decision making. The growing body of research on red tape clearly attests to its importance.

Red tape is defined as 'bad rules'; that is, when rule making goes wrong and rules shift from actions intended to increase organizational performance to actions that stifle and inhibit it. Red tape is, therefore, associated with the proliferation of bad rules which result in various maladies. It is, consequently, universally seen as something problematic that must be overcome. In fact, the concept seems to be fundamentally based on the notion that it has corrosive effects on governmental performance. Bozeman's (2000) widely cited definition of red tape (see above) captures the essence of the concept and illustrates this view of its harmful nature.

Several other definitions and measures of red tape have been employed in previous research, but they too are predicated on the belief that red tape has negative effects – especially on the lives of public servants and citizens, and on governmental performance. These definitions are typically associated with constraints and rigidity in rules and procedures, for example, excessive business regulation (Organisation for Economic Co-operation and

Development [OECD] 2001), administrative complexity (OECD 2003), excessive paperwork (US Office of Management and Budget 1979), excessive rules and task delays (Bozeman *et al.* 1992), formalization (Bozeman and Scott 1996), personnel system constraints (Rainey *et al.* 1995; Brewer 2005, 2006), and stifling bureaucracy (Brewer and Selden 2000).

Attention has been focused on the ways in which red tape differs from other organizational constructs, notably formalization (Bozeman and Kingsley 1998; Pandey and Scott 2002). Bozeman (1993) suggests that red tape is pathological, whereas formalization is a neutral attribute of organizations. Yet Brewer and Walker (2010a) found that different types of red tape can have varying (i.e. positive or negative) effects on organizational performance at the sub-dimensional level. Their study was based on perceptual measures of red tape which, while defined as burdensome rules and regulations, might produce slightly less harmful effects than more objective measures of the concept. Their findings also call into question the viability of concept definitions that hinge on red tape having all good or all bad outcomes. This produces tautological theoretical expectations that may not be sustainable in social science or the real world. Nevertheless, over the past fifteen years, scholars have not seriously challenged or tried to revamp Bozeman's definition of red tape.

Two different types of red tape have been identified by Bozeman (2000): organizational and stakeholder red tape. Organizational red tape is defined as 'a rule that remains in force and entails a compliance burden for the organization but makes no contribution to achieving the rule's functional objective' (Bozeman 2000: 82). Two sub-dimensions of organizational red tape are discussed in the literature: internal and external. Internal red tape refers to constraints imposed within an organization which suppress the individual effort of organizational members and dampen organizational performance. External red tape is imposed on an organization by outside entities and it can make life difficult for stakeholders (i.e. users, clients and citizens) who try to interact with the organization (Baldwin 1990). External red tape can also undercut organization performance.

Internal rules can mutate into red tape in one of two ways (Bozeman 2000): rules can be *born badly* because rule makers wrongly predict organizational behaviour, try to frustrate or hobble an agency, aim to centralize power within the agency, or exert excessive managerial or political control. Rules may *go bad* when the implementation process alters the rule in a counterproductive way, the need for the rule changes so that it becomes useless or less effective, or rule strain occurs as the number of rules increases and places a compliance burden on the organization. Thus, some rules are congenitally bad, while others are functional or inert at first and evolve into bad rules over time.

External red tape is the product of intensive external control (often for accountability purposes) and large numbers of diverse stakeholders (Bozeman 2000). These factors can apply to public and private organizations, but seem especially prevalent in the former. Moreover, most of the discussion of red tape by business firms relates to this type of red tape and suggests that it is something out of the organization's control – often identified as governmental regulation of business – stifling product innovation, slowing service delivery, and harming performance (Center for International Private Enterprise 2001; OECD 2001, 2003). Here, government is portrayed as the source of red tape, business firms are the intermediate victims, and citizens (as consumers) are the long-term losers.

The external red tape model assumes that a main determinant of red tape occurring is the extent to which rules are external in origin. Two factors can influence this: the way in which external bodies monitor rules and subsequently their distance from those they oversee, and the numbers of stakeholders, especially diverse stakeholders. Figure 5.1 presents a model of the external control of red tape. Red tape is argued to increase for three reasons. First, the likelihood of red tape increasing is in proportion to the number of organizational units imposing rules on the organization. This is because the opportunity for the misapplication of rules grows. Second, if the communication loop is large there are more opportunities for communication entropy. Third, externally imposed rules are likely to be misunderstood, resented and undermined, in comparison to those 'owned' by an organization. Red tape is expected to be reduced by frequent and high-quality communication from clients and between managers with responsibility for the formulation of rules and those who implement them.

Most of the literature examines organizational red tape, and is typically concerned with internal red tape. However, red tape comes in many different forms and has many different meanings for various stakeholders. Stakeholder red tape is 'a rule that remains in force and entails a compliance burden, but serves no objective valued by a given stakeholder group' (Bozeman 2000: 83). This echoes Waldo's (1946: 396) observation that 'one man's red tape is another man's system' and Kaufman's (1978: 4) view that 'one person's red tape is another's treasured safeguard'. In other words, a variation of Miles' law may be operative in public organizations: various stakeholder groups may define red tape differently and hold different views about its causes and effects, in part because of their different stations in the governmental process.

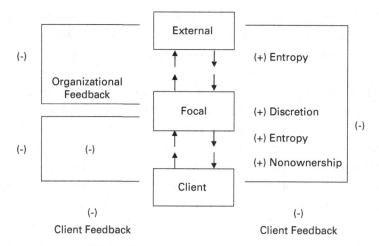

Figure 5.1: External control model of red tape

Source: adapted from Bozeman (1993: 292).

This suggests that red tape is a subject-dependent concept and more complex than research has hitherto shown. The notion of stakeholder red tape has far-reaching implications for defining and measuring the construct, which essentially compounds the difficulty of the task (Brewer and Walker 2010a).

Measurement and sampling difficulties have also been addressed in the red tape literature. Two dominant approaches have been adopted to operationalize red tape: as a behavioural artefact or by perceptions. The behavioural approach asks survey respondents about administrative processes, procedures, or delays, and gauges how many steps are involved in a specified process, or how long it takes to get certain things done, such as hiring a new employee. Examples include Pandey and Bretschneider's (1997) conceptualization of red-tape-based administrative delays, and Bozeman and colleagues' (1992) study that measured red tape as the amount of time required for the performance of core organizational tasks. The perceptual approach typically asks survey respondents about perceived difficulties in performing tasks and about the extent of red tape in their organization. The effort to measure red tape as a behavioural artefact also relies on perceptual measures in most instances, but these measures are based on a metric – passage of time – that may be easier for respondents to gauge accurately than more generalized questions about the amount or degree of red tape in their organization.

Red tape has many sub-dimensions. The measurement of red tape has followed best methodological practices and all recent studies measure it as an index (for exceptions see Brewer and Walker 2010a). Some indexes measure overall red tape, implicitly drawing upon a number of sub-dimensions. Other studies focus on measuring sub-dimensions associated with key organizational processes: human resources, communication, procurement, information systems and budgeting (see, for example, Coursey and Pandey 2007; Pandey *et al.* 2007). These sub-dimensions typically tap the internal organizational red-tape construct, overlooking external red tape. A few studies aim to examine both types of measures, and these studies have shown that they are distinctive (Brewer and Walker 2010a, 2010b; Walker and Brewer 2008, 2009b).

The proposed ills of red tape

Presumptions about the pervasive negative effects of red tape are seen around the globe, whether drawn from rigorously designed studies or casual observations from politicians, policy-makers and service users. From the perspective of politicians and policy-makers, either from individual countries or international organizations, red tape uniformly harms governmental performance. Organizations such as the OECD, International Monetary Fund and World Bank regularly report on the problems of red tape, both relative to its association with corruption, loss of transparency, reduced levels of trust in government, and through case-study examples of its divisive and harmful effects within particular countries or policy sectors (e.g. Center for International Private Enterprise 2001; OECD 2001, 2003). Much of the evidence presented by these agencies concerns external red tape which can be defined as governmental regulation of business. However, public organizations may have other forms of external red tape; in this case, the source may be overhead political authorities or governmental regulators such as the General Accountability Office and the Office of Management and Budget in the USA, the Audit Commission in the UK, and ombudsmen in Western European countries.

In the USA, the term red tape has been used to denote formalization, structural complexity, burgeoning paperwork, excessive rules and task delays. Attempts to eliminate red tape date back to paperwork reduction efforts in the late 1970s (Kaufman 1978; US Office of Management and Budget 1979). Ironically, these efforts often produced more paperwork and increased red tape at the street level. Nevertheless, efforts to curb red tape have intensified in recent years and have been a central plank in governmental reform efforts for both Democrats and Republicans in the USA (Gore 1993; Richardson and Ziebart 1994; US Office of Management and Budget 2001). The political left proposes to combat red tape by decentralizing the public services, empowering public employees, and instilling an entrepreneurial spirit in government (Osborne and Gaebler 1992; Gore 1993). The political right, in contrast, offers a harsher set of remedies that includes wholesale deregulation of business and increased contracting and privatization of public services (US Office of Management and Budget 2001; Heritage Foundation 2005).

In the UK, red tape was previously the preserve of the Conservative Party which sought to 'roll back the state' and introduce market mechanisms and streamlined processes (Walsh 1995). More recently, this agenda has been exploited by the Labour Party, which has made public service improvement a central facet of its domestic policy agenda. A key aspect of this reform agenda is the perceived necessity to cut red tape: 'More effort is needed to cut back further on red tape, which steals valuable time from doctors, nurses, teachers, the police and other public servants' (Office of Public Service Reform (OPSR) 2002: 18). Thus, the Labour administration has taken the problem of red tape to heart. It established the Better Regulation Executive (BRE) in the Cabinet Office soon after taking office in 1997. Within public organizations, the BRE targets reductions in internal red tape: 'The BRE's Public Sector Team works closely with the five key delivery areas within the public sector (health, education, criminal justice, local government and transportation) to understand and minimize unnecessary bureaucracy, or "red-tape" that prevents front-line staff from carrying out their core duties' (BRE 2005). Similarly, the BRE seeks to ease the burden of external red tape – or regulation – by reducing the regulatory requirements government places on business. Prime Minister Blair was explicit about the need to reduce 'bureaucratic demarcations, restrictive practices and red tape' (OPSR 2002: 18; also see Blair 2002) in the delivery of local government services. To resolve the problem of red tape, local governments are encouraged to innovate and find new ways to respond to customer demands. Reductions in red tape are expected to boost governmental performance.

These political, policy and practice dictums generally treat all red tape equally and do not differentiate between organizational or stakeholder red tape, internal or external red tape or different forms of internal red tape. Similarly it is seen to affect all types of performance. As explained in the introductory chapter of this volume, performance is a multidimensional construct. In practice, this means that performance involves concern about a family of service delivery characteristics that include efficiency, effectiveness, fairness, equity, justice, timeliness, consumer satisfaction and other criteria. Theory and anecdotal evidence generally suggests that all types of red tape are harmful to all elements of performance; yet Brewer and Walker (2010a) found that the effects are variable: they range from positive to negative effects and include some null findings. Moreover, the pattern of evidence was somewhat counterintuitive. Red tape in English local government did not seem to hamper efficiency and effectiveness, for example, but it did exert a positive impact on fairness and equity.

This again draws attention to the traditional view of red tape as always being harmful. There is, in fact, an a-priori assumption that red tape is inextricably associated with poor organizational performance. Thus, there has been little formal discussion and hypothesizing about its impact on performance. One notable gap in the literature is that scholars have not carefully analysed and offered hypotheses about the varying impacts of internally and externally created red tape on performance. Another missing link in the literature is discussion of individual and organizational conceptualizations of red tape, save Walker and Brewer's study (2008) that showed clear differences in how organizational stakeholder groups view red tape, and their follow-on study (Brewer and Walker 2010a) that presented evidence of different stakeholders' views of red tape and how it impacts governmental performance. Yet these studies are more suggestive than conclusive; more work needs to be done on this topic.

Empirical evidence on red tape and performance

Very few empirical studies have examined the relationship between red tape and governmental performance, or between the dimensions of the concept. The majority of studies can be grouped into two sets. The first set examines differences in red tape between public and private organizations (Buchanan 1975; Baldwin 1990; Bozeman *et al.* 1992; Bretschneider 1990; DeHart-Davis and Pandey 2005; Rainey *et al.* 1995). The second set of research aims to identify the determinants of red tape, and thus treats the concept as a dependent variable (see, for example, Chen and Williams 2007; Moon 1999; Turaga and Bozeman 2005; Walker and Brewer 2009b, 2010b).

A number of studies include red tape as one of several independent variables that are postulated to affect performance. As we note above, some of these studies seek to explain individual performance while others focus on organizational performance. The range of evidence is interesting but not altogether consistent. Studies of individual managers find that positive work attitudes overcome red tape constraints (Pandey and Welch 2005). Other studies explicitly associate red tape with organizational performance and conduct analyses that aim to explain varying levels of red tape while assuming that the concept is linked to declining performance. For example, DeHart-Davis and Pandey (2005: 134) define red tape as 'managers' perceptions that rules and procedures have a negative effect on organizational performance'. They examine the effects of work alienation indicators (organizational commitment, job involvement and job satisfaction) on perceived organizational and personnel red tape and find that red tape is negatively associated with seven of the eight work alienation measures. Using experimental research methodologies Scott and Pandey (2005) show how higher levels of red tape result in the allocation of lower benefits to clients. The results of the simulation amongst social work students were, however, strongly moderated by the respondents' perceptions of the client. At the individual level these studies skirt around the edge of the issue of red tape and performance. Studies such as DeHart-Davis and Pandey somewhat conflate red tape and organizational performance while Scott and Pandey's results imply that red tape changes behaviour and that this could have implications for the distribution of resources or equity.

Other studies examine red tape as one of several independent variables that affect organizational performance. In some instances, these studies are not primarily focused on red tape as the variable of interest but include it among their explanatory variables. For instance, Brewer and Selden (2000) included a measure of red tape described as 'excessive management levels' in their study of organizational performance in US federal agencies. In another study, Brewer (2006) included a measure of personnel red tape in his study of organizational performance and found that it produced large and statistically significant effects in US federal agencies. In other words, low levels of personnel red tape were associated with high levels of organizational performance, and high levels of personnel red tape were associated with low levels of organizational performance. These studies have not focused on red tape as such in their primary research question but, along with the other studies described here, they shed light on its effects on performance.

A small number of studies have examined the performance impact of red tape at the organizational level. These studies draw upon the American NASP II and the English local government datasets. Given that the literature only sees red tape as harmful to performance, the results of these studies offer some quite startling findings. First, red tape can indeed inflict damage on the performance of public agencies. Red tape, when measured as an aggregate variable, is negatively associated with performance (Brewer and Walker 2010a, Walker and Brewer 2009b).

Second, these results diminish when the sub-dimensions of red tape are examined. Pandey and Moynihan (2006) and Pandey et al. (2007) show that human resource management and information systems red tape is harmful to mission effectiveness but that there are no statistically significant relationships for procurement red tape, budgetary red tape and communication red tape. When the dependent variable is service quality, only procurement red tape is negatively associated. Brewer and Walker (2010a) extend this analysis by examining five dimensions of red tape (internal, remove poor manager, reward good manager, reorganization and external red tape) and ten measures of performance taken from two stakeholder groups – central government as represented by the Audit Commission and public managers in the organizations being analysed. The measures of performance in their analysis include an external perceptual aggregate measure known as core service performance in internal perceptions of quality, value for money, efficiency, effectiveness, equity, customer satisfaction, staff satisfaction and social, economic and environmental performance. Their results paint a more complex picture, noting not only negative and non-significant effects but also positive associations. For example, the external measure of performance had a positive statistical relationship with external red tape, as did quality and equity as measured by public officials. Rather unexpectedly, internal red tape assisted effectiveness and social, economic and environmental performance. These results raise a number of important questions about the effects of red tape on organizational performance and suggest that the hypotheses developed to date, in the academic literature and practice, are overly simplistic and do not delve into the possible effects that different dimensions of red tape may have for different dimensions of performance.

Third, internal management strategies and practices have been shown to mitigate the negative effects of red tape at the level of the overall construct and amongst its sub-parts. Walker and Brewer (2009b) draw upon Miles and Snow's (1978) strategy content typology to show that prospectors (innovative outward-looking organizations) can mitigate the negative effects of red tape as an organizational construct and that reactors (organizations that await their strategy clues from the external organizational environment and agencies) may compound the already harmful effects of red tape. These tests are undertaken on cross-sectional internal perceptions of performance and a lagged model using the external core service performance score mentioned above as the dependent variable. The results are similar in both cases.

In two linked studies Pandey and colleagues (Pandey and Moynihan 2006; Pandey et al. 2007) show how developmental culture, 'a cultural orientation that places high value on a focus on the organization (rather than people), flexibility, readiness, adaptability and growth' (Pandey and Moynihan 2006: 134) mitigates the negative effects of certain subsystem measures of red tape. Again, what is interesting in these studies is that developmental culture reduces the harmful effects of red tape on several management subsystems (human resources, information systems and communication) but not on others (procurement, budgetary and mission effectiveness) (Pandey et al. 2007: 411). In their prior study Pandey and Moynihan (2006) also demonstrate the positive effects that political support can have on human resources red tape (when the dependent variable is mission effectiveness) and procurement red tape (when the dependent variable is service quality).

These studies, while not modelling the origins of red tape (internally or externally generated), show that management action can be a force of good in the battle against red tape. These findings reflect those of other studies that show how internal management – integration and strategy management – can overcome red tape, some of which was externally generated or at least beyond the control of public managers (Walker and Brewer 2009a). Broadly, these findings on the mitigating effect of proactive management strategies show that there is much in the armoury of the public manager that can be used to combat the negative effects of red tape. The results also raise questions about the complexity of the relationships between red tape and performance. We now turn to these questions and propose directions for future research.

Research agenda

Our search for academic writing on red tape uncovered less than forty articles along with several books and numerous governmental and quasi-governmental reports. As we noted above, only a handful of these articles directly dealt with the topic of this book: organizational performance. Given the widespread presumption in the literature that red tape is harmful to performance, the lack of precise theorizing and empirical studies on the topic is surprising. What is particularly noteworthy is that the empirical findings of these studies cast some doubts on the severity and one-way nature of the red tape–performance hypothesis.

The studies we have cited in this chapter have some important limitations. We will initially focus on these methodological concerns before outlining our propositions. First, the majority of studies undertaken draw their evidence from the National Administration Studies Project (NASP) I and II, with the balance substantially favouring the second phase of the study. NASP I examined chief executive officers in public, private and voluntary organizations, and if the organization employed more than 500 personnel the immediate subordinates of the chief executive officer were included. NASP II focused upon managers involved in 'information management activities' in US state health and social services programmes, and reports an N of 273. The more recent studies by Brewer and Walker draw upon the English local government dataset. Measures of red tape were recorded in 2004 amongst 135 local authorities, using multiple informant survey techniques to garner information from the senior management team and middle managers. Other studies, undertaken by faculty at Syracuse University in the early 1990s, include R&D labs and information technology departments as the unit of analysis (for example see Bretschneider 1990; Bozeman and Bretschneider 1994). The first priority for new research is thus to develop and examine some new datasets.

While some progress has been made in the measurement of red tape, the use of limited datasets means that the number of survey items drawn upon is quite limited. Indeed much of our knowledge stems from a relatively limited number of survey questions. New datasets present the opportunity to measure red tape in different ways. One fruitful line of inquiry would be to use both behavioural (e.g. measures of administrative time delays or the number of steps required to complete a process) and perceptual (e.g. my organization seems to have a lot of red tape) measures, and to systematically tease out a more ideal measure of red tape. Within the existing datasets there has been only limited coverage of different dimensions of performance, and the majority have been recorded within the organization by the same public officials who complete the survey on other items of management and organization. While the prospects of common-source bias are not as extensive as perhaps thought (Brewer 2006), there is, nonetheless, a possibility that these findings are compromised.

Throughout this chapter we have made a number of observations about the nature of red tape and its relationship to organizational performance. We now turn our attention to some key propositions on these relationships.

Our first observation is based upon the nature of red tape itself. We noted that red tape could be internal, external and stakeholder. The evidence reviewed points toward the veracity of the notion of stakeholder red tape – variations in its impact on performance were noted within organizations and by different actors (Brewer and Walker 2010a; Walker and Brewer 2008).

Given that the majority of research has been undertaken on organizational or internal red tape, we note the urgent need for research on external and stakeholder red tape. Our first propositions relates to the way red tape is conceptualized:

> *Proposition 1*: Red tape is a subject-dependent construct.

One important observation we have made in reviewing the evidence is upon the differential impact of red tape when measured as an aggregate variable compared with when composed of its parts. From this inspection we derive a further three propositions. It is not possible to offer propositions on the likely effects of different types of red tape on different dimensions of performance because the evidence basis remains limited. Thus:

> *Proposition 2*: Red tape (as an aggregate construct) has a negative effect on public service performance.
> *Proposition 3*: Different dimensions of red tape do not always or consistently have a negative effect on public service performance.
> *Proposition 4*: Different dimensions of red tape will have varying effects on different dimensions of performance.

One area of merit to explore in the red tape–performance hypothesis is the point at which red tape starts to harm performance – or assist it if other studies support our proposition that red tape can benefit performance. Understanding 'red tape points' would advance our knowledge of the field and, like answers to many of these propositions, would lead to useful findings for the world of policy and practice.

A small number of studies have examined the joint effects of other management practices upon the red tape–performance relationship. These studies indicate that the negative effects of red tape can be offset by adroit management practices, thus we propose:

> *Proposition 5*: The negative effects of the red tape construct can be mitigated by a range of management practices.

Variables to include in these relationships are many. But research could usefully focus on questions of organizational structure, and in particular the extent to which decision making is centralized or decentralized (see Chapter 4). Questions of leadership, human resource management practices and organizational size also require examination, while additional tests are required on strategy and culture. In examining external red tape, network structure and behaviour could be explored as strategies to mitigate the potentially harmful effects of this form of red tape, while study of the model would require the development of knowledge on internal and external communication strategies.

An ideal study of the performance consequences of red tape should, therefore, be longitudinal; include different stakeholders who offer ratings on the levels of red tape in a public agency; collect some behavioural measures of the construct; include robust measures of management and organization; and include a range of performance measures. The study should also cut across different public service sectors, both vertically and horizontally, to boost its external validity. Another question that can be addressed by such a study is to what extent findings are generalizable across different countries. So far, empirical research on red tape has been confined to a handful of studies in the USA and UK. These studies often use different measures of key constructs and address different research questions. Cross-country replications are almost nonexistent. Thus, other countries need to enter the fray, and scholars in various countries need to focus intently on core research questions.

Good work is clearly being undertaken on the red-tape–performance hypothesis. This is an important area of investigation for public management scholars, given its home-grown status. We must, however, necessarily conclude that we still have some considerable distance to travel to obtain robust evidence on the impact of red tape on public service performance.

REFERENCES

Baldwin, J. Norman. 1990. 'Perceptions of public versus private sector personnel and informal red tape and their impact on motivation', *American Review of Public Administration*, 20, 1, 7–28.

Better Regulation Executive. 2005. 'BRE and the public sector team'. Available online: www.cabinetoffice.gov.uk/regulation/public_services/ (accessed 8 October 2007).

Blair, Tony. 2002. 'The courage of our convictions: why reform of the public services is the route to social justice', Fabian Ideas 603, London: Fabian Society.

Bozeman, Barry. 1993. 'A theory of government "Red Tape"', *Journal of Public Administration Research and Theory* 3, 3, 273–303.

2000. *Bureaucracy and Red Tape*. Upper Saddle River, NJ: Prentice Hall.

Bozeman, Barry, and Stuart Bretschneider. 1994. 'The "Publicness Puzzle" in organization theory: a test of alternative explanations of differences between public and private organizations', *Journal of Public Administration Research and Theory*, 4, 2, 197–223.

Bozeman, Barry, and Gordon Kingsley. 1998. 'Risk culture in public and private organizations', *Public Administration Review*, 58, 2, 109–118.

Bozeman, Barry, Pamela Reed, and Patrick G. Scott. 1992. 'Red tape and task delays in public and private organizations', *Administration & Society*, 24, 3, 290–322.

Bozeman, Barry, and Patrick G. Scott. 1996. 'Bureaucratic "red tape" and formalization: untangling conceptual knots', *American Review of Public Administration*, 26, 1, 1–13.

Bretschneider, Stuart. 1990. 'Managing information systems in public and private organizations: an empirical test', *Public Administration Review*, 50, 5, 536–45.

Brewer, Gene A. 2005. 'In the eye of the storm: frontline supervisors and federal agency performance', *Journal of Public Administration Research and Theory*, 15, 4, 505–27.

   2006. 'All measures of performance are subjective: more evidence on US federal agencies', in George A. Boyne, Kenneth. J. Meier, Laurence J. O'Toole, Jr. and Richard M. Walker (eds.) *Public Service Performance*. Cambridge University Press.

Brewer, Gene A., and Sally Coleman Selden. 2000. 'Why elephants gallop: assessing and predicting organizational performance in federal agencies', *Journal of Public Administration Research and Theory*, 10, 4, 685–711.

Brewer, Gene A., and Richard M. Walker. 2010a. 'The impact of red tape on organizational performance: an empirical analysis', *Journal of Public Administration Research and Theory*, 20, 1, 233–57.

   2010b. 'Explaining variations in perceptions of red tape: a professionalism-marketisation model', *Public Administration*, 82, 2 (DOI: 10.1111/j.1467–9299.2010.01827.x).

Buchanan, Bruce. 1975. 'Red tape and the service ethic: some unexpected differences between public and private managers', *Administration & Society*, 6, 4, 423–44.

Center for International Private Enterprise. 2001. 'Red tape ranking'. Available online: www.cipe.org/programs/informalsector/redtaperanking/ (accessed 4 March 2005).

Chen, Greg, and Daniel W. Williams. 2007. 'How political support influences red tape through developmental culture', *The Policy Studies Journal*, 35, 3, 419–36.

Coursey, David H., and Sanjay K. Pandey. 2007. 'Content domain, measurement, and validity of the red tape concept. A second-order confirmatory factor analysis', *The American Review of Public Administration*, 37, 3, 342–61.

Crozier, Michel. 1964. *The Bureaucratic Phenomenon*. University of Chicago Press.

DeHart-Davis, Leisha, and Sanjay K. Pandey. 2005. 'Red tape and public employees: does perceived rule dysfunction alienate managers?', *Journal of Public Administration Research and Theory*, 15, 1, 133–48.

Gore, Albert. 1993. 'From red tape to results: creating a government that works better and costs less', Report of the National Performance Review. Washington, DC: Government Printing Office.

Heritage Foundation. 2005. *Mandate For Leadership: Principles to Limit Government, Expand Freedom, and Strengthen America*. Washington, DC: Heritage Foundation.

Kaufman, Herbert. 1978. *Red Tape: its Origins, Uses, and Abuses*. Washington, DC: Brookings Institution.

March, James G., Martin Schulz, and Xuenghang Zhou. 2000. *The Dynamics of Rules: Changes in Written Organizational Rules*. Stanford University Press.

Merton, Robert K. 1957. 'Bureaucratic structure and personality', in Robert K. Merton (ed.) *Social Theory and Social Structure*. New York: Free Press.

Miles, Raymond E., and Charles C. Snow. 1978. *Organizational Strategy, Structure and Process*. New York: McGraw-Hill.

Moon, M. Jae. 1999. 'The pursuit of managerial entrepreneurship: does organization matter?', *Public Administration Review*, 59, 1, 31–43.

Office of Public Service Reform (OPSR), 2002. *Reforming our Public Services: Principles into Practice*. London: the Prime Minister's Office of Public Service Reform.

Organisation for Economic Co-operation and Development (OECD). 2001. *Businesses' Views on Red Tape: Administrative and Regulatory Burdens on Small- and Medium-sized Enterprises*. Paris: OECD.

Organisation for Economic Co-operation and Development. 2003. *From Red Tape to Smart Tape: Administrative Simplification in OECD Countries*. Paris: OECD.

Osborne, David, and Ted Gaebler. 1992. *Reinventing Government: How the Entrepreneurial Spirit is Transforming the Public Sector*. Reading, MA: Addison-Wesley.

Pandey, Sanjay K., and Stuart I. Bretschneider. 1997. 'The impact of red tape's administrative delay on public organizations' interest in new information technology', *Journal of Public Administration Research and Theory*, 7, 1, 113–30.

Pandey, Sanjay K., David H. Coursey, and Donald P. Moynihan. 2007. 'Organizational effectiveness and bureaucratic red tape: a multimethod study', *Public Performance and Management Review*, 30, 3, 398–425.

Pandey, Sanjay K., and Donald P. Moynihan. 2006. 'Bureaucratic red tape and organizational performance: testing the moderating role of culture and political support', in George A. Boyne, Kenneth J. Meier, Laurence J. O'Toole, Jr. and Richard M. Walker (eds.) *Public Service Performance*. Cambridge University Press.

Pandey, Sanjay K., and Patrick G. Scott. 2002. 'Red tape: a review and assessment of concepts and measures', *Journal of Public Administration Research and Theory*, 12, 4, 553–80.

Pandey, Sanjay K., and Eric W. Welch. 2005. 'Beyond stereotypes. A multistage model of managerial perceptions of red tape', *Administration & Society*, 37, 5, 542–75.

Rainey, Hal G., Sanjay K. Pandey, and Barry Bozeman. 1995. 'Research note: public and private managers' perceptions of red tape', *Public Administration Review*, 55, 6, 567–574.

Richardson, Craig E., and Geoff C. Ziebart. 1994. *Red Tape in America: Stories from the Front Line*. Washington, DC: Heritage Foundation.

Scott, Patrick G., and Sanjay K. Pandey. 2005. 'Red tape and public service motivation: findings from a national survey of managers in state health and human services agencies', *Review of Public Personnel Administration*, 25, 2, 155–80.

Turaga, Rama M. R., and Barry Bozeman. 2005. 'Red tape and public mangers' decision-making', *American Review of Public Administration*, 35, 4, 363–79.

US Office of Management and Budget, 1979. 'Paperwork and red tape: new perspectives, new directions', A Report to the President and the Congress from the Office of Management and Budget. Washington, DC: US Government Printing Office.

US Office of Management and Budget. 2001. *The President's Management Agenda, FY 2002*. Washington, DC: Government Printing Office.

Waldo, Dwight. 1946. 'Government by procedure', in Fritz Morstein Marx (ed.) *Elements of Public Administration*. Englewood Cliffs, NJ: Prentice-Hall.

Walker, Richard M., and Gene A. Brewer. 2008. 'An organizational echelon analysis of the determinants of red tape in public organizations', *Public Administration Review*, 68, 6, 1112–27.

2009a. 'Can managers reduce red tape? The role of internal management in overcoming external constraints', *Policy & Politics*, 37, 2, 255–72.

2009b. 'Can management strategy minimize the impact of red tape on organizational performance?', *Administration & Society*, 41, 4, 423–48.

Walsh, Kieron. 1995. *Public Services and Market Mechanisms: Competition, Contracting and the New Public Management*. Basingstoke: Macmillan.

Weber, Max. 1988. *The Protestant Ethic and the Spirit of Capitalism*. Gloucester, MA: Peter Smith.

Managerial networking, managing the environment, and programme performance: a summary of findings and an agenda

Kenneth J. Meier and Laurence J. O'Toole, Jr.

Introduction

The public management of networks and managerial efforts to interact with the interdependent environments surrounding public organizations are frequent themes in the current governance literature (for extensive documentation see Rainey 2003; see also Provan and Kenis 2008). Organizations, of course, are open systems and must either adapt to environmental pressures or seek to alter the environment (Thompson 1967; Pfeffer and Salancik 1978). Interactions with the environment and attempts to manage them almost inevitably involve networks of other actors outside the control of the manager (Agranoff and McGuire 2001). By networks we mean 'structures of interdependence involving multiple organizations, where one unit is not just the formal subunit or subordinate of the other in some larger hierarchical arrangement' (O'Toole 1997b: 117). At times networks arise out of formal government mandates (Hall and O'Toole 2000); at other times they are created to help solve implementation problems (O'Toole 1997b; Blair 2002); they can also arise from self-organized efforts at collaboration (Bardach 1998; Mandell 2001; O'Leary 2008); and sometimes the stimuli may be multiple. In contemporary public policy, the management of networks and

This chapter is part of an ongoing research agenda on the role of public management in complex policy settings. That agenda has benefited from the helpful comments of George Boyne, Stuart Bretschneider, Gene Brewer, Amy Kneedler Donahue, Sergio Fernández, H. George Frederickson, Carolyn Heinrich, Peter Hupe, Patricia Ingraham, J. Edward Kellough, H. Brinton Milward, Sean Nicholson-Crotty, David Peterson, Hal G. Rainey and Bob Stein on various aspects of this research programme. Needless to say, this chapter is the responsibility of the authors only.

of the interdependent environment is perceived to be crucial to programme success.

Fully analysing such patterns of interdependence involves estimating the impact of networks as structures and also determining the influence of the networking in which managers engage (Walker *et al.* 2007). In this chapter we focus on the latter issue (for an explanation of its importance see Rhodes 2002). Studies exploring the networking of public managers consider managerial efforts to shape the actions of an entire network or the externally oriented, networking behaviour of managers as they operate outside their own organization but within their interdependent environment. Kickert and Koppenjan (1997) sketch various strategies for 'network management', whereas Agranoff and McGuire (2003) outline a set of managerial functions in networked settings. We examine this externally directed networking by managers, which can be considered one aspect of management in interdependent settings.

The subjects of networks and managerial efforts to operate in and influence the interdependent organizational setting are especially prominent among researchers in Europe (for instance, Kickert *et al.* 1997; Rhodes 1997; Stoker 1999) and North America (Provan and Milward 1995; Agranoff and McGuire 2003; Berry *et al.* 2004; Rethemeyer 2005; Herranz 2008). The broad research questions implied by networks and networking are multiple (for detailed treatment see O'Toole 1997b). Most prominent are three sets of issues: (1) to what extent are networks a key part of the context in which public management operates? In which governance settings and which policy fields? (2) What values do networked settings facilitate, or impede, and thus how can traditionally important concerns like responsiveness and accountability be addressed in such complex institutional settings? And (3) how can we understand the operations of networks and public managers in networked settings, with a view toward explaining observed patterns and possibly predicting behaviour in networked contexts? How do such patterns shape public programme performance?

While additional research may be valuable on all of these matters, some progress has been made on the first set of issues, which is primarily focused on description of the extant public management settings (for instance, Agranoff and McGuire 2003; Hall and O'Toole 2000, 2004). Similarly, the second theme, one focused on normative theory, has begun to be addressed by researchers (O'Toole 1997a; Behn 2001). The third set of concerns raises the question of empirical theory. This subject too has seen attention in recent years. Scholars based in social network analysis have developed a detailed conceptual apparatus to characterize networks and their features, although this line of work has been less successful at parsimonious theoretical advance. Others, based in public management, have begun to offer partial theoretical explanations for observed patterns. Nonetheless, relatively few of these researchers have developed explicit theoretical and empirical links between networks or networking and performance (an exception is Provan and Milward 1995; other investigations which begin to examine this link include Bardach 1998; Johnston and Romzek 2008; Weber and Khademian 2008; and Schneider 2009).

Our own emphasis has been in empirical theory, although we have also contributed to the normative debate (for instance, Meier and O'Toole 2006). How public managers operate in networked environments, how they and their organizations respond to environmental pressures and opportunities, and how these behaviours contribute to programme performance are questions at the centre of a major research agenda we launched several years ago that has emphasized large-N quantitative research rather than the more commonly found work involving qualitative assessment and/or small-N investigations. While the latter type of study can be valuable, particularly for validating the full networked environment of a public organization and discerning some of the fine-grained managerial and interactive details of operations in such settings, we have emphasized large-N empirical studies for the considerable advantages that they offer, such as the opportunity to explore patterns across hundreds or thousands of cases and the chance to include numerous control variables to isolate managerial impacts on performance (for detailed treatment of the methodological advantages of this approach, see Meier and O'Toole 2005). The objectives of our research programme in this regard have been to (1) distil the available knowledge concerning public management, including managing in networks and interacting with the environment, into a concise and testable format, and (2) assess the empirical validity of the available theoretical formulations via systematic tests. That research agenda has produced a series of empirical and theoretical papers by the authors as well as additional papers by a second generation of scholars.

In this chapter we provide a concise summary of this work. To set the study of networks and public organizational environments in the broader context of public management, we begin by sketching our base model and its central elements. We then define and discuss the key concepts and their operationalization. After reviewing the current research findings, we sketch an agenda for future research.

The base model

Although theoretical ideas about how public organizations manage in networks and the broader environment are many, much of that work is ambiguous in character and unsystematic in sketching causal links between public management and public programme performance. Only careful efforts at validation make it possible to tell which ideas provide important insights and which, although plausible, are actually dead-ends. In an effort to provide a solid starting point for analysis and to trim productively the overabundance of theory via empirical research, we have inductively developed a formal model of such relationships – a model constructed from our examination of the farrago of theoretical and empirical (mostly case-study) material on public management and performance, as well as on some of the prominent notions of how management might matter in complex, or networked, institutional settings (see O'Toole 2000). To understand the relationship among public management, institutional arrangements and public programme performance, we begin with the following:

$$O_t = \beta_1(S + M_1)O_{t-1} + \beta_2(X_t/S)(M_3/M_4) + \varepsilon_t$$

where
O is some measure of outcome,
S is a measure of stability,
M denotes management, which can be divided into three parts
   M_1 management's contribution to organizational stability through additions to hierarchy/structure as well as regular operations,
   M_3 management's efforts to exploit the environment of the organization,
   M_4 management's effort to buffer the unit from environmental shocks,
X is a vector of environmental forces,
ε is an error term,
the other subscripts denote time periods, and
β_1 and β_2 are estimable parameters.
The model incorporates three basic principles with regard to public management and administrative systems for delivering public programme results. First, such arrays are autoregressive systems – that is, they create processes and operating procedures that tend to reproduce the same outputs over time. Second, the model is non-linear rather than strictly additive. At times variables interact in a multiplicative manner, at times the interaction is with a

reciprocal function, and at other times terms add together and then interact with another variable to generate their overall impact on public programme performance. Third, the model is contingent in order to reflect our view that what works in terms of public management is contingent on a variety of other factors. Among the most interesting contingencies are those involving networks, managerial networking and the environment.

In the model, S can be considered a composite of the various kinds of stability in an organizational setting. Some stability is induced by structure; other forms of stability have their origins in management processes and procedures. While stability contributes greatly to the autoregressive nature of the organization, it is distinct conceptually because it is composed of specific actions intended to induce autoregression. A wide variety of other factors, some outside the organization (e.g. political expectations, budget patterns), can also contribute to the autoregressive aspect of organizations.

The model contains three different functions of management. They are efforts to manage the internal operations of the organization (M_1), efforts to exploit opportunities in the interdependent environment (M_3), and efforts to limit the negative impact of environmental perturbations on the administrative system (M_4). The latter two functions in the second, or environmental, portion of the model, are often combined as M_2 – defined as the ratio of M_3 to M_4. Our concern in this essay is M_2, the ability to manage in the network (thus, managerial networking) along with an aspect of M_1, internal management in the organization. The facet of M_1 that we consider in this chapter is the managerial effort to handle impacts or potential impacts from the environment, particularly in difficult situations.

Our objective in presenting the original formal model, and the impetus behind this research agenda, is to be precise about our ideas regarding how public management might relate to performance directly and how it might interact with other factors to affect performance. We have stated from the outset of this work that we care less about being right in the final analysis than about being precise in what is being said (O'Toole and Meier 1999: 523). An unfalsifiable theory is of little use in a scientific effort to understand phenomena, including such a complex and important phenomenon as public management. As our empirical agenda has proceeded, the model has been refined in certain respects, as evidence has accumulated regarding the various elements and relationships in the model. Further refinements can be expected as the research programme moves ahead (for some possibilities see Meier and O'Toole 2004b).

Defining key terms

The theory of public management and programme performance that we have been developing is highly parsimonious; it contains only four variables, or variable clusters: performance, management, stability and the environment. At the same time testing the entire theory with an existing dataset would be extremely difficult, if not impossible, since multiple measures for each of the variable clusters would need to be developed and validated, the test would have to be performed over a variety of different performance indicators, and the theoretical specification itself is highly complex. We have therefore opted for an incremental strategy that focuses on the link between management and performance in general – and specifically on developing reliable and valid measures of management. Within this strategic approach, we have proceeded by testing discrete portions of the model and building on the results in subsequent rounds of analysis.

We have identified and operationalized eight different elements of management – managerial networking, managerial quality, managerial stability, workforce stability, managerial strategy, managerial buffering, crisis management, and human resources management. This chapter will focus on managerial networking and those aspects of internal management that permit the organization to deal with environmental demands (managerial buffering, managerial stability, workforce stability and managerial capacity). In most cases we have conducted these studies in a pooled time-series analysis of Texas school districts.[1] Unless otherwise noted, the empirical findings are generated from this database (for a scientific justification of the extensive use of this database see Meier and O'Toole 2007).

Managerial networking is an effort to operationalize our M_2 term, the actions of the manager in the networked environment of a public agency. This measure assumes that managers cannot engage in network-like behaviour with other actors in the environment without coming into contact with them. Using the Texas School District dataset, we asked top managers to rate how frequently, from daily to never, they interact with each of a set of environmental actors (five actors in a 2000 survey, eight actors in 2002 and 2005

---

[1] School districts in the United States are generally independent local governments with their own taxing powers. All districts in the analyses discussed in this chapter are of this type. Independent means that the school district is not subordinate to another unit such as a city. Independent districts have their own elected board, have the ability to tax and set budgets, and acquire bonding authority by a vote of the residents. There are roughly 14,000 school districts in the US, approximately one thousand of which are in Texas.

surveys, and ten in the 2007 survey). These items have been factor analysed and consistently produce a first factor that is a general networking measure with all positive loadings (at times one factor only is produced). A factor score which indicates that the manager interacts more with environmental actors is taken as the measure of M_2.

Both *management stability* (S_m) and *workforce stability* (S_w) were originally constructed as measures of stability, but indeed they reflect aspects of management and might be considered as much a management element as a stability component – or, alternatively, as management's contribution to personnel stability in the administrative system. Management stability is a simple measure of how long the superintendent has been employed by the organization in any capacity. Workforce stability measures the stability of the core production personnel, the teachers. The measure is 100 minus the teacher-turnover rate.

Buffering is a key element in managing the environment and can take several forms, including shielding the organization from environmental influences, creating structures to deal with environmental turbulence, and dissipating the environmental shocks that penetrate the organization (Meier and O'Toole 2009b). The proposed measure of buffering reflects, in our view, both managerial efforts to dissipate shocks and also structural arrangements that do the same. Hence the buffering term is designated with SM_4 to indicate it is both a structural and a managerial measure. Buffering in this view is similar to an organization being loosely coupled so that any environmental influences that penetrate to the organization get dampened down and do not continue to permeate through the autoregressive aspect of the organization. Meier and O'Toole (2008) measure buffering by taking organizational outputs at time t and correlating them with outputs at t – 1, for the time period 1986 to 1994 (a time period prior to the time period [1995–2002] when the actual analysis of buffering was done). This correlation coefficient is then subtracted from 1.0 so that high numbers mean a loosely coupled (highly buffered) organization.[2]

The focus on the management of organizational crises emanating from the environment grew out of the buffering agenda and led to the creation of a managerial capacity measure (O'Toole and Meier 2009; Meier *et al.* 2010). The empirical question was what do organizations do after experiencing a serious environmental shock. Two shocks were assessed – a 10 per cent or greater budget cut and the problems generated by Hurricanes Katrina and

---

[2] We also are working on the development of an attitudinal measure of buffering based on questions about managers seeking to buffer the organization from environmental disruptions.

Rita on the US Gulf Coast (an influx of students from Katrina and class closures from Rita). The crisis management studies and follow-up investigations (O'Toole and Meier 2009) have generated measures of *managerial capacity*, essentially the stockpiling of managerial slack for times of need. Management capacity is tapped simply as the percentage of central office administrators of total employment. We stress central office administrators because most other managers have line responsibilities and thus cannot be easily shifted to other tasks in a crisis.

What do we know? Managerial networking M_2

Because the concepts of performance and management in networked settings figure heavily in our theory of public management, examining efforts by managers to interact with key stakeholders in the environment was a task at the core of our first empirical studies. The relevant investigations can be divided into two parts: those focused on the relationship of M_2 to performance and those concerned with measurement validity.

Performance questions

The first task was to show that the measure of managerial networking was related to the performance of public organizations while controlling for the resources and constraints that also affect performance (Meier and O'Toole 2001: 285 and subsequent papers showed that managerial networking was positively related to student performance on standardized tests and on high-end indicators for college-bound students. Qualitative data suggested that high network scores meant that managers were dealing with environmental problems, particularly political ones, and keeping such distractions from affecting the organization's production personnel.

Two papers (Meier and O'Toole 2001, 2003) probed the non-linear aspects in the relationship between managerial networking and performance (see also Hicklin *et al.* 2008). Of great interest was the relationship between managerial networking and the autoregressive character of the administrative system. Although the inertial nature of such a system can be a positive thing (it creates the patterns of efficiency we associate with organization), an excessive level of autoregression means a rigid institution that cannot adapt to change. Meier and O'Toole (2003: 696) found that at high levels of managerial networking (more than 1.5 standard deviations above the mean), the degree of autoregressivity declines precipitously. This relationship suggests that managing in the networked setting can provide an agency with some flexibility and allow it to break away from sub-optimal routines when useful. This networking-autoregressive interaction could well be associated with managers generating additional support for the organization and thus enhancing its capacity to be flexible. We found greater efforts to manage externally were associated with more support from the clientele of the organization, more support from political sovereigns and greater levels of community support (Meier and O'Toole 2003: 693).

Nicholson-Crotty and O'Toole (2004) extended the managerial networking studies to US local police departments. They created an external management scale that combined measures of contact with measures of public feedback systems and with community-oriented policing activities. They found a strong positive relationship between this measure of networking and environmental management and performance measured as crime clearance rates.

Our theory suggests that management should interact with various resources and constraints in a non-linear manner. The non-linear element implies that under certain conditions management should magnify or enhance the positive impact of resources well above normal or be able to mitigate the negative influences of constraints. Meier and O'Toole (2001: 289) showed that network management can reduce the negative impact of black and Hispanic students (task difficulty is greater when dealing with more disadvantaged students) as well as of noncertified teachers on organizational performance; in other words, increasing the level of managerial networking can reduce the negative correlation between disadvantaged student characteristics and overall organizational performance (for conceptualization of the variety of forms of buffering that management may be able to employ to support the core production in a public programme, see O'Toole and Meier 2003b; for empirical studies see Meier and O'Toole 2008; Meier et al. 2007). Similarly, managerial networking selectively interacts with resources and can produce much larger gains for a unit increase in resources. The impact of increases in teachers' salaries, for example, is 3.27 times greater and the impact of smaller classes is 8.6 times greater (Meier and O'Toole 2003: 696) in organizations with high levels of managerial networking. Not all of the relationships between resources and constraints (the X variables) and M_2 are non-linear, however; management exercises choice in selecting the levers that might connect to performance. This choice means that some relationships will be characterized by interactions and non-linearity and others will not.

M_2 also interacts with organizational performance in non-linear ways. When the data were split into quintiles based on the level of organizational performance, the relationship between management and performance changed in different quintiles. Managerial networking matters more for units at the extremes of performance – that is, it matters more for organizations in the highest performing quintile and those in the lowest performing quintile (Meier and O'Toole 2001: 695). The former case is likely the more important one, since almost anything management is likely to do will improve the sorry performance of organizations in the bottom quintile. Managerial networking also has a greater impact on performance in organizations that have very high and very low levels of management quality (O'Toole and Meier 2003a: 58).[3]

Hicklin *et al.* (2008) investigated whether non-linearity applied to M_2 taken by itself. Their theoretical hypothesis was that there had to be limits to managerial networking that would eventually result in diminishing marginal returns from additional networking actions. Their analysis showed exactly that pattern and also demonstrated that talented managers (measured as those scoring high on the quality measure) seemed to be cognizant of the limits of networking, since they restricted their own efforts before they reached the point of negative marginal returns.

Additional work distinguished between, and estimated the relative impacts of, managing in the networked setting (M_2), a behavioural manifestation, and network-like structures themselves. The latter involve the formal and sometimes informal regularized ties that link a core public agency to a set of other key actors in the environment, or link a set of coproducing units together. M_2, in contrast, is the behavioural actions that managers take to deal with the various nodes in the organization's setting. This distinction was examined empirically in O'Toole and Meier (2004a). The structural aspect of the network was defined in financial terms, via the degree to which the school district had to depend on others for monetary support (state and federal governments). Although managerial networking is important and positively linked to performance both when the organization is financially dependent on others and when it is financially independent, it is more important for performance among organizations that are dependent on others for financial

---

[3] Management quality is a salary-based residual measure that incorporates all the factors that should influence salaries and considers the residual as correlated with some judgement as to quality (Meier and O'Toole 2002). The interaction of high-quality managers and networking makes intuitive sense. Why low-quality managers benefit from networking is unclear unless the networking compensates for the lack or expertise of the manager (but see Gonzalez Juenke 2005).

support. In short, managerial networking matters more in structural networks (O'Toole and Meier 2004a: 487–8).

Managing outward into the networked setting involves managers interacting with others in sets of exchange relationships. The logic of viewing managerial networking as an exchange relationship or as a set of games (see Scharpf 1993) implies that the external actors – the network nodes – also expect to receive something of value from the interaction. Because actors in the regular pattern of interdependence are likely to over-represent the better organized, they are also likely to represent especially well the more privileged elements in the managerial setting. This logic suggests that managerial networking will have distributional consequences – that network interactions will benefit the more advantaged clientele at the expense of the less well off. Because school systems have multiple goals and the performance-appraisal system includes data on different types of students and different outcomes, O'Toole and Meier (2004b) were able to investigate the distributional consequences of managerial networking. They found that networking was positively related to higher test scores for Anglo students (as well as overall test scores) and three measures of performance for college-bound students. In contrast, managerial networking was not related to pass rates for Latinos, blacks, or low-income students (O'Toole and Meier 2004b: 688).[4] These findings suggest the operation of a politics of public management whereby the more powerful political forces are likely to exert greater influence on management as managers increase their activities in the network (see Hawes 2008).

Managerial networking also appears to interact with managerial capacity (see Meier and O'Toole 2009a). As the size of the central office bureaucracy increases, the impact of managerial networking on Texas Assessment of Academic Skills (TAAS) exams increases by about 40 per cent. Such increases in central office staff appear to double the impact of managerial networking on student attendance and increase it by a factor of four on the percentage of students scoring at the top of college board exams. These results make intuitive sense; to get the most out of network interactions, management needs the capacity to determine which actors to approach and what types of exchanges could benefit the organization.

Goerdel (2006) extended the work on managerial networking by including a strategic element. She argued that managerial networking would matter

---

[4] Networking was associated with lower dropout rates, a disadvantaged indicator, but was not related to attendance rates, another low-end indicator.

more when managers initiated the interactions (proactive networking) rather than when they passively responded to the initiatives of others (reactive networking). In general she found positive correlations for proactive networking and negative correlations for reactive networking.

Gonzalez Juenke (2005) linked managerial stability with managerial networking. He argued that to exploit network opportunities fully, the manager needed extensive experience. His research corroborated this hypothesis; more experienced managers gained greater benefits from managerial networking than did less experienced managers.

Measurement questions

Measurement issues in regard to network management are important, simply because this research programme is one of the first efforts to create measures of management for use in a large-N quantitative set of studies. The argument for M_2 as a reliable and valid measure of management activities rests on several grounds. First, the factor analysis of networking items reveals that contact with environmental actors forms a consistent pattern across nodes. Such contacts are all correlated with each other, and always produce a generic first factor with positive loading regardless of how many nodes are included in the analysis.[5]

Second, M_2 is positively correlated with a manager's time estimates of how much of their effort is focused outside the organization (as opposed to focused on internal matters, see Meier and O'Toole 2003: 698 n4).[6] In addition, the strong results in various linkages to performance with a wide variety of indicators (O'Toole and Meier 2003a: 54, 56) reveal a concept with a great deal of empirical import and external validity.

Third, by comparing survey results in 2000 with those in 2002, Meier and O'Toole (2005) provided a systematic evaluation of the concept's reliability and validity. This assessment revealed that the exact number of nodes included in the measure was not especially crucial; the five-node measure correlated strongly with the eight-node measure (as did the four- and seven-node measures). We have replicated these findings with the 2005 and 2007 surveys and get similar results. This finding does not mean that scholars can

---

[5] In subsequent analysis with local managers in the United Kingdom, we also consistently find a first factor with a set of positive loadings (Walker *et al.* 2007: 750). A preliminary analysis with US college presidents also shows a single significant factor.

[6] In this regard, findings in a recent study of English local government managers, designed around a similarly constructed measure, mirror those obtained from the Texas dataset. See Walker *et al.* (2007: 752).

select just any set of nodes to create this measure, but rather they need to select the most common nodes that occupy a manager's time. Given careful selection, the total number of nodes becomes less relevant; researchers should stress getting information on the most common nodes rather than worrying about information on all nodes.

The 2000-to-2002 comparisons, as well as comparisons for later surveys, also revealed that M_2 is very much a managerial choice. Networking measures for a given organization at the two time points were essentially uncorrelated if the organization had changed top managers. When the same manager was in place in both years, there was a strong positive correlation between the two measures of M_2. Despite there being distributional consequences to networking, therefore (O'Toole and Meier 2004b), networking itself is driven largely by managers' decisions. It is not an epiphenomenon forced on managers by the external actors.

Networking also appears to be an effective long-term strategy of managers. After the destruction and displaced students generated by a couple of hurricanes in the autumn of 2005, school superintendents were forced to interact with emergency response networks of law enforcement officials, social service providers, and nonprofit groups. One of the best predictors of post-hurricane networking with various organizations was the extent of networking measured in normal times by the previous survey. In short, networks cannot be created instantly; they need to be developed in anticipation of future use (Hicklin *et al.* 2009).

The need to create managerial networks appears to be a generic phenomenon, but it is influenced by context. O'Toole *et al.* (2007) compare the networking behaviour of Texas school superintendents with those of UK local government managers. In both cases a strong first factor with positive loadings is generated. The actual networking patterns differ somewhat in terms of the variation in the local context. For example, trade unions receive far more contact in the UK where they flourish compared to Texas where they are weak. Similarly, US superintendents interact more with local business leaders than do all the UK managers except those at the very top level of management.

Walker *et al.* (2007) asked whether networking was an activity that occurred throughout the organization. Their study of UK local governments surveyed top management (corporate level), middle management (chief operating officers), and lower management (service level managers) with a similar set of network nodes. Again the results showed that the broad pattern of networking across the groups was very similar. At the same time, interactions with the individual nodes varied by hierarchical level – a pattern consistent with the notion that the overall network activity is shared with some specialization across the levels. What was not investigated was whether or not networking at these various levels affected performance.[7]

What we know: managing the environment

Our studies of managing the organizational environment were designed in accord with a belief that we could learn the most about organizations under situations of duress. This led us initially to study a series of crises triggered by shocks emanating from the organizational environment that affected the core unit to determine how such crises were managed. The first such study involved a moderately predictable crisis, a budget cut (Meier and O'Toole 2009b). Using the criterion that a budget cut of 10 per cent or more was enough to create a significant organizational perturbation, we examined how school districts over an eight-year period responded to the cuts. The budget cut itself had only a modest impact on the core performance criterion, the TAAS (a decline of one-half point in the first year and an additional point in the second year), but had a more significant impact on college-bound students – particularly in terms of taking the college board exams and in scoring well on those exams. The impact on college board exams rather than TAAS was easily explained by the superintendents' own stated goals (more than 70 per cent stated that TAAS was their primary goal).

How did superintendents protect TAAS scores from these budget cuts? They made a series of rational decisions that resulted in a set of minor adjustments in funding and subtle shifts in the allocation of personnel in the system. Instructional expenditures were generally protected (they suffered smaller cuts than other areas). Among instructional resources the reallocations were made in predictable ways. Superintendents held down teachers' salaries and let class sizes grow. When teachers left, more expensive teachers (those with bilingual or special education specialties) were replaced by less expensive teachers (regular education teachers). The sum of these minor decisions protected most of the instructional function from the budget cuts and allowed the district to maintain its relative performance on the TAAS exam.

---

[7] In another study, Andrews et al. (2010) did not find a positive impact of networking overall on government performance. However, it appeared that low levels of performance generated greater contact by elected officials and that managers responded by increasing their contacts with user groups and other clientele to try to improve performance.

Although budget cuts can often be somewhat predictable and certainly can be expected in most public organizations on occasion, natural disasters are not. In 2005 the Gulf Coast of the United States was hit by two major hurricanes within a few weeks. Hurricane Katrina displaced some 45,000 students from Louisiana to Texas school districts (of these, 36,000 remained the full academic year). Hurricane Rita then led to a massive evacuation of the Texas gulf coast; the evacuation and the hurricane damage resulted in districts losing 1,200 total class days. Both hurricanes had a negative impact on district performance, but not all districts suffered equally; many were able to weather these two shocks and score as well as or better than predicted (from an autoregressive model).

Analysis of the more than 700 districts with at least 500 students each showed two key factors that mitigated the negative impact of the hurricanes (Meier *et al.* 2010). First, *managerial capacity*, a variable that reflects both internal management and internal structures (M_1 and S), was measured by the percentage of employees that were in central office administration. Greater management capacity meant that districts had the ability to quickly sort incoming students and to make decisions on how to make up for missing classes. Managerial capacity interacted with the impact of the disasters. At low levels of managerial capacity, the impact of both hurricanes was negative and statistically significant. At higher levels of managerial capacity, the impact of the hurricanes essentially dropped to zero. Our measure of *workforce stability* had a similar impact on the negative relationship. In districts with higher turnover among teachers, both the influx of Katrina students and days missed due to Rita reduced TAKS [8] scores by a statistically significant amount. As teacher turnover declined, and thus as human capital in the organization increased, these negative impacts became smaller until they were essentially zero.

These findings with regard to the response to the hurricanes are generally supported by a second analysis of budget cuts. O'Toole and Meier (2009) examined whether central office staff and teacher stability interacted with a budget cut to mitigate its negative impact. We found that organizations with larger central office staffs were able to overcome both the first and second year negative impacts of a budget cut. We found similar interactive results for teacher stability.

In a non-crisis-focused examination of the impact of managerial capacity on organizational performance, we examined the interaction of capacity

---

[8] The Texas Assessment of Knowledge and Skills (TAKS) replaced the TAAS in 2003.

with managerial networking (Meier and O'Toole 2009a). Central office bureaucracy appears to have no impact on student TAAS scores in normal times,
a strong positive impact on attendance, and a negative impact on high college
board scores. As managerial networking increases, however, managerial capacity positively affects the standardized test scores, increases its impact on
attendance by about 30 per cent, and reduces its negative impact on college
board scores by about 56 per cent.

The overall findings for managerial capacity, given that its impact is positive on indicators for disadvantaged students but negative for high-end
performance, suggest that managerial capacity may be related to a key organizational trade-off. School systems can either invest their slack resources in
managerial capacity (which will address one set of problems) or commit
these resources to dealing with high-end performance (advanced placement
instructors, etc.). Neither option is inherently incorrect; the choice between
central capacity versus front-line human resources reflects a decision by public managers to address one set of challenges rather than another.

Other aspects of change in public organizational environments and the
management of that change have also been addressed. Hicklin (2004) examined two other forms of environmental stress – changes in the political system and shifts in the organization's revenue base. She found that the impact
of managerial networking on performance increased when there were lower
levels of political stability and lower levels of resource stability. She interpreted instability in these environmental factors as generating opportunities
that managers can then exploit.

A different examination of the political environment generated analogous
results. Using the normative logic of the politics – administration dichotomy,
Meier and O'Toole (2004a) argued that when the political institutions fail to
perform their vital role of representation, managers must not only do their
own job but must also take up the slack for the political failings. Their contention was that in the presence of under-performance by the political system
(measured as failure to represent the diversity of the community), the impact of
management would be greater, but only on politically salient issues. Using data
from eight years, they found that in situations where the school board, as the
elected political body, did not represent the diversity of the population well, the
overall magnitude of public management's impact on performance increased.
This increase occurred, however, only on salient issues, that is, on those issues
where one might expect the political system to make a contribution.

Instances of political instability or political failure represent only one type
of case from among the array of challenges posed by public organizations'

environments. Boyne and Meier (2009) introduced a general measure of environmental turbulence or instability based on unpredictable changes in revenues, enrolments and the composition of the student population. Turbulence of this type negatively affects the performance of the organization. Boyne and Meier (2009) then examined whether turbulence can be managed via structural decisions. They found that stable organizational structures, both vertical and horizontal, were able to mitigate the negative impact of turbulence on the organization.

The role that structural stability plays in managing the organizational environment raises the question about the impact of stability on performance. Both managerial stability and workforce stability are associated with higher levels of public organizational performance even with controls for other factors that influence results (O'Toole and Meier 2003a: 56), employee stability in eight of ten cases and managerial stability in five of ten cases.[9]

Although the measures of stability are generally uncorrelated with the measures of managerial networking and managerial quality, they do interact with each other to influence the relative impact of the four factors. As an example, managerial stability matters more when managerial quality is lower (O'Toole and Meier 2003a: 59). For another example, greater workforce stability is associated with a decline in the impact of managerial networking (O'Toole and Meier 2003a: 60). In terms of the interaction of stability with the environment, managerial stability and workforce stability matter in both diverse and less diverse networks, as well as financially dependent and financially independent environments (O'Toole and Meier 2004a: 482–6). Both factors, however, have more influence on organizational performance when an organization is dependent on others for funds; in short, stability matters more in interdependent (network-like) settings. So rather than following the general injunction in the management literature that one needs to make the organization complement the environment (e.g. rigid hierarchies in stable environments), the empirical findings suggest that organizational stability can substitute for environmental stability and thus influence performance (see also Boyne and Meier 2009).

Meier and O'Toole (2008) attempted to ascertain two things about organizational buffering – did it matter in terms of performance, and what was the appropriate functional form? Our theory of public management hypothesizes that the relationship of buffering with performance should take the

---

[9] As noted above, workforce stability also ameliorated the deleterious consequences resulting from Hurricanes Katrina and Rita and from the negative impacts of budget cuts. See also Gonzalez Juenke (2005) for the interaction of experience with managerial networking.

form of a reciprocal function and it should interact with both management (M_3) and the environment. In terms of the first question, in the US schools studies organizational buffering is positively associated with organizational performance in seven of ten cases (only for SAT scores, ACT scores and percentage of high scores showed no significant relationships). An interesting pattern is that the impact is higher for more disadvantaged students (poor students and black students) and lower for more advantaged clientele (much the opposite of the relationships for managerial networking).

To determine if the relationship between buffering and performance is linear and additive or, rather, takes the more complex reciprocal form that interacts with other variables, as predicted by our model, we applied the principle of Occam's razor – unless the more complex specifications were demonstrably superior, we would accept the simpler linear, additive form as correct. Estimating a reciprocal function, a reciprocal function that interacted with management, and a reciprocal form interacting with the environment did not produce results that were consistently better than the linear additive form. While we concluded that the evidence most supported a linear additive model for buffering, we qualified that conclusion because we only specified a single form of buffering and applied it to only one set of cases. More empirical tests are needed before rejecting the rich qualitative literature that suggests buffering affects performance in a highly non-linear, interactive format.[10]

An agenda for research

Of the several broad research questions regarding networks, managerial networking, and public programme performance, as sketched at the outset of this chapter, we have devoted attention here to the development and testing of empirical theory. Theory development and theory testing quite clearly must go hand in hand as information about the way the world operates feeds back into our models of public management and public programme performance. This point certainly holds for that portion of the research agenda focused on networks, managerial networking, and managerial efforts to deal with and, when appropriate, buffer public organizations from the environment with which they are

---

[10] We have also investigated whether our attitudinal measures of M_3 and M_4 interact with managerial networking, either directly or as a reciprocal as the theory predicts. We found no evidence that the interactive relationship added any more explanation than a strictly linear one. These findings, however, are preliminary at the present time and should be taken as suggestive at best.

interdependent. In the course of developing this research agenda, we have often made some theoretical assertions that seemed likely to be true, even if we did not have much information on which to base such expectations. In other cases we were required to develop what Lynn *et al.* (2001) refer to as a convincing causal story – that is, a plausible and explicit logic by which the empirical relationships we were able to uncover could be explained. At still other times we have worked primarily at the theoretical level in an effort to clear out more underbrush for our empirical work (see Meier and O'Toole 2004b).[11]

This section sets out an agenda for future research. It is based on our focus on empirical theory and its testing, and our concentration on large-N research approaches as an especially useful vehicle for advancing the work. The objective in the remainder of this chapter is to specify places where key theoretical issues might be resolved via empirical research. Six of these hypotheses deal with managing in the network, two with management in general, three with structure and organization, and one with scholarship on management.

> *Network Proposition 1*: Networking occurs at all levels of the organization. That is, M_2 is an organizational function, which is likely to be greater at the top but can operate at all organizational levels (Meier *et al.* 2004; but see Walker *et al.* 2007). Although with the Texas dataset we have only examined networking behaviour by the top manager, it is quite likely that organizations delegate different network interactions.[12] Perhaps such decisions reflect the priority of the actor at a particular node or, alternatively, the degree of expertise needed (preliminary evidence and discussion of networking at other levels in English local governments is available in O'Toole *et al.* 2007; and Walker *et al.* 2007). What we do not know at the present time is what the impacts of networking are from anywhere other than the top management of the organization. Nor do we know if top management and middle management networking are substitutes for each other, augment the influence of each other, or work at cross purposes.

---

[11] This chapter does not recount the range of conceptual and theoretical issues we believe deserve explication as the research programme continues to advance. Such a list would include many additional topics, such as: estimating the performance impacts of other types of stability, exploring public management at the network (rather than organizational) level, examining overall impacts of management from multiple managerial positions, and analysing interactions with and relative influence of political overseers. For coverage of many such parts of the agenda see Meier and O'Toole (2004b).

[12] Hicklin (2006) also has data on networking activities of both university presidents and college deans.

Network Proposition 2: Management can selectively choose which resources to exploit in an organization, particularly in regard to networking. One should not expect that increases in all resources will all carry the same performance effects, or even that there will be positive effects at all from certain resources (Meier and O'Toole 2003). What determines the ability to exploit resources or dampen constraints? How much of this is a conscious choice by top management?

Network Proposition 3: Managerial networking is subject to diminishing marginal returns (Hicklin *et al.* 2008). How is it that good managers know when to stop? Is there an optimal balance of networking with other activities? Are other management variables also subject to diminishing marginal returns?

Network Proposition 4: Managerial networking in routine times facilitates the ability of the organization to network with new nodes in unprecedented or crisis situations (Hicklin *et al.* 2009). Can one develop an investment theory of networking? Under what conditions should managers maximize networking?

Network Proposition 5: Greater managerial capacity increases the impact of managerial networking across all types of management indicators (Meier and O'Toole 2009a). Networking has a similar impact on management capacity. Does this mean that investments in capacity necessarily will generate greater network impacts?

Network Proposition 6: Public organizations operate in a political environment and, therefore, must work to manage political forces. Managerial networking is one way to create political cover for organization members so that they can perform jobs without interference of politics on core production (Meier and O'Toole 2001). Are there upper limits to such managerial actions? Can management contribute to the overall stability of the political system (via effective performance or via cultivation of network ties)? Can it endanger the democratic nature of the overall governance regime (Meier and O'Toole 2006)?

Management Proposition 1: Managerial capacity is especially useful in a crisis situation (Meier *et al.* 2007; O'Toole and Meier 2009). What permits organizations to create managerial capacity? There is a trade-off in terms of performance in building managerial capacity versus investing in the improvement of street-level skills. How can the trade-offs of adding to managerial capital in terms of performance in non-crisis times be overcome?

Management Proposition 2: Managerial capacity facilitates the ability of an organization to buffer environmental shocks (Meier *et al.* 2007). Is management capacity generic in this regard? Can it deal with other types of shocks? How can management legitimate the need for managerial capacity given that some politicians will associate managerial capacity with bloated bureaucracy?

Structural Proposition 1: Not all organizational clientele are the same. Factors that contribute to greater stability of organizations are likely to benefit more disadvantaged clientele (O'Toole and Meier 2003a: 57). Managerial networking frequently favours the better-off (O'Toole and Meier 2006). Are there management activities that can alter these relationships? Can some organizations serve all clientele without making trade-offs?

Structural Proposition 2: Internal loose coupling of an organization can be a structural or behavioural way to buffer the organization from environmental turbulence (Meier and O'Toole 2008). What are the managerial processes that create loose coupling? When might management opt for tight or loose coupling when choice is possible?

Structural Proposition 3: Organizations in more diverse structural networks are inherently less manageable (O'Toole and Meier 1999; 2004a). To test this relationship, one needs a dataset that contains both behavioural and structural measures of networks. Networks can vary greatly on numerous dimensions, including size or complexity. Scholarly breakthroughs, however, will likely come more quickly by focusing on simple networks (n = 2, n = 3) where the research problems are more tractable.

Scholarship Proposition 1: One can learn more about organizations when they are under significant stress. Studying how organizations deal with environmental shocks, as a result, should be a productive enterprise (Meier and O'Toole 2009b; Meier *et al.* 2007; O'Toole and Meier 2009). Most of our work has been on major shocks, but much could be gained by looking at general levels of organizational turbulence and how organizations manage that turbulence (see Boyne and Meier 2009). Similarly, not all environmental shocks are the same, so we might expect the managerial responses to vary contingent on the type of shock (O'Toole and Meier 2003b).

These twelve propositions do not exhaust the future agenda. We are well aware that this large body of research rests primarily but not exclusively on one exceptionally rich dataset. One of our disappointments is that others have not taken up our challenge to develop similar datasets capable of answering a wide variety of important questions of public management. Ultimately, the theoretical notions developed in this and other related research agendas must be examined and tested in many and varied settings for the field to be able to offer valid insights to public managers and researchers across organizational types and governance regimes of various sorts.

Conclusion

All organizations must deal with their environments; in many cases this necessity requires managers to operate in networks of other actors over whom the manager has no direct control. This study has documented the results of a series of large-N studies of managerial networking and other related management actions that interface between the organization and its environment. While a great deal of knowledge has been gained, the brief sketch of an agenda for the future indicates that there is still much to learn.

REFERENCES

Agranoff, Robert, and Michael McGuire. 2001. 'Big questions in public network management research', *Journal of Public Administration Research and Theory*, 11, 3, 295–326.
—— 2003. *Collaborative Public Management: New Strategies for Local Governments*. Washington, DC: Georgetown University Press.
Bardach, Eugene. 1998. *Getting Agencies to Work Together*. Washington, DC: Brookings Institution.
Behn, Robert D. 2001. *Rethinking Democratic Accountability*. Washington, DC: Brookings Institution.
Berry, Frances S., Ralph S. Brower, Sang Ok Choi, Wendy Xinfang Goa, HeeSoun Jang, Myungjung Kwon, and Jessica Word. 2004. 'Three traditions of network research: what the public management research agenda can learn from other research communities', *Public Administration Review*, 64, 5, 539–52.
Blair, Robert. 2002. 'Policy tools theory and implementation networks: understanding state enterprise zone partnerships', *Journal of Public Administration Research and Theory*, 12, 2, 161–90.
Boyne, George A., and Kenneth J. Meier. 2009. 'Environmental turbulence, organizational stability, and public service performance', *Administration & Society*, 40, 8, 799–824.
Goerdel, Holly T. 2006. 'Taking initiative: proactive management and organizational performance in networked environments', *Journal of Public Administration Research and Theory*, 16, 3, 351–67.

Gonzalez Juenke, Eric. 2005. 'Management tenure and network time: how experience affects bureaucratic dynamics', *Journal of Public Administration Research and Theory*, 15, 1, 113–31.

Hall, Thad E., and Laurence J. O'Toole, Jr. 2000. 'Structures for policy implementation: an analysis of national legislation, 1965–1966 and 1993–1994', *Administration and Society*, 31, 6, 667–86.

2004. 'Shaping formal networks through the regulatory process', *Administration and Society*, 36, 2, 1–22.

Hawes, Daniel P. 2008. 'Political institutions, public management, and bureaucratic performance: political-bureaucratic interactions and their effect on policy outcomes', unpublished Ph.D. dissertation, Department of Political Science, Texas A&M University.

Herranz, Joaquin, Jr. 2008. 'The multisectoral trilemma of network management', *Journal of Public Administration Research and Theory*, 18, 1, 1–31.

Hicklin, Alisa K. 2004. 'Network stability: opportunity or obstacle?' *Public Organization Review*, 4, 121–33.

Hicklin, Alisa K., Laurence J. O'Toole, Jr., and Kenneth J. Meier. 2008. 'Serpents in the sand: managerial networking and nonlinear influences on organizational performance', *Journal of Public Administration Research and Theory*, 18, 2, 253–74.

Hicklin, Alisa K., Laurence J. O'Toole, Jr., Kenneth J. Meier, and Scott E. Robinson. 2009. 'Calming the storms: collaborative public management, Hurricanes Katrina and Rita, and disaster response', in Rosemary O'Leary and Lisa Bingham (eds.) *The Collaborative Manager*. Washington, DC: Georgetown University Press, pp. 95–114.

Johnston, Jocelyn M., and Barbara S. Romzek. 2008. 'Social welfare contracts as networks: the impact of network stability on management and performance', *Administration & Society*, 40, 2, 115–46.

Kickert, W. J. M., E.-H. Klijn, and J. F. M. Koppenjan (eds.). 1997. *Managing Complex Networks: Strategies for the Public Sector*. London: Sage.

Kickert, W. J. M., and J. F. M. Koopenjan . 1997. 'Public management and network management: an overview', in Walter J. M. Kickert, Erik-Hans Klijn and Joop F. M. Koppenjan (eds.) *Managing Complex Networks: Strategies for the Public Sector*. London: Sage, pp. 35–61.

Lynn, Laurence E., Carolyn J. Heinrich, and Carolyn J. Hill. 2001. *Improving Governance: A New Logic for Empirical Research*. Washington, DC: Georgetown University Press.

Mandell, Myrna P. (ed.). 2001. *Getting Results Through Collaboration: Networks and Network Structures For Public Policy and Management*. Westport, CT: Quorum Books.

Meier, Kenneth J., and Laurence J. O'Toole, Jr. 2001. 'Managerial strategies and behavior in networks: a model with evidence from US public education', *Journal of Public Administration Research and Theory*, 11, 3, 271–95.

2003. 'Public management and educational performance: the impact of managerial networking', *Public Administration Review*, 63, 6, 675–85.

2004a. 'Unsung impossible jobs: the politics of public management', Paper presented at the annual meeting of the American Political Science Association.

2004b. 'Conceptual issues in modeling and measuring management and its impacts on performance', in Patricia Ingraham and Laurence E. Lynn, Jr. (eds.) *The Art of*

Governance: Analyzing Management and Administration. Washington DC: Georgetown University Press, pp. 195–223.

2005. 'Managerial networking: issues of measurement and research design', *Administration & Society*, 37, 5, 523–41.

2006. *Bureaucracy in a Democratic State: A Governance Perspective*. Baltimore, MD: the Johns Hopkins University Press.

2007. 'Modeling public management: empirical analysis of the management–performance nexus', *Public Management Review*, 9, 6, 503–27.

2008. 'Management theory and Occam's Razor: how public organizations buffer the environment', *Administration & Society*, 39, 8, 931–59.

2009a. 'Beware of managers not bearing gifts: how management capacity augments the impact of managerial networking', *Public Administration* (forthcoming).

2009b. 'The dog that didn't bark: how public managers handle environmental shocks', *Public Administration*, 87,3, 485–502.

Meier, Kenneth J., Laurence J. O'Toole, Jr., and Alisa K. Hicklin. 2010. 'I've seen fire and I've seen rain: public management and performance after a natural disaster', *Administration & Society*, 41 (January 2010), 979–1003.

Meier, Kenneth J., Laurence J. O'Toole, Jr., and Sean Nicholson-Crotty. 2004. 'Multilevel governance and organizational performance: investigating the political bureaucratic labyrinth', *Journal of Policy Analysis and Management*, 23, 1, 31–48.

Nicholson-Crotty, Sean, and Laurence J. O'Toole, Jr. 2004. 'Public management and organizational performance: the case of law enforcement agencies', *Journal of Public Administration Research and Theory*, 14, 1, 1–18.

O'Leary, Rosemary (ed.). 2008. *The Collaborative Public Manager*. Washington, DC: Georgetown University Press.

O'Toole, Laurence J., Jr. 1997a. 'The implications for democracy in a networked bureaucratic world', *Journal of Public Administration Research and Theory*, 7, 3, 443–59.

1997b. 'Treating networks seriously: practical and research-based agendas in public administration', *Public Administration Review*, 57, 1, 45–52.

2000. 'Different public managements? Implications of structural context in hierarchies and networks', in Jeffrey L. Brudney, Laurence J. O'Toole and Hal G. Rainey (eds.) *Advancing Public Management*. Washington, DC: Georgetown University Press, pp. 19–32.

O'Toole, Laurence J., Jr. and Kenneth J. Meier. 1999. 'Modeling the impact of public management: the implications of structural context', *Journal of Public Administration Research and Theory*, 9, 3, 505–26.

2003a. 'Plus ça change: public management, personnel stability, and organizational performance', *Journal of Public Administration Research and Theory*, 13, 1, 43–64.

2003b. 'Bureaucracy and uncertainty', in Barry C. Burden (ed.) *Everything but Death and Taxes: Uncertainty and the Study of American Politics*. New York: Cambridge University Press, pp. 98–117.

2004a. 'Public management in intergovernmental networks: matching structural networks and managerial networking', *Journal of Public Administration Research and Theory*, 14, 3, 469–95.

2004b. 'Desperately seeking Selznick: cooptation and the dark side of public management in networks', *Public Administration Review*, 64, 6, 681–93.

2006. 'Networking in the penumbra: public management, cooptative links, and distributional consequences', *International Public Management Journal*, 9, 3, 271–94.

2009. 'In defense of bureaucracy: public managerial capacity, slack, and the dampening of environmental shocks', *Public Management Review* (forthcoming).

O'Toole, Laurence J., Jr., Richard M. Walker, Kenneth J. Meier, and George A. Boyne. 2007. 'Networking in comparative context: public managers in the US and UK.' *Public Management Review*, 9, 3, 401–20.

Pfeffer, Jeffrey, and Gerald R. Salancik. 1978. *The External Control of Organizations*. New York: Harper and Row.

Provan, Keith G., and Patrick Kenis. 2008. 'Modes of network governance: structure, management, and effectiveness', *Journal of Public Administration Research and Theory*, 18, 2, 229–52.

Provan, Keith G., and H. Brinton Milward . 1995. 'A preliminary theory of interorganizational network effectiveness', *Administrative Science Quarterly*, 40, 1, 1–33.

Rainey, Hal G. 2003. *Understanding and Managing Public Organizations*, 3rd edn. San Francisco: Jossey-Bass.

Rethemeyer, R. Karl. 2005. 'Conceptualizing and measuring collaborative networks', *Public Administration Review*, 65, 1, 117–21.

Rhodes, Roderick A. W. 1997. *Understanding Governance: Policy Networks, Reflexivity and Accountability*. Buckingham, UK: Open University Press.

2002. 'Putting people back into networks', *Australian Journal of Political Science*, 37, 3, 399–416.

Scharpf, Fritz W. (ed.). 1993. *Games in Hierarchies and Networks*. Frankfurt am Main: Campus/Westview.

Schneider, Anne L. 2009. 'Why do some boundary organizations result in new ideas and practices and others only meet resistance? Examples from juvenile justice', *American Review of Public Administration*, 39, 1, 60–79.

Stoker, G. (ed.). 1999. *The New Management of British Local Governance*. Basingstoke: Macmillan.

Thompson, James D. 1967. *Organizations in Action*. New York: McGraw-Hill.

Walker, Richard, Laurence J. O'Toole, Jr., and Kenneth J. Meier. 2007. 'It's where you are that matters: an empirical analysis of the networking behaviour of English local government officers', *Public Administration*, 85, 3, 739–56.

Weber, Edward, and Anne M. Khademian. 2008. 'Managing collaborative processes: common practices, uncommon circumstances', *Administration and Society*, 40, 5, 431–64.

7 Public service motivation and performance

Gene A. Brewer

Public administration is a hybrid field of study that has borrowed heavily from other disciplines such as management, political science and economics. One mark of the field's vitality and sustainability is how well it has leveraged this interactive knowledge base to create new insights and lines of inquiry that advance the state of knowledge overall. Public service motivation (PSM) is one example of a native public management concept that represents this type of progress. (Another example is red tape which is covered in Chapter 5 of this volume.)

The relationship between PSM and performance is a matter of utmost importance to scholars and practitioners in the field of public administration. Scholars want to identify predictable linkages between what motivates individuals and drives organizational performance. Practitioners, in turn, are searching for ways to achieve goals and produce results in public organizations. PSM may thus be a way to improve individual and organizational performance. But is PSM related to performance in fact?

Brewer (2008) recently noted the importance of the relationship between PSM and performance and conducted a comprehensive review of empirical studies on the topic. He turned up only a handful of studies and found that the evidence was inconclusive. He then called for more research. Fortunately, scholars have been responsive to this call; they have published several additional studies in recent years that help to clarify the relationship between PSM and performance. That work is brought current in this chapter, which assesses the current state of knowledge on the PSM–performance relationship and seeks to advance our understanding of it. The chapter begins with an introductory section on the origin and development of the PSM concept, followed by a discussion of the theoretical and practical bases for expecting a positive relationship between PSM and performance. Evidence from previous research is then reviewed in detail. Implications and suggestions for future research are presented, and the chapter closes with some propositions about the relationship between PSM and performance.

Origin and development of the PSM concept

The notion that public life involves self-sacrifice, devotion to duty and commitment to the public interest dates back at least to the ancient Greek city-states (Brewer 2003; Holzer 1999). In the 1960s, social researchers began conducting sectoral-based comparisons that showed that public servants and other citizens held slightly different attitudes on some of these characteristics. These early studies, and others that followed, provided the impetus for formalizing the PSM concept.

Rainey (1982) made a seminal contribution by asking a sample of public and private sector managers to rate their 'desire to engage in meaningful public service'. Rainey reasoned that asking individuals directly was the best way to assess their motives, and he found that public managers reported significantly higher scores than private managers. However, Rainey acknowledged several problems with asking this type of survey question. Respondents may tend to provide socially desirable responses rather than the truth. Also, private managers may be equally public spirited, but they may not associate their work activities with public service. Rainey (1982: 298–9) set the stage for future research with this pioneering study, but he also pointed out some limitations that would hinder researchers: PSM is a broad, multifaceted concept that varies over time, changes with the public image of government service, and takes different forms in different agencies and service areas. Rainey concluded that public service is an elusive concept much like the public interest.

Perry and Wise (1990: 368) followed on Rainey's work by defining PSM as 'an individual's predisposition to respond to motives grounded primarily or uniquely in public institutions and organizations'. They described three potential bases of PSM: rational, norm-based and affective. Rational motives are grounded in enlightened self-interest. The individual believes that his or her personal interests coincide with those of the larger community. Such motives can lead individuals to participate in the policy process, show commitment to public programmes or policies because of personal identification with them, or serve as advocates for a special interest. Norm-based motives involve dedication to a cause and desire to serve the public interest, however one perceives it. These motives include patriotism, duty and loyalty to the government. Affective motives are grounded in human emotion, and they are characterized by a desire and willingness to help others.

Perry and Wise (1990: 370–1) then formulated three hypotheses to guide future research:

1. The greater an individual's PSM, the more likely the individual will seek membership in a public organization.
2. In public organizations, PSM is positively related to performance.
3. Public organizations that attract members with high levels of PSM are likely to be less dependent on utilitarian incentives to manage individual performance effectively.

As this review will show, empirical research has tended to confirm their predictions.

In another sectoral-comparison study, Wittmer (1991) reported that public sector employees place a higher value on helping others and performing work that is worthwhile to society. These findings were consistent with the PSM concept and they confirmed results from a number of public and private sector surveys which had been conducted since the early 1960s showing that public employees are generally more altruistic and prosocial than other members of society (for details, see Rainey 1991). But as yet, there was no acceptable way to measure PSM.

Perry (1996) then began a pioneering effort to develop a more sensitive and complete measure of PSM. He translated the theory into a measurement scale and tested it with confirmatory factor analysis. Perry derived four factors: public policy making, public interest, compassion and self-sacrifice. The first three factors corresponded to the theoretical framework proposed by Perry and Wise (1990), and the fourth added self-sacrifice – a factor frequently mentioned in the literature and anecdotal accounts of public service. These four factors were represented in twenty-four measurement items. Perry's final instrument had strong face validity and desirable mathematical and sociometric properties. In a follow-up study, Perry (1997) identified several antecedents of PSM and reported their correlations to the measurement scale, thus providing further evidence of construct validity.

Next, Brewer and Selden (1998) focused attention on the consequences of PSM and linked the concept to a broad range of work-related attitudes and behaviour. In a multivariate analysis, they showed that lowered concern for job security and heightened concern for the public interest were the most important differences between federal employee whistle-blowers and other employees who observed wrongdoing but chose to remain silent. Further comparing these two groups, the authors found that whistle-blowers reported significantly higher levels of job commitment, achievement and job satisfaction; they received higher job performance ratings; and they reported working for higher performing organizations.

Importantly, Brewer and Selden (1998) were concerned that efforts to study PSM through public and private sector difference studies were limiting the vast potential of the concept. Like Rainey (1982: 297–8), they agreed that PSM has special significance in the public sector, but they also felt that it transcends the public sector. People in all walks of life can perform meaningful public, community and social service. Brewer and Selden (1998: 418) sought to resolve this tension in PSM theory by formulating two independent premises:

1. PSM is the motivational force that induces individuals to perform meaningful public, community and social service.
2. PSM is more prevalent in the public sector than in the private sector and elsewhere.

The first premise rests on the belief that PSM is part of a behavioural process in which altruistic motives lead to prosocial behaviour. The second premise implies that PSM is more prevalent in the public sector than elsewhere.

Naff and Crum (1999) examined 1996 Merit Principles Survey data that included several measures of PSM from Perry's original instrument. They found significant relationships between PSM and federal employees' job satisfaction, performance, intention to remain with the government and support for government reinvention efforts. In light of these findings, Naff and Crum (1999: 14) urged researchers to focus attention on the role of PSM in the recruitment and retention of federal employees.

Brewer, Selden and Facer (2000) bored deeper into the PSM concept and sought to understand how individuals who perform public service view these activities. They utilized Perry's measurement items in a Q methodology study of a small but varied sample of current and prospective public servants. The researchers uncovered four distinctive roles or self-concepts: Samaritans, communitarians, patriots and humanitarians. This research showed that individuals with similar levels of PSM might perceive the ways and means of performing public service quite differently. For example, some individuals linked self-preservation with their conceptions of PSM, while others reported that self-sacrifice – a willingness to place the common good and public interest ahead of one's self-interest – has had an important element in how they perceive their roles. Overall, these findings suggested that PSM is far more complex than previously suggested.

Taking a different tack, Crewson (1997) constructed a measure of PSM based on Deci's (1975) framework of intrinsic and extrinsic motivation.

Crewson operationalized PSM as the difference between an individual's service orientation (preference for intrinsic rewards) and economic orientation (preference for extrinsic rewards). On this differential measure, Crewson found that public sector employees reported higher scores than those in the private sector.

Crewson's study was systematic and thorough. He examined three types of datasets to answer additional research questions: General Social Surveys (1989 and 1973–1993), the 1979 Federal Employee Attitude Survey, and the 1997 Survey of Electrical Engineers. The across-time data showed that public servants consistently rank 'feeling of accomplishment' higher than private sector employees, and the cross-sectional datasets showed that PSM is positively related to organizational commitment but not related to attitudes favouring government growth. Thus, Crewson concluded that a service orientation is real and stable among public sector employees, and that it makes them more productive without biasing their attitudes toward the role of government.

In another well-executed study, Houston (2000) used Crewson's measure of PSM to perform a multivariate analysis on pooled 1991, 1993 and 1994 General Social Survey data. He found that public employees tended to value intrinsic rewards such as doing important work and having a feeling of accomplishment, while private sector employees tended to value extrinsic rewards such as earning higher incomes and working fewer hours.

These empirical studies by Crewson (1997) and Houston (2000) use different measures of PSM than other studies reviewed here (which, incidentally, also use slightly different measures on occasion). This raises an important question. Are these researchers measuring different things? Or, are they all measuring parts of the same underlying or overarching construct? Since all of these studies use measures of PSM that are well grounded in theory and anecdotal accounts of public service, and since they tend to produce similar results on PSM, the latter explanation seems likely. Still, it is important to differentiate between these different measures and sets of findings to develop a clearer understanding of PSM.

Recently, researchers have been exploring the role of PSM in larger theoretical and empirical frameworks. For example, Rainey and Steinbauer (1999: 23–7) proposed a theory of effective government organizations that included three different types of employee motivation: public service, mission and task motivation. Brewer and Selden (2000) tested this theory with archival data from the twenty-nine largest federal agencies in the USA. The researchers found that measures of public service and task motivation were moderately related to organizational performance, but they could not come up with any suitable measures to test mission motivation.

This relatively consistent pattern of findings, and growing effort to link PSM with other phenomena, provides a good foundation for developing a more comprehensive theoretical framework that can more clearly articulate the relationship between PSM and performance. Also note that Perry's measurement scale is the dominant way to measure the PSM construct as evidenced in most of the studies reviewed below. Several scholars have utilized different measures in the past (for example, see Rainey 1982; Crewson 1997; Brewer and Selden 1998; Houston, 2000; Alonso and Lewis 2001; Lewis and Frank 2002), and others are working to improve on or refine this scale (for example see Coursey and Pandey 2007; Coursey *et al.* 2008; Vandenabeele 2008; Kim 2009). But as yet, most empirical studies continue to utilize Perry's measurement scale in whole or part. The next section explores the theoretical and practical bases for expecting a positive relationship between PSM and performance.

Theoretical and practical bases

One of the most compelling arguments for PSM is its alleged association with high performance (for example, see Perry and Wise 1990; Brewer and Selden 1998). Reflecting on the power of this argument, the economist Patrick François (2000) entitled an article 'Public Service Motivation as an Argument for Government Provision'. The PSM–performance relationship is thus an important cornerstone of PSM theory and efforts to improve public service performance.

PSM is a set of values and attitudes that influence behaviour. The most important result of PSM is its behavioural outcomes, which may include choosing public service-oriented employment, increased job involvement and organizational commitment, and ultimately higher employee and organizational performance. Perry and Wise (1990: 368) emphasized the relationship between PSM and public institutions, defining the concept as 'an individual's predisposition to respond to motives grounded primarily or uniquely in public institutions' (370–1). These authors were among the first scholars to posit a positive relationship between PSM and performance. Brewer and Selden (1998: 417) sought to expand the definition of PSM by describing it as 'the motivational force that induces individuals to perform meaningful ... public, community, and social service', thus emphasizing the concept's behavioural implications and applicability beyond the public sector. Brewer and Selden (1998: 425) also emphasized the performance-related implications of PSM, saying that high performance is central to the theory of PSM. Various other scholars have implicitly and explicitly expressed support for this hypothesis, suggesting that a consensus exists within the small but growing PSM research community.

The growing strength of this consensus has prompted numerous scholars to propose that public organizations are higher performers than similar organizations in the private sector, and that PSM may help make government provision of public services more efficient and desirable than other arrangements such as contracting and privatization, which rely heavily on non-governmental organizations and extrinsic rewards for service delivery (e.g. see Brehm and Gates 1997; Brewer 2004; Brewer and Selden 2000; François 2000; Perry 2000; Rainey and Steinbauer 1999).

Of particular importance is recent research showing that public employees are more likely than average citizens to perform extra-role behaviours such as voting, participating in politics, making charitable contributions, giving blood, and devoting their personal time to worthwhile social causes (Blais et al. 1990; Brewer 2001, 2003; Clerkin et al. 2009; Houston 2006, 2008; Kim 2005, 2006). These findings transcend the traditional view of employee and organizational performance, and suggest that some public employees may also be both high achievers and 'good citizens' in a variety of extra-organizational contexts. Indeed, it can be argued that public sector employment places greater responsibility on the individual to be ethical and contribute more to society.

In recent years, a growing number of public management scholars have focused intently on empirical research aimed at improving governmental performance (e.g. see Boyne et al. 2006; Heinrich and Lynn 2000). This research effort is very important because good government benefits everyone in the long run. Since existing theory and empirical evidence suggest that high levels of PSM can improve employee and organizational performance in government, researchers need to probe these relationships more carefully. Unfortunately, empirical research on governmental performance is limited (for reviews, see Boyne 2003; and Chapter 1 of this volume), and research on the PSM–performance relationship is even more scarce (Brewer 2008).

An important caveat applies here. The performance concept is fundamentally different in public organizations compared with nonprofit organizations and commercial enterprises. For instance, in business firms, individual performance is often considered the same as job- or task-goal performance.

Ethical behaviour is often beyond the narrow operational definition of performance that is used for performance appraisals or assessments of organizational effectiveness. These and other forms of ethical conduct or organizational citizenship behaviour are desirable but they are considered 'extra-role'. Similarly, most business firms are by necessity more concerned with financial performance than with accountability and achieving equity and fairness in service delivery, at least when compared with most public organizations. Nonprofit organizations are the proverbial 'middle-man': they are typically more exposed to market pressures than public organizations, and they are expected to be more ethical and sensitive to a wider range of performance targets than business firms.

We have far more difficulty specifying what 'extra-role behaviour' is in the public sector. For instance, a strong case can be made that whistle-blowing is not only 'in role' but that it is also a moral and legal obligation for public employees. Similarly, public organizations must strive to perform well on many different dimensions of performance – some of which are considered peripheral in private organizations. One example is discursive and inclusive public hearings which are often required in the public sector; in contrast, most nonprofit organizations focus on a narrower band of stakeholders, while most private sector organizations prefer to formulate strategy and make decisions in closed forums.

One implication is that researchers should strive for broader definitions of public service performance. Indeed, if we frame the discussion around more generalized notions of PSM (including altruism and prosocial motivation) and expanded notions of performance (including organizational citizenship behaviour and prosocial organizational behaviour such as whistle-blowing, voting, and donating time, blood and money for the betterment of society), there is much more evidence and support for the PSM–performance relationship than the following section suggests. Yet expanding the definition of performance to include almost everything of importance to society is also problematic: it is far easier for public organizations to achieve goals when those goals are clear and attainable (see Chapter 2 in this volume on goal ambiguity).

Empirical evidence

Does empirical evidence support the assertion that PSM is related to perform-ance? Below, I review two sets of studies that address this question directly. The first set provides evidence on employee performance at the individual level of analysis, and the second set provides evidence on organizational performance at the organization-wide or collective level.

Evidence on employee performance

Several studies have examined the relationship between PSM and employee performance. For example, Naff and Crum (1999) examined data collected by the US Merit Systems Protection Board (1996) which included responses from nearly 10,000 federal employees. The survey instrument included several measures of PSM taken from Perry's (1996) original instrument. The authors found significant relationships between PSM and federal employees' job satisfaction, performance, intention to remain with the government, and support for government reinvention efforts. In light of these findings, Naff and Crum (1999: 14) urged researchers to focus attention on the role of PSM in the recruitment and retention of federal employees.

These findings were not conclusive, however. In the first stage of analysis, the authors created two groups representing high and low PSM, and excluded a number of cases that lay near the breaking point. Performance was measured via the employee's most recent performance appraisal score (on a Likert scale ranging from 1 = unacceptable to 5 = outstanding) as reported by the employee. A bivariate analysis showed that members of the high PSM group reported receiving higher performance appraisal ratings than members of the low PSM group. In the next stage, the authors utilized multivariate analysis. They recoded performance ratings because the data were heavily skewed toward high performance. The recoded variable was bivariate: 1 (formerly coded 5) = high performers and 0 (formerly coded 4 or below) = all others.[1] Logistic regression was then utilized in the ensuing multivariate analysis. In that analysis, the effect of PSM on performance was estimated while controlling for race, gender, education, age, tenure, grade level, and job type (white collar or other). The results showed that PSM exerted a positive, statistically significant effect on employees' self-reported performance ratings. In the third stage of analysis, Naff and Crum (1999) held all covariates constant by inserting the characteristics of an 'average federal employee' responding to the survey (i.e. the modal responses on the control variables) and varying only the level of PSM. The results showed that an individual with a low PSM score would have a 29 per cent probability of receiving an outstanding

---

[1] The authors reported testing an alternative model using a different recoding scheme for the performance variable that produced virtually the same results.

performance rating, compared to a 42 per cent probability for an individual with an average level and a 52 per cent probability if the level were high. In this case, however, some of the control variables proved to be better predictors of performance than PSM.

These findings seem fairly consistent, but several mitigating factors may limit their import. The PSM scale consisted of six items – somewhat less than Perry's twenty-four-item scale, and subsequent research by Brewer and Selden (2000: 700) utilizing the same dataset showed that one of these items did not factor-load with the others or contribute to an acceptable alpha reliability score. However, Naff and Crum (1999) did not analyse the same number of cases or report alpha reliability coefficients so an assessment cannot be made about comparability of findings. Moreover, in their multivariate analysis, Naff and Crum transformed the interval-level measure of PSM into a nominal-level variable: high and low public service-motivation groups. A similar transformation occurred in the third stage of analysis – transforming the interval-level measure into a categorical variable: high, average and low PSM. The supervisor's performance rating of the employee is also suspect in that such ratings are often biased, and they are so inflated that the resulting variable does not have sound mathematic and sociometric qualities for multivariate analysis (Alonso and Lewis 2001). The authors were thus forced to recalibrate the measure into a blunt nominal-level variable consisting of high and low performing employees.

Like most other research on PSM and performance, Naff and Crum (1999) relied upon employee self-reports, thus introducing the possibility of memory lapses, judgemental errors, socially desirable responses and common source bias. Self-reports are considered a major problem in behavioural research because they are thought to bias the results. While such reports are often more accessible than other types of measures, they are considered inferior by some. Researchers tend to place a premium on more objective or at least externally derived measures. For example, rather than asking employees to report their most recent performance ratings, the ratings could be obtained from archival personnel records; and instead of asking employees to report on their organizations' performance, researchers could utilize performance measures created by government authorities for management and budgeting purposes. These measures, while still possibly incomplete, are at least externally derived and arguably more objective than employee self-reports. The implication is that Naff and Crum's (1999) research does not provide a conclusive answer to the PSM–performance question. It does, however, weigh positively and confirm the need for further research.

In two other studies, Alonso and Lewis (2001) have examined the role of PSM in individual performance and Lewis and Frank (2002) have investigated individuals' desire to work for the government. In both instances, the researchers used archival data and employed novel research designs and innovative tests to examine their hypotheses. Most importantly, Lewis and Frank (2002) found that public employees reported working slightly harder than their private sector counterparts, but Alonso and Lewis (2001) found contradictory evidence on the PSM–performance relationship in two samples of US federal government employees: the 1996 Merit Principles Survey conducted by the US Merit Systems Protection Board (1996), which was also analysed by Naff and Crum (1999), and the US Office of Personnel Management's Survey of Federal Employees 1991. The findings showed that PSM was positively related to self-reported performance ratings in one sample, but not in the other. The authors concluded that 'flaws and cross-dataset differences in the key measures allow for multiple interpretations of our findings, but the links between PSM and performance were clearly not robust' (Alonso and Lewis 2001: 376).

Alonso and Lewis (2001) essentially replicated Naff and Crum's (1999) finding of a fairly strong, positive relationship between PSM and performance ratings using the same dataset but a different model specification. Yet when using different measures, the results did not hold up. They found no evidence that federal employees who highly valued 'service to others' achieved higher performance ratings in the 1991 dataset. Furthermore, when they utilized the employee's grade level as a proxy measure of performance, they found that PSM had no apparent impact on grade level in the 1996 dataset, while placing a high value on service to others was *negatively* related to grade level in the 1991 dataset.

A close review of the databases and measures used in the above research may help explain these inconsistent findings. First, Alonso and Lewis' (2001) results for the 1996 database, where they had a more complete measure of PSM, were more positive than their results for the 1991 database, where they were forced to use a more inferior measure of the concept. That single-item measure merely plumbed the extent to which respondents valued 'service to others' – which is an incomplete measure of PSM. Also, the 1996 database provided a measure of individual performance that was more similar to Naff and Crum's (1999) measure, while the 1991 data was limited to a proxy measure of dubious validity – the employee's pay-grade level. Highly performing employees may not always seek promotions and related pay increases, and public organizations may not always do a good job of identifying and promoting highly performing employees.

Several other weaknesses common to other studies of PSM are present in the Alonso and Lewis (2001) study. These weaknesses include utilizing employee self-reports of key concepts, cross-sectional research designs to study causal relationships, and questionable measures of important variables (such as using a single-item measure of PSM and the employee's pay-grade level as a proxy measure of individual performance). It should also be noted that Alonso and Lewis's (2001) positive finding when replicating Naff and Crum's (1999) research on the 1996 Merit Principles Survey database is dampened by the same problems affecting the latter study.

In another study, Bright (2007) used structural equation modelling to investigate whether person–organization fit (P–O Fit) mediates the relationship between PSM and the self-reported performance of public employees. P–O Fit is congruence between individuals and organizations. Bright (2007) analysed survey results from a sample of 205 public employees randomly drawn from three public organizations in the United States – a public healthcare agency, a city government and a county jurisdiction – located in the states of Indiana, Kentucky and Oregon. In the study, PSM was measured using Perry's (1996) twenty-four-item revised scale. The respondents were asked to rate their agreement with the twenty-four questions posed. Their responses ranged from 1 (highly disagree) to 7 (highly agree) on the Likert-type scale that was utilized in the survey. Employee job performance was measured via one question asking respondents to report their most recent performance appraisal rating on their current job during the year. The response categories ranged from 1 (poor) to 5 (excellent). The results showed that P–O Fit fully mediated the relationship between PSM and employee performance. In other words, after taking P–O Fit into account, PSM had no direct, significant impact on performance. It should be noted that PSM was an important contributor to P–O Fit; therefore, it was shown to be an indirect contributor to employee performance.

These findings are relevant and intriguing. They suggest that other factors may mediate or moderate the relationship between PSM and performance, and that PSM may have indirect contributions to make. The findings are not utterly convincing, however, since Bright's study sample was so small and his measures of PSM and performance so incomplete. The author was therefore cautious about his findings.

Two additional studies have examined the relationship between PSM and employee performance in recent years – both occurring outside of the United States. Leisink and Steijn (2009) surveyed Dutch civil servants representing various segments of the Dutch public sector (N = 4,130, weighted) to examine the relationship between PSM and three performance-related behavioural-outcome variables: affective commitment, willingness to exert effort and perceived job performance. The authors used an abridged version of Perry's measurement scale for PSM, adapted from Coursey and Pandey's (2007) slimmed-down version and altered slightly to fit the Dutch context. Responses were in the form of a 5-point Likert scale (1 = 'completely disagree' to 5 = 'completely agree'). Leisink and Steijn (2009) also constructed a mediating variable called PSM-Fit, derived from theories of person–environment fit, which measures the opportunity a person has to exercise commitment to the public interest in his or her job. Individual performance was again measured through self-reports: employees were asked to evaluate their own job performance relative to their colleagues in a single-item response. Only 1.4 per cent of those responding admitted poor performance, whereas 39.6 per cent claimed to be above average. Leisink and Steijn (2009: 42) converted these responses into a dichotomous variable distinguishing those who perceive themselves as above average performers from the rest.

The authors had hypothesized that PSM-Fit would mediate the relationship between PSM and the three outcome variables which included employee performance, but this did not happen. Both PSM and PSM-Fit had a positive effect on employee reports of their commitment, willingness to exert effort and job performance. The results, then, provide additional support for the PSM–performance hypothesis. The weaknesses of this research are also apparent based on our previous discussion of the American studies. The authors utilized a shrunken and altered version of Perry's (1996) measurement scale, and more important, their measure of employee performance is suspect.

In another study, Wouter Vandenabeele (2009) analysed a survey sample of 3,506 Flemish civil servants working in central government ministries and related agencies. With these data, he tested the relationship between PSM and employee performance, and estimated the mediating effects of job satisfaction and organizational commitment. The latter variable included three forms of commitment identified in past research: normative, affective and continuance. Vandenabeele (2009) used an eighteen-item measurement scale for PSM that included five dimensions: the four identified by Perry (1996) (politics and policies, public interest, compassion and self-sacrifice) and one added by himself (democratic governance). Vandenabeele (2009) utilized these five dimensions as separate variables in the subsequent analysis rather than consolidating them as some past researchers had done. Respondents were asked to give Likert-type responses to survey questions ranging from 1 – 'totally disagree' to 5 – 'totally agree'. The dependent variable was a four-item measurement scale of perceived performance – also self-reported by the respondents. Vandenabeele (2009) confirmed a positive relationship between PSM and performance on four of the five dimensions of PSM tested (the exception was the compassion dimension); thus, he concluded that PSM is positively related to performance via a 'robust link'. The mediating effects of job satisfaction and organizational commitment were also confirmed, but the effects varied across the dimensions of PSM. There were also differing effects for affective, normative and continuous commitment. Vandenabeele (2009: 28) concluded that more research is needed to explain these mediating effects and develop an encompassing theory of PSM and performance.

One study conducted by Andersen (2009) has failed to confirm this result, but a close inspection of the measures and methods utilized in the study helps to explain this contrarian finding. Andersen (2009) focused her research on health professionals in the public and private sectors in Denmark. She conducted semi-structured interviews with twelve surgeons, six general practitioners, and six dentists, some of whom were moonlighting in both sectors. Through these interviews and other means (i.e. surveys of patients and employees, and examination of health registry data), she investigated the effects of PSM, professional norms and economic incentives on their behaviour and performance. If health professionals prioritized the wellbeing of patients and/or general societal concerns in their work, this was interpreted as an indicator of PSM. Her performance measures were occupation-specific: for dentists, they included toothbrush instruction as evidenced by the number of cavity-free children, and fissure sealings as evidenced by the number of decaying tooth surfaces; for surgeons, they included the percentage of patients re-hospitalized after receiving prophylactic pharmacy for hip operations, and hip surgery patient selection waiting times; and for general practitioners, they included patient satisfaction with clinical care rendered through ordinary consultations, and patient satisfaction with accessibility to talk therapy consultations. The analysis indicated that PSM as measured by Andersen (2009) was at the same high level for public and private sector health professionals, so it did not explain differences in their behaviour or performance. The key finding she reported is that firm professional norms make a difference: when these norms are present, different economic incentives do not produce different behaviour or performance among health professionals.

Andersen's (2009) study includes a different measure of PSM than most studies reviewed here. The validity, reliability and sensitivity of this measure are questionable. In addition, her several measures of performance have strong face validity, but they are limited in scope and do not comport with the call for multidimensional measures of performance found in the literature. It can be argued that single-item 'global measures' of performance are more encompassing. Moreover, lack of variation in the PSM variable and difficulty in isolating cause and effect between PSM and performance variables cast doubt on the study's findings – or lack thereof – relative to the PSM-performance relationship. The findings on professional norms, economic incentives and performance seem much better grounded.

In summary, all of these studies have measurement problems and other concerns that make their results somewhat inconclusive. Measures of PSM and/or employee performance are potentially problematic in each study, and the three partially inconsistent findings (i.e. Alonso and Lewis 2001; Bright 2007; and Andersen 2009) raise questions which beg further research. Nevertheless, the weight of the evidence suggests that PSM is positively and significantly related to employee performance. This includes Bright's (2007) study which essentially confirms the relationship but suggests that PSM is an indirect rather than a direct driver of performance, and several other studies which confirm that the PSM–performance relationship at the individual employee level is more complex than previously envisioned. The next section looks at evidence on the relationship between PSM and organizational performance.

Evidence on organizational performance

Three studies have examined the relationship between PSM and organizational performance (Brewer and Selden 2000; Kim 2005; Ritz 2009). All of these studies reported a positive and consistent effect.

First, Brewer and Selden (2000) developed a theoretical model predicting organizational performance and utilized the 1996 Merit Principles Survey dataset (the same one used by Naff and Crum 1999 and Alonso and Lewis 2001) to test the model. The authors utilized the PSM items included in the survey to create a measurement scale (dropping one item to achieve an acceptable alpha reliability score as mentioned above). They also developed a multidimensional measure of organizational performance from the employee self-reports contained in the survey. The model produced relatively strong results, with PSM emerging as a modestly important predictor of organizational performance. (The standardized regression coefficient for the relationship was 0.071.) Yet several factors may limit the validity of their findings.

Organizational performance is one of the hardest concepts to measure in public management research (Boyne 2003; Boyne *et al.* 2006; Brewer 2004; Brewer and Selden 2000; Kim 2006). Brewer and Selden (2000) constructed a measure of performance based on internal and external dimensions of efficiency, effectiveness and fairness, which was robust but may have overlooked some aspects of performance such as the level of citizen satisfaction and compliance with the law. Perhaps more important, the authors drew their measures from employee self-reports, which are considered problematic, as we have already discussed. Moreover, the authors utilized the pared-down six-item measurement scale of PSM provided in the survey, and were subsequently forced to drop one of the items/dimensions to achieve an acceptable alpha reliability score. They also utilized cross-sectional data to assess the impact of PSM on organizational performance, which is a purported causal relationship. Longitudinal data are normally required for this purpose because time-order is an important element of causality and it cannot be established without across-time data.

Kim (2005) used a different dataset but a similar research design to replicate Brewer and Selden's (2000) work in Korea (N = 1,739 public employees at different levels of government). His measures of PSM and performance were similar to Brewer and Selden's (2000) measures, but the model specification was slightly different as Kim (2005) was mainly interested in the impact of individual-level factors on organizational performance. His results showed that four traits increased organizational performance: job satisfaction, affective commitment, PSM, and organizational citizenship behaviour. The standardized regression coefficient for the PSM–performance relationship was 0.073 – very similar to the effect size documented in Brewer and Selden's (2000) study. Thus, empirical evidence from the two studies is consistent and positive.

Another recent study has added to this growing body of evidence. Ritz (2009) examined the effects of PSM, organizational commitment and job satisfaction on perceived performance in a 2007 survey sample of 13,532 Swiss federal government employees. Only two dimensions of PSM were included in the study – commitment to the public interest and attraction to public policy-making – and the measure of performance was limited to what Brewer and Selden (2000) termed 'internal efficiency' with a strong focus on procedural efficiency, and measured with a three-item index. All of these measures were self-reported on Likert-type scales with 1 being the lowest and 6 being the highest rating. Through a multivariate analysis, Ritz (2009: 66) found that the 'commitment to the public interest' dimension of PSM had a significant, positive relationship with perceived performance (the standardized effect size was 0.068 – very similar to the effect size documented in the two previous studies), but the second dimension of PSM, 'attraction to policy-making', did not produce large results or achieve statistical significance. These findings mostly mirror those reported by Brewer and Selden (2000) and Kim (2005), which are described above. Therefore, Ritz (2009: 69–71) concluded that to increase performance, it is important to have sound public management and employees who are committed to the public interest.

On the downside, these studies share many of the same weaknesses noted in the previous section. They utilize somewhat incomplete measures of PSM, and their organizational performance measures are possibly incomplete as well. In addition, they utilize employee self-reports to measure key concepts and cross-sectional databases to make causal attributions. These studies are also aggregating individual-level measures of PSM to test the relationship between organizational-level PSM and the dependent variable – organizational performance. Researchers may need an organizational-level measure of PSM to test this relationship more rigorously. That is, researchers need to establish more clearly the propriety of 'aggregating up' individual-level data to the organizational level. Another possibility is to reformulate the PSM measurement items into an organizationally relevant set of measures. Then elite survey respondents or other informants could report on the organization's level of PSM, as they do on other organizational attributes. Another potential weakness of these studies involves the measurement validity of their organizational performance metric. As explained above, organizational performance is a multidimensional concept that is very hard to define and measure in the public sector. These studies utilized the same theoretical framework of organizational performance set out in Brewer and Selden (2000), and similar measures of PSM and organizational performance. But their efforts were not necessarily complete. Alternative frameworks and measures might produce slightly different results.

In summary, these studies have examined the PSM–performance relationship in very similar ways, and they have produced very similar results. This permits us to conclude within the limited experience of these studies that PSM is positively related to organizational performance.

Implications and suggestions for future research

Results from the studies reviewed here seem sensitive to the definitions and measures of the key concepts (PSM and performance), the populations studied and the statistical techniques utilized. For example, most studies have utilized scaled-down versions of Perry's twenty-four-item measurement scale and incomplete, self-reported measures of performance. Yet it is hard to determine the impact of this lack of measurement precision on the findings reported. Certainly, studies utilizing downsized versions of Perry's scale have produced positive results while studies measuring PSM as a more generalized altruistic trait, such as Alonso and Lewis's (2001) 'service to others' measure, have produced less positive results. Similarly, several studies reviewed here analysed 1996 Merit Principles Survey data, which consists of survey responses from US federal government employees at one point in time, and these studies often produced slightly different results. Questions naturally arise about generalizing these and other findings reviewed in this chapter. Finally, most studies of individual performance have encountered problems because some key variables failed to meet normality assumptions. The researchers often tried to overcome this problem by reconstituting the variables' values and moving from ordinal to nominal levels of measurement. This forced the researchers to use weaker statistical methods – such as contingency-table analysis and logistic regression – in their subsequent analyses.

Studies of organizational performance have utilized multivariate regression analysis, which is arguably a stronger method of analysis, but these studies were testing complex model specifications that may require even more advanced statistical methods such as structural equation or hierarchical linear modelling (see Chapter 11) to gauge the true impact of PSM on organizational performance. In addition, we have noted the similarity of the study designs which has both good and bad implications for interpreting the findings. On one hand, it is reassuring to see that similar research designs have produced consistent findings, thus providing evidence of reliability. On the other hand, we could have greater confidence in the findings if they were derived from a more diverse set of study designs and thus were more robust.

To summarize, there is a growing body of empirical evidence on the PSM–performance relationship. Studies utilizing similar measures, study samples and statistical methods have produced fairly consistent results – whether positive or negative. The preponderance of evidence seems to support the view of a modest positive relationship between the variables. Yet the evidence remains slightly inconsistent in the case of PSM and individual performance. There are several possible explanations for these inconsistencies, and several ways to interpret the contrarian evidence consistent with PSM theory. Rather than moving toward closure on the PSM–performance question, these explanations actually suggest the need for further research.

The first explanation for these apparent inconsistencies is straightforward. Since its inception, scholars have observed that PSM is a 'multidimensional construct with dynamic properties' (Brewer and Selden 1998: 424; also see Perry 1996; Rainey 1982). Rainey (1982: 298–9) wrote that PSM is a broad, multifaceted concept that may be conceived many different ways. Perry (1996) identified four dimensions of the construct: attraction to policy-making, compassion, commitment to the public interest and self-sacrifice. Other scholars have proposed additional dimensions. Going forward, a question of some consequence is whether empirical researchers should attempt to consolidate the several dimensions of PSM into an aggregate measure, as past research has often done, or whether the dimensions should be retained and entered as separate variables in empirical analyses. As this chapter shows, researchers are following both conventions and this seems to further cloud the findings.

Researchers need to consider seriously the implications of PSM being a dynamic, changeable concept. For example, Brewer *et al.* (2000) followed up on Rainey's observation that PSM can be conceived in many different ways and showed that there are at least four distinct conceptions of PSM among public service practitioners: they were described as Samaritans, communitarians, patriots and humanitarians.[2] Each conception had unique content, covariates and probable outcomes. In other words, some conceptions of PSM may be more strongly linked to some dimensions of individual and organizational performance (which are also multidimensional constructs), and it follows that the strength and direction of these relationships may vary.

The implication is that researchers should unpack the PSM and performance concepts and explore their sub-dimensional relationships. A somewhat overdrawn example may help to illustrate this point. On the Brewer *et al.* (2000) framework described above, nurses were described as Samaritans who work in social service settings where performance involves rendering care for others, while soldiers are described as patriots who serve in military organizations where performance often involves doing harm to others. The omnibus PSM and performance concepts that have been used in previous research may not be sensitive enough to explain these fine-grained differences.

Another implication is that PSM is highly variable. As Rainey (1991: 155) explained, it involves many different dimensions and 'appears to vary over time, with changes in the public image of government service, and to take

---

[2] Brewer *et al.* (2000) showed that individuals can be high on one dimension and low on another, suggesting that combined indexes may mask individual differences and effects.

different forms in different agencies and service areas'. Brewer suggested that PSM 'may vary across individuals and situations, and it may be moderated by characteristics of the organization or service area such as policy type, goal crispness, and red tape' (Brewer 2001: 79). Perry (2000) added that PSM appears to be strongest in the most difficult circumstances – a finding that echoed from Brewer and Selden (1998). Extant research has confirmed many of these assertions, but PSM's inherent dynamism and variability continues to pose challenges for theoreticians and empirical researchers. These challenges have made research on the PSM and performance relationship difficult, as explained in this chapter.

As the above discussion suggests, conflicting findings on the PSM–performance relationship are actually consistent with the view that PSM is a dynamic concept that changes in ways that we do not fully understand yet. It may be present in some settings but not others. Performance is also a moving target, with various concerns such as economy and fairness ebbing and flowing in their importance. Mapping out this larger theoretical model probably represents the greatest need for future research on PSM, in part because it will also help unravel other mysteries about the nature, antecedents and consequences of PSM, and its relationship to individual and organizational performance in the public sector.

Moreover, researchers may need to bring in other theoretical frameworks such as goal theory, psychological contracts, and P–O Fit (Bright 2007; Castaing 2006; Coyle-Shapiro and Kessler 2003; Wright 2004). Fresh theoretical frameworks may illuminate our understanding of the PSM–performance relationship.

Although Perry and Wise (1990) argued that PSM and performance are related, they did not provide a detailed theoretical rationale, that is, they did not specify the cause–effect relationships, including mediating and moderating variables. What does the complete model look like? This question is beyond the scope of this review, but it is a central topic for future research.

Propositions for future research

Several propositions for future research are now presented. Much of the groundwork for these propositions has been laid earlier in the chapter, so they are merely summarized here in no particular order of importance.

PSM and performance are related, but incomplete measurement and associated problems, such as conflating individual and organizational performance or failing to acknowledge their connection, have tended to obscure the relationship. We therefore stipulate:

> *Proposition 1*: On the whole, PSM is positively related to individual performance, and the relationship will be stronger when the construct measures are more complete.
>
> *Proposition 2*: On the whole, PSM is positively related to organizational performance, and the relationship will be stronger when the construct measures are more complete.
>
> *Proposition 3*: PSM will be more positively related to individual and organizational performance when the latter two constructs are found to be more strongly related.

PSM and performance are multidimensional constructs and researchers should explore linkages between the sub-dimensions of the constructs. For example, there is reason to believe that:

> *Proposition 4*: The PSM dimension of compassion is positively related to the organizational performance dimensions of fairness, justice, equity and client satisfaction.
>
> *Proposition 5*: The PSM dimension of attraction to policy-making is positively related to the organizational performance dimensions of economy and efficiency.
>
> *Proposition 6*: The PSM dimension of concern for the public interest is positively related to the organizational performance dimensions of quality, effectiveness, accountability and transparency.

Various dimensions of PSM may work in concert to affect performance. One such moderator or mediator is self-sacrifice. For instance:

> *Proposition 7*: The PSM dimension of self-sacrifice works in concert with other PSM dimensions to positively affect individual and organizational performance, but its effect is variable across these dimensions.

Various dimensions and conceptions of PSM are related to various organizational missions and service types. For example, we can observe that Samaritans (as defined by Brewer *et al.* 2000) often exhibit compassion and are more likely to work in social welfare agencies where their individual orientations are consistent with their organizations' goals, missions and aspirations. Another example is patriots (as defined by Brewer *et al.* 2000) who often exhibit concern for the public interest and are more likely to work in public safety or front-line military organizations. As a result, we can say:

Proposition 8: The relationship between individual and organizational performance will be stronger when individuals' conceptions and forms of PSM are closely matched to their organization's goals, missions and aspirations.

There is continuing concern that PSM should not be Balkanized in the public sector. This concern grows out of the fact that increasingly, many people are employed by private and nonprofit organizations such as government contractors who do socially important work that impacts the public interest. What are the implications of this spillover from the public to the private and nonprofit sectors for PSM and performance? We can speculate that:

Proposition 9: Individuals employed in private and nonprofit organizations that have government sponsored and public-regarding missions will exhibit levels of PSM similar to public employees engaged in like activities.

Proposition 10: PSM among individuals employed in private and nonprofit organizations will be positively related to individual and organizational performance, to the extent that performance is defined as service to the public and public-regardedness.

These propositions are meant to be illustrative and not exhaustive. Many other propositions could be formulated about the relationship between PSM and performance. Moreover, some of these propositions may be confirmed through future research while others may be rejected. The important point is for researchers to utilize the scientific method to advance the state of knowledge on the relationship between PSM and performance.

Conclusion

Research on PSM and performance is reaching a critical mass in which it is possible to make some inferences about the direction and strength of the relationship. Based on the articles reviewed, it appears that PSM is positively related to employee and organizational performance. However, it can be added that the latter relationship seems to be supported by more consistent evidence than the former. The strength of the relationship is, however, modest in both instances. Another caveat is that the PSM and performance variables do not operate in a vacuum: researchers are already identifying a number of mediating and moderating variables, and suggesting that some of PSM's impact on performance may be indirect.

This chapter has sought to investigate the relationship between PSM and two main types of performance: employee and organizational. An increasing number of empirical studies are examining this relationship, but they are employing many different measures and producing some mixed findings, particularly on PSM's relationship with employee performance. At the individual level, the majority of empirical studies that employ relatively good measures of PSM and performance confirm the relationship, while several studies with blunter and less complete measures have disconfirmed it. At the organizational level, three empirical studies employing similar theoretical frameworks and measures of PSM and performance have produced remarkably similar results. These studies show that PSM is positively related to organizational performance, given the inherent limitations of the studies that have been conducted.

My previous review of empirical research on the PSM–performance relationship was fraught with doubts and difficulties because there were so few empirical studies to draw from (Brewer 2008; also see Hondeghem and Perry 2009).[3] Several new studies have now emerged, making it easier to draw inferences about the relationship and speak with a measure of confidence. Given the importance of PSM and performance as separate concepts, and the desirability of having them work in concert, it seems that extending this line of research should be one of the most important priorities for public management researchers. Indeed, researchers need to mount a full-bore research effort to understand the relationship between PSM and performance.

Scholars and practitioners should remain optimistic about the relationship between PSM and performance. As this volume shows, research has accumulated over the past decade and researchers have made progress in identifying the drivers of high performance in public organizations. Policymakers and public managers increasingly recognize the importance of public service motives and high performance, and they surely want to leverage these motives to improve performance at the individual and organizational levels. The empirical evidence suggests that the relationship between PSM and performance is positive, but the relationship is more nuanced and complex than Perry and Wise (1990) originally envisioned. Thus, the relationship

---

[3] Hondeghem and Perry (2009) recently edited a symposium on PSM and performance in the *International Review of Administrative Sciences*. The four studies published address the impact of PSM on either individual employee performance or organizational performance. They are reviewed earlier in this chapter.

between PSM and performance remains a central concern of public management scholarship and practice.

REFERENCES

Alonso, Pablo, and Gregory B. Lewis. 2001. 'Public service motivation and job performance: evidence from the federal sector', *American Review of Public Administration*, 31, 4, 363–80.

Andersen, Lotte Bøgh. 2009. 'What determines the behaviour and performance of health professionals? Public service motivation, professional norms and/or economic incentives', *International Review of Administrative Sciences*, 75, 1, 79–97.

Blais, André, Donald E. Blake, and Stéphane Dion. 1990. 'The public/private sector cleavage in North America: the political behavior and attitudes of public sector employees', *Comparative Political Studies*, 23, 3, 381–403.

Boyne, George A. 2003. 'Sources of public service improvement: a critical review and research agenda', *Journal of Public Administration Research and Theory*, 13, 3, 367–94.

Boyne, George A., Kenneth J. Meier, Laurence J. O'Toole, Jr., and Richard M. Walker. (eds.). 2006. *Public Service Performance: Perspectives on Measurement and Management*. Cambridge University Press.

Brehm, John, and Scott Gates. 1997. *Working, Shirking and Sabotage: Bureaucratic Response to a Democratic Public*. Ann Arbor: University of Michigan Press.

Brewer, Gene A. 2001. 'A portrait of public servants: empirical evidence from comparisons with other citizens', unpublished Ph.D. dissertation, University of Georgia.

2003. 'Building social capital: civic attitudes and behavior of public servants', *Journal of Public Administration Research and Theory*, 13, 1, 5–26.

2004. 'Does administrative reform improve bureaucratic performance? A cross-country empirical analysis', *Public Finance and Management*, 4, 3, 399–428.

2008. 'Employee and organizational performance', in J. L. Perry and A. Hondeghem (eds.) *Motivation in Public Management: the Call of Public Service*. Oxford and New York: Oxford University Press, pp. 136–56.

Brewer, Gene A., and Sally Coleman Selden. 1998. 'Whistle blowers in the federal civil service: new evidence of the public service ethic', *Journal of Public Administration Research and Theory*, 8, 3, 413–39.

2000. 'Why elephants gallop: assessing and predicting organizational performance in federal agencies', *Journal of Public Administration Research and Theory*, 10, 4, 685–711.

Brewer, Gene A., Sally Coleman Selden, and Rex L. Facer II. 2000. 'Individual conceptions of public service motivation', *Public Administration Review*, 60, 3, 254–64.

Bright, Leonard. 2007. 'Does person-organization fit mediate the relationship between public service motivation and the job performance of public employees?', *Review of Public Personnel Administration*, 27, 4, 361–79.

Castaing, Sebastien. 2006. 'The effects of psychological contract fulfilment and public service motivation on organizational commitment in the French civil service', *Public Policy and Administration*, 21, 1, 84–98.

Clerkin, Richard M., Sharon R. Paynter, and Jamie Kathleen Taylor. 2009. 'Public service motivation in undergraduate giving and volunteering decisions', *The American Review of Public Administration*, 39, 6, 675–98.

Coursey, David H., and Sanjay K. Pandey. 2007. 'Public service motivation measurement: testing an abridged version of Perry's proposed scale', *Administration and Society*, 39, 5, 547–68.

Coursey, David H., James L. Perry, Jeffrey L. Brudney, and Laura Littlepage. 2008. 'Psychometric verification of Perry's public service motivation instrument: results for volunteer exemplars', *Review of Public Personnel Administration*, 28, 1, 79–90.

Coyle-Shapiro, Jacqueline A. M., and Ian Kessler. 2003. 'The employment relationship in the UK public sector: a psychological contract perspective', *Journal of Public Administration Research and Theory*, 13, 2, 213–30.

Crewson, Philip E. 1997. 'Public-service motivation: building empirical evidence of incidence and effect', *Journal of Public Administration Research and Theory*, 7, 4, 499–518.

Deci, Edward L. 1975. *Intrinsic Motivation*. New York: Plenum Press.

François, Patrick. 2000. '"Public service motivation" as an argument for government provision', *Journal of Public Economics*, 78, 3, 275–99.

Heinrich, Carolyn J., and Laurence E. Lynn Jr. 2000. *Governance and Performance: New Perspectives*. Washington, DC: Georgetown University Press.

Holzer, Marc. 1999. 'Communicating commitment: public administration as a calling', *Public Administration and Management: an Interactive Journal*, 4, 2, 184–207.

Hondeghem, Annie, and James L. Perry. 2009. 'EGPA symposium on public service motivation and performance: Introduction', *International Review of Administrative Sciences*, 75, 1, 5–9.

Houston, David J. 2000. 'Public service motivation: a multivariate test', *Journal of Public Administration Research and Theory*, 10, 4, 713–27.

  2006. '"Walking the walk of public service motivation": public employees and charitable gifts of time, blood, and money', *Journal of Public Administration Research and Theory*, 16, 1, 67–86.

  2008. 'Behavior in the public square', in J. L. Perry and A. Hondeghem (eds.) *Motivation in Public Management: The Call of Public Service*. Oxford and New York: Oxford University Press, pp. 177–202.

Kim, Sangmook. 2005. 'Individual-level factors and organizational performance in government organizations', *Journal of Public Administration Research and Theory*, 15, 2, 245–61.

  2006. 'Public service motivation and organizational citizenship behavior', *International Journal of Manpower*, 27, 8, 722–40.

  2009. 'Revising Perry's measurement scale of public service motivation', *The American Review of Public Administration*, 39, 2, 149–63.

Leisink, Peter, and Bram Steijn. 2009. 'Public service motivation and job performance of public sector employees in the Netherlands', *International Review of Administrative Sciences*, 75, 1, 35–52.

Lewis, Gregory B., and Sue A. Frank. 2002. 'Who wants to work for the government?', *Public Administration Review*, 62, 4, 395–404.

Naff, Katherine C., and John Crum. 1999. 'Working for America: does public service motivation make a difference?', *Review of Public Personnel Administration*, 19, 4, 5–16.

Perry, James L. 1996. 'Measuring public service motivation: an assessment of construct reliability and validity', *Journal of Public Administration Research and Theory*, 6, 1, 5–22.

1997. 'Antecedents of public service motivation', *Journal of Public Administration Research and Theory*, 7, 2, 181–97.

Perry, James L., and Lois R. Wise. 1990. 'The motivational bases of public service', *Public Administration Review*, 50, 3, 367–73.

Rainey, Hal G. 1982. 'Reward preferences among public and private managers: in search of the service ethic', *American Review of Public Administration*, 16, 4, 288–302.

1991. *Understanding and Managing Public Organizations*, 1st edn. San Francisco: Jossey-Bass.

Rainey, Hal G., and Paula Steinbauer. 1999. 'Galloping elephants: developing elements of a theory of effective government organizations', *Journal of Public Administration Research and Theory*, 9, 1, 1–32.

Ritz, Adrian. 2009. 'Public service motivation and organizational performance in Swiss federal government', *International Review of Administrative Sciences*, 75, 1, 53–78.

US Merit Systems Protection Board. 1996. *Merit Principles Survey, 1996*. Washington, DC: US Merit Systems Protection Board.

Vandenabeele, Wouter. 2008. 'Development of a public service motivation measurement scale: corroborating and extending Perry's measurement instrument', *International Public Management Journal*, 11, 1; 143–67.

2009. 'The mediating effect of job satisfaction and organizational commitment on self-reported performance: more robust evidence of the PSM-performance relationship', *International Review of Administrative Sciences*, 75, 1, 11–34.

Wittmer, Dennis. 1991. 'Serving the people or serving for pay: reward preferences among government, hybrid sector and business managers', *Public Productivity and Management Review*, 14, 4, 369–83.

Wright, Bradley E. 2004. 'The role of work context in work motivation: a public sector application of goal and social cognitive theories', *Journal of Public Administration Research and Theory*, 14, 1, 59–78.

8 Organizational diversity and public service performance

David W. Pitts

Introduction

Public organizations in developed countries are becoming more and more diverse, particularly along racial, ethnic and gender lines. Globalization, technology, and shifting cultural norms have contributed to increased percentages of women and people of colour in the workforce worldwide. In European countries, EU guidelines on immigration have led to marked increases in the numbers of foreign nationals living in many member countries (OECD 2003). The workforces of countries formerly under apartheid rule, such as Namibia and South Africa, are seeing fast, significant increases in the representation of ethnic minorities (Balogun 2001). In the United States growing immigration has led to sharp increases in non-native-English-speaking residents (Rubaii-Barrett and Wise 2007). This surge in workforce diversity has created challenges for public managers who are accustomed to managing in a homogeneous environment. Diversity provides both opportunities and struggles for organizations with shifting demographic profiles, but research on managing diversity is still in its infancy. As this literature develops, it is becoming clear that employee diversity creates implications for both the sociology of organizations and the human resources management strategies that best address employee differences. These two lenses – one behavioural, one managerial – have provided the foundation for much of the work on organizational diversity and its consequences for performance.

Diversity-oriented research on public organizations frequently consists of arguments made on normative grounds, but since New Public Management and market-based reforms have hit the public sector, organizations are increasingly tasked to make diversity a strategic, performance-oriented issue. For public sector organizations, the emphasis on diversity has historically been in compliance with the laws and regulations governing recruitment, selection and separation (for a review, see Riccucci 2002). However, the general management environment in the public sector over the past twenty years has shifted to focus more on strategy, performance and efficiency (Osborne and Gaebler 1992; Kettl 2000; Radin 2006). As public sector organizations are challenged to adopt the for-profit norms of performance measurement and strategic planning, the emphasis on diversity has shifted increasingly to a focus on management strategy (Kellough and Naff 2004; Pitts 2006; Riccucci 2002; Wise and Tschirhart 2000). Many believe that workforce diversity makes organizations more competitive – if an organization is diverse, then it is in the best position to respond to various target population needs and formulate creative solutions to complex problems. Ignored in these arguments, however, is the increased likelihood that these organizations will suffer from communication, collaboration and conflict problems stemming from diversity. Just as it creates the potential for innovation and creativity, diversity often leads to decision-making delays, communication struggles and heightened conflict between employees.

The purpose of this chapter is to reflect upon the state of research on diversity in public organizations, particularly research that connects diversity to performance. I will begin with a discussion about the definition and measurement of diversity, followed by a review of the three theoretical frameworks that tend to be used in the literature: social categorization and similarity/attraction theories, decision-making/information theory, and the business case for diversity. I will then discuss diversity management initiatives that have been developed by public managers tasked to solve diversity-related problems and exploit diversity's benefits. The chapter will continue by reviewing the empirical research on organizational diversity and diversity management in public organizations, assessing the extent to which the field may be confident in its findings and identifying questions that warrant further inquiry. The chapter will conclude by issuing recommendations for future research.

Defining organizational diversity

Diversity is a social-psychological phenomenon based in a sense of 'likeness' and 'otherness'. In a group of two or more people, diversity refers to the ways in which the individuals vary on some dimension (McGrath *et al.* 1995). Research has established that humans tend to be ethnocentric, such that intergroup relationships tend to involve categorization based on available attributes, no matter how seemingly minor (Triandis *et al.* 1994). As such, members of a group tend to categorize all of the other members of the group in different ways – by sex, by race, by physical attraction and many other dimensions. This process of categorization results in behaviours that are modified, depending on the level of diversity present among the categories. Individuals act differently in the presence of a homogeneous group than they would in the presence of a heterogeneous group (Turner 1987). In addition to process-oriented changes in behaviour, diversity can result in some substantive changes in group outcomes. Simply put, the more differences present in a group of people, the more ideas that group will have to solve a problem, create a product, or serve a population of people (Adler 2003). Diversity is a complicated concept in the context of organizations because it affects *individual*-level behaviour within *groups* of employees. It is very difficult to avoid atomistic and ecological fallacies in diversity research, because diversity by definition requires that there be a group of two or more employees, but the behavioural consequences are ideally measured at the individual level.

Diversity exists on many different dimensions. A surface-level dimension is one that can be discerned after only a short interaction, typically either by sight or hearing. Race and sex are surface-level indicators, since they tend to be evident upon sight. A deep-level dimension is one that may not be apparent until after further contact. For example, one may not learn about the educational background, political ideology or religious beliefs of another person until he or she chooses to disclose them in conversation. Many dimensions of diversity straddle the two categories. For example, a person's language is surface level if one is introduced to him or her immediately through sound, but it is deep level if interaction does not involve talking or writing. As a concept of 'likeness' and 'otherness', diversity measures the extent to which a group is composed of individuals who are similar on relevant dimensions, whether surface level or deep level (Gruenfeld *et al.* 1996; Harrison *et al.* 1998, 2002).

The most common type of diversity encountered in the organizational setting is workforce diversity, which tends to encompass three distinct elements (Ospina 2001):

- *Occupational diversity*, or the heterogeneity of occupations that are present in the organization
- *Professional diversity*, or the certification and education required for the organization's occupations
- *Social diversity*, or the various ways that employees are different along racial, ethnic, gender, language, cultural, or other lines

Understanding these characteristics of the diversity concept is important for those tasked with managing public services. Diversity is simply the number of variations among parts of a whole. When many people hear the word 'diversity' they think of dyads: majority vs. minority, black vs. white, or domestic vs. foreign. However, diversity is much more nuanced, and the most important differences are often found between minority groups who might otherwise be lumped together as 'nonwhite' or 'minority'. Moreover, the diversity that is most salient to one organization may be utterly irrelevant to another (Wise and Tschirhart 2000). For example, social caste diversity might be most relevant to the workings of an Indian government agency, whereas language diversity might present the most challenges to a Belgian organization. Research on one dimension of diversity does not necessarily apply to another dimension, so managers must be careful not to generalize too broadly. For example, research finding that racial diversity in a US firm benefits performance cannot be used to theorize about how gender diversity would affect performance for a government agency in Mexico.

Diversity can be considered through two distinct lenses: behavioural and managerial. The *behavioural lens* focuses on how employee diversity affects the ways that members of the organization communicate, collaborate and engage in conflict with one another. Diversity has serious implications for the sociology of organizations, specifically in how efficiently and effectively workgroups are able to function. On the other hand, the *managerial lens* is a more practice-oriented way to think about diversity, and it focuses more on how organizations can use management strategies and programmes to address the sociological consequences stemming from employee diversity. Given its position as a professional and applied field, public management has historically viewed diversity as it affects management (for a review, see Riccucci 2002). While the most visible diversity issues typically arise in the context of human resources management, there are broader organizational implications as well. As an organization diversifies along functional and professional lines, it by necessity restructures itself and is forced to consider whether its core strategies are properly aligned to the environment in which it operates. Employee diversity affects public organizations in multiple ways that go beyond individual employee incentives and productivity. Increasing the ways in which employees are different – even if by function or task – inevitably complicates broad management processes related to strategy, decision making and structure. As a result, the relationship between organizational diversity and performance is a complicated one that is contingent upon a variety of forces both internal and external to the organization.

Both scholars and practitioners frequently confuse diversity with representation, but there are distinctions that are important in both concept and practice. While a diverse organization has large variation among employees on a particular demographic dimension, a representative organization simply *matches* the target population that it serves on these demographic dimensions. In the public services context, representation has historically been explored in conjunction with the field of representative bureaucracy, which has demonstrated that minority service recipients often benefit when they interact with bureaucrats of the same background (for a review see Dolan and Rosenbloom 2003). A representative match between bureaucrat and service recipient does not necessarily indicate that the organization as a whole is diverse. On the contrary, it is much easier to achieve representation in scenarios of low diversity, since there are fewer groups to 'match' (Pitts 2005).

Measuring organizational diversity

Confusion between diversity and representation is often manifested through problems in social science measurement. Researchers interested in diversity have a number of measurement options at their disposal, but many of them lack basic face validity if examined in detail. For example, a very common means of measuring racial diversity is to take the percentage of the organization or population that is nonwhite. While this measure may be a very accurate reflection of diversity in cases of only one nonwhite race, it distorts reality in those with multiple nonwhite groups. For example, assume two English cities: one is 50% White and 50% Asian, and the other is 50% White, 15% Asian, 15% Black, 10% Indian and 10% Pacific Islander. Both are 50% nonwhite, but the second is much more diverse than the first because there is more variation among parts of the whole. Treating these as equivalently diverse cities can result in inappropriate management strategies and policy recommendations.

The best means of measuring diversity in categorical variables is the Blau (1977) Index of Dissimilarity or the related Herfindahl-Hirschman Index (HHI). Both are measures of heterogeneity that range from 0 to 1 (Blau) or 10,000 (HHI), and they are perfect inverse correlates. A value of 0 on the Blau Index represents an organization where all employees are identical on the dimension of interest, while a value of 1 is an organization where all employees are *different* on the dimension of interest. This formula, outlined in detailed in Figure 8.1, demonstrates the extent to which there is variation on the analysed dimension. It improves upon more basic percentage-based measures by taking into account the size *and* number of minority groups. Organizations with employees from many different minority groups will score higher on the Blau Index than those with a large number of employees

$$D = 1 - \Sigma p_i^2$$

where

p = Proportion of organizational employees in each group
i = The number of different categories

<u>Example</u>

An organization comprises 80% whites, 10% African-Americans, 5% Hispanics, and 5% from all other categories. As a result, $D = 1 - [0.80^2 + 0.10^2 + 0.05^2 + 0.05^2]$, or **0.345**. When four categories of race/ethnicity are used, the values of the variable range from 0 perfect homogeneity to 0.75 perfect heterogeneity.

Figure 8.1:   Measuring organizational diversity

from one particular minority group. The Blau Index or HHI has been used extensively in public administration research on diversity (e.g. Amirkhanyan 2007; Andrews *et al.* 2005; Pitts 2005).

Some argue that the Blau Index and HHI are inappropriate for research in public administration and policy because they obscure the identity of the groups being explored (Rushton 2008). The Blau Index is agnostic about the characteristics of the individuals classified into its different categories. For example, it does not distinguish between 'advantaged' and 'disadvantaged' groups. Rushton's argument is that, under the Blau Index, an organization that is 90% black and 10% white is scored identically to one that is 90% white and 10% black, which are certainly very different environments. For researchers interested in the substantive experiences of particular racial or ethnic groups, the Blau Index is indeed not the best approach to measurement. This is because the researcher is not really interested in *diversity* at all, but rather in the experiences of a particular group or in the presence of a particular pattern of groups. By contrast, the theories and issues related to organizational diversity stem from the consequences of organizational *variation*, whatever that variation might look like (Williams and O'Reilly 1998).

As a concept of variation, diversity must be measured at a level where multiple 'parts' are present. An individual cannot be diverse, since she or he cannot vary from her or himself, and in the context of organizations, employee diversity is typically measured at the workgroup or organizational levels. Research almost exclusively uses the Blau or Herfindahl Index described above (Andrews *et al.* 2005; Bantel and Jackson 1989; Jackson *et al.* 1991; Pitts

2005; Pitts and Jarry 2007, 2009). While this is the best means of measuring diversity from a mathematical perspective, there are two potential complications. First, this strategy assumes that the diversity measured at the group or organizational level trickles down to all subparts. Since much of the theory about diversity and performance focuses on the impact of diversity on interpersonal relationships, one must assume that diverse employees interact in some way (Wise and Tschirhart 2000). If diversity is measured at the organizational level, but employees are segregated into distinct sub-organizations on dimensions like race/ethnicity or sex, the theory cannot hold since the interpersonal relationships will rarely span two employees who are different from one another.

Second, there is often a mismatch between the unit of analysis on the independent and dependent variables. If organizational diversity is the primary independent variable and performance is the dependent variable, it is rare that both are measured at the same level of analysis. For example, diversity must be measured at the organizational level, and if the dependent variable is employee turnover intention or job satisfaction, then it must be aggregated to the agency level in order to make a reasonable comparison. Aggregating individual-level outcomes like job satisfaction muddies the causal waters, since both random and non-random measurement error is likely to be introduced on the right-hand side of the equation. One alternative is to measure employee diversity at the organization level and then disaggregate the score down to the individual level, which is the unit of analysis at which a dependent variable like turnover intention or job satisfaction is ideally measured (e.g. Choi 2009; Pitts 2009). A better alternative, and one that has not yet appeared in the public management literature on diversity, would be to use multilevel modelling that explicitly accounted for forces at different levels of analysis. Much of the research on diversity and performance has relied upon experimental data that are inappropriate for such an analysis (Williams and O'Reilly 1998; Wise and Tschirhart 2000), but in the US context, individual-level surveys like the Federal Human Capital Survey could be combined with agency-level performance indicators to create a dataset that would be adequate for such an undertaking.

Frameworks for understanding organizational diversity and performance

A large share of the theoretical underpinnings relating organizational diversity to performance stems from basic in-group/out-group psychology (Williams and O'Reilly 1998). Three areas of theory have developed: (1) social categorization and similarity/attraction theories, (2) information and decision-making theory, and (3) the business case for diversity. The bulk of diversity-performance research in these literatures has viewed employee diversity through a behavioural lens, focusing on how interpersonal relationships are more complicated when employees are different from one another.

Much of the research guiding these theories was developing in the research literature on private sector firms, but there has been recent attention toward applying them in the public sector context (Choi 2009; Foldy 2004; Pitts and Jarry 2007, 2009). Public organizations are distinct from private organizations in various ways, even if the sectors often seem blurred (Rainey 2003). For instance, studies have shown that public organizations often have goals that are more ambiguous, multiple and occasionally conflicting than those in private organizations (Rainey 1993; Chun and Rainey 2005). Individual managers in the private sector frequently have more discretion over the goals that they set for their units, while goals in the public sector are commonly set at least partially by mandate and are monitored by political overseers. These differences between the sectors are likely to create variations in the nature of the relationship between any phenomenon and performance. Moreover, the environment in which public organizations operate is one of limited and tightly monitored resources (Meier and Bohte 2007). Consequently, pay structures for employee performance cannot have the same flexibility in public organizations, causing key motivational differences between employees in each of the sectors (Perry 1997). These differences in public and private organizations are likely to lead to different research findings about connections between diversity and performance, but given the relative youth of the public management literature, it still relies upon theories that were generated primarily on for-profit firms. The relationship between diversity and performance is undoubtedly contingent upon a number of internal and external factors, so the extent to which public–private distinctions matter is a direct function of the extent to which mediating and moderating forces (vis-à-vis diversity and performance) differ between the sectors. I outline the tenets of these three approaches in the following sections, and a summary appears in Table 8.1.

Social categorization and similarity/attraction theories

Social categorization theory predicts that as an organization becomes more diverse, breakdowns in communication, coordination and cohesion make it harder for members to work together effectively. These process-oriented

Table 8.1: Theories and frameworks linking diversity and performance

Theory/Framework	Consequences for performance	Foundational studies
Social categorization and similarity/attraction theories	*Negative*; weaker communication and cooperation, lower trust	Burt and Regans 1997; Byrne *et al.* 1966; Lincoln and Miller 1979; Tajfel 1981; Turner 1982, 1987
Information/decision-making theory	*Positive*; more information for decision making, more innovative solutions to problems	Gruenfeld *et al.* 1996; Wittenbaum and Stasser 1996
Business case for diversity	*Positive*; more responsiveness to clients, better recruitment from labour market	Cox and Blake 1991; Kochan *et al.* 2003; Konrad 2003; Robinson and Dechant 1997

difficulties prevent the group from producing a final product, solution or idea that is on a par with one that would be produced by a group that did not fall prey to the same procedural difficulties (e.g. Tajfel 1981; Turner 1982, 1987). While some might argue that organizational diversity should generate benefits via new ideas and perspectives, social categorization theory suggests that the substantive benefits will be outweighed by process-oriented drawbacks. As diversity leads to a variety of new ideas and perspectives, then it must also lead to different approaches to work and problem-solving. Those differences will occasionally lead to conflict.

The mechanics of social categorization are fairly straightforward. The first step is social identification, which begins with the assumption that each individual wishes to maximize his or her self-esteem. In order to ensure high self-esteem, individuals engage in a series of social comparisons with others. These self-comparisons involve individuals placing themselves, and others, into a series of categories along organizational, religious, gender, ethnic and socioeconomic lines, among others. This process leads each individual to establish his or her social identity, with that identity defined as one's membership in a given group of different categories. Given the initial assumption – that an individual does all of this in order to maintain a high level of self-esteem – it follows that individuals will deem the categories in which they belong as 'good' (often called the in-group) and the categories in which others belong as 'bad' (the out-group). Empirical research has shown that individuals often (falsely) attribute negative characteristics to out-group members as part of this process, believing the out-group to be comprised of individuals who are less trustworthy, honest, cooperative or intelligent (Brewer 1979; Stephan and Stephan 1985; Tajfel 1982).

The process of categorization often involves physical traits such as sex, race and age (Messick and Massie 1989). Given that membership in the out-group is seen as a deficiency, this classification often results in individuals assuming those from different racial backgrounds are either inherently 'worse' than they are, or, at the very least, untrustworthy (Loden and Rosener 1991). Social categorization theory, then, assumes that individuals quickly stereotype and make judgements about those from other groups. In a diverse organization, there are many more out-groups than in-groups, a pattern which is expected to cause heightened problems with trust, communication and cooperation. As a result, work processes will be made much more difficult, thus causing the final product, idea or solution to be weaker. This theory, then, suggests a negative relationship between organizational diversity and work-related outcomes.

Like social categorization theory, similarity/attraction theory suggests that organizational diversity will detract from performance. It is predicated on the notion that similarity in attributes, particularly demographic variables, increases interpersonal attraction and liking (Byrne et al. 1966). Individuals with similar backgrounds may find that they have more in common with each other than with others from different backgrounds, making it more comfortable for them to work together and collaborate toward producing a product or solving a problem. Similarity allows one to have his or her values and ideas reinforced, whereas dissimilarity causes one to question his or her values and ideas, a process that is likely to be unsettling. Research has shown that in a situation where an individual has the opportunity to interact with one of a number of different people, he or she is most likely to select a person who is similar (Burt and Regans 1997; Lincoln and Miller 1979). The dimension on which a person judges another as similar or dissimilar varies by context. In some cases, race or sex may be most important, but in many cases, it is likely to be a 'hidden' dimension of diversity, like educational background, religion or sexual orientation.

That one is likely to be most attracted to those with similar attributes yields clear predictions for the relationship between organizational diversity and work-related outcomes. Early research using the similarity/attraction concept found that dissimilarity led to a lack of 'attraction' to others that manifested itself through decreased communication, message distortion and communication error (Barnlund and Harland 1963; Triandis 1960). As with social categorization theory, similarity/attraction research would predict that high levels of diversity in an organization are likely to lead to faulty work processes. These faulty work processes will, in turn, lead to weaker performance.

There is evidence in the literature, however, that the process-oriented problems related to social categorization and similarity/attraction will dissipate over time. As group members get to know one another, the impact of surface-level diversity dissipates, with deeper-level factors like educational background, personality traits and values becoming more relevant (Gruenfeld *et al.* 1996; Harrison *et al.* 1998, 2002). Employees begin to get a better idea of what other employees are like, beyond surface-level features, and form more complex opinions.

For research linking diversity to performance, the element of time becomes a crucial connection between the theories of diversity and the anticipated empirical relationship. While it may be the case that one would anticipate a negative relationship between diversity and performance based on social categorization and similarity/attraction theories, one might argue that correct specification of the model requires a time element to take into account the mediating effect of employees getting to know each other. While research on ethnic diversity in public organizations has only recently taken this element into account (Pitts and Jarry 2009), a small proportion of the private sector literature has explored the mediating effect of time.

Empirical research indeed shows that surface-level diversity *initially* has a negative impact on group functioning (see Harrison *et al.* 2002: 1031). However, the studies' findings indicate that the impact of surface-level diversity on team outcomes tends to lessen with group longevity. Harrison *et al.* (1998) found that time weakens the negative effects of surface-level diversity on group social integration. Similarly, Harrison *et al.* (2002) hypothesized and found that increasing collaboration over time weakens the impacts of surface-level diversity on team outcomes but strengthens those of deep-level diversity.

In an earlier study, Watson *et al.* (1993) questioned whether newly formed culturally diverse groups would perform less well on complex problem-solving tasks than would newly formed culturally homogeneous groups. They found support for this hypothesis, but they discovered that the diverse groups resolved their process issues over time and the initial differences in group effectiveness diminished. Pelled *et al.* (1999) examined diversity's impact on emotional conflict in workgroups, which in turn has a negative effect on performance. Race was one of the diversity variables that the authors found to increase emotional conflict in the groups. They found that group longevity reduces the effects of diversity on workgroup emotional conflict. In their study of student workgroups, Mohammed and Angell (2004) also found that the negative impact of surface-level diversity on relationship conflict decreased with the passage of time. Their study is somewhat different, because the researchers purposefully introduced team orientation and a focus on team process to the groups as moderating effects. Team orientation reduced the impact of surface-level diversity, while team process decreased the impact of deep-level diversity.

Information and decision-making theory

The stream of research on information and decision making in groups is predicated on the notion that the composition of the workgroup will affect how the group processes information and makes decisions (Gruenfeld *et al.* 1996; Wittenbaum and Stasser 1996). One might expect, given the orientation of the first two theories, that this theory would also predict a negative relationship between diversity and outcomes. If social categorization and similarity/attraction theories tend to argue that diversity will cause breakdowns in collaboration and communication, then it would seem to follow that diversity would specifically cause problems in information generation and decision making.

However, the literature on information and decision making in groups tends to show that, for these two specific functions (producing information and making decisions), the faulty processes that result from high levels of heterogeneity are overcome by benefits gained by more creativity, a larger number of ideas and a larger pool of knowledge (Tziner and Eden 1985). Research has shown that, even in situations where diversity has a clearly negative impact on work processes, the increase in information available to the group that comes from diversity is enough to offset process problems (Ancona and Caldwell 1992; Jehn *et al.* 1997; Zenger and Lawrence 1989). The idea that diversity brings a number of new perspectives to the table, making it possible for an organization to be more effective, has served as the basis for a number of claims that diversity is a strength and resource for organizations (e.g. Adler 2003; Dobbs 1996; Thomas 1990).

The theory is not quite so straightforward, however, and it is important to consider the type of task when determining whether one might rely on information and decision-making research to predict a positive relationship between diversity and outcomes. For example, a routine task that involves little discretion or group interaction is likely not to benefit from diversity (Adler 2003). Since more information, knowledge and creativity are likely to be of little use for such a task, it seems most probable that these substantive benefits will not be enough to offset the faulty work processes that will result from group heterogeneity. Rather, diversity is most likely to provide positive results when the task is to solve a complex problem, generate a set of creative ideas or innovations, or produce a new product. In these cases, the more information and viewpoints that are present, the more likely the group will be to come to an optimal solution.

A second caveat is that most of the research on information and decision making in groups is based on deep-level dimensions of diversity, such as education and function (Ancona and Caldwell 1992; Bantel and Jackson 1989; Pelled *et al.* 1999). Research on surface-level diversity that uses this theoretical framework is sparse. Cox *et al.* (1991) use the individualism/collectivism value divide to suggest that racial/ethnic diversity creates a variety of perspectives that will benefit organizations and produce synergies. A handful of other studies use the same framework – differences in values that run along racial/ethnic lines – to test hypotheses related to information and decision making, but the literature is fairly shallow in this area (McLeod and Lobel 1992; Watson *et al.* 1993). While this theoretical stream does suggest a positive relationship between diversity and performance, it is a weak hypothesis and one that should be approached with caution.

The business case for diversity

The business case for diversity argues that organizations wishing to maximize their performance must recruit a staff that is as heterogeneous as possible. It is much more applied and practical than the three theories described above, but it is very common in both the public and private management literatures. Also called the 'value in diversity' approach (Cox and Blake 1991), the business case for diversity arose in the early 1990s as managers became increasingly aware of shifting workforce demographics. The core argument of the business case is that organizations must diversify as a means of responding to the overall environmental shift toward greater diversity in the labour market (Cox and Blake 1991; Konrad 2003; Robinson and Dechant 1997). As white men make up a smaller and smaller percentage of the workforce, organizations must look to other demographic groups in order to ensure that they hire the most talented individuals in the labour market (Rubaii-Barrett and Wise 2007). Moreover, as labour markets shift toward greater diversity, so too do client bases, and diverse organizations are arguably better positioned than homogeneous ones to respond to changing customer needs (Richard 2000). Finally, the theory of a 'market place of ideas' suggests that increasing the diversity of perspectives in an organization can lead to creative solutions and better end-products. The argument is similar to that forwarded by information and decision-making theory.

The business case for diversity is a politically powerful argument. It assumes that increasing employee diversity will lead to an increase in the perspectives and solutions considered by a group or organization, with these substantive benefits leading to performance gains (Gardenswartz and Rowe 1998). This permits organizations to obtain the buy-in of multiple constituent groups. For example, the business case for diversity satisfies those who are interested in improving social equity, since it speaks to the intrinsic value of the perspectives held by groups that have historically been disadvantaged. It also satisfies those who have an opposing view of equity and are opposed to affirmative action programmes on the grounds that they constitute reverse discrimination. These employees will accept the business case for diversity because a rational relationship can be demonstrated between diversity and performance, something that ultimately benefits all employees regardless of demographics. For-profit firms are not the only organizations that have used the business case as an argument for diversity. Public sector organizations were quick to adopt this philosophy as well, since it was politically defensible in ways that affirmative action never was, and it also fitted in with the performance-based reforms of the 1990s (Kellough and Naff 2004).

A key contingency in the diversity–performance relationship: diversity management programmes and policies

As outlined above, the three theoretical frameworks linking organizational diversity and performance are split as to whether diversity creates gains or drawbacks. Social categorization and similarity/attraction theories predict a negative relationship, while information/decision-making theory and the business case for diversity suggest a positive relationship. While these theories are rarely combined into a comprehensive framework for understanding diversity, research has established that they might all apply in the case of an organization that takes steps to *manage* organizational diversity. In this case, diversity may create problems in communication, collaboration and trust, while also creating benefits stemming from better information and more innovative services and solutions. If the organization manages its diversity properly, it will simultaneously buffer itself from process-oriented drawbacks and exploit the substantive benefits from diversity (Adler 2003; Pitts 2007,

2009). As such, diversity management is inherently a *strategic* response to diversity (Wise and Tschirhart 2000). The relationship between employee diversity and performance is likely to be contingent upon the extent to which the organization manages for diversity, making management a key variable in any study attempting to link organizational diversity to performance outcomes (Choi 2009; Pitts 2009).

A number of organizations have initiated such management strategies under the umbrella terms 'diversity management' or 'managing *for* diversity'. R. Roosevelt Thomas (1990) was one of the first to bring attention to diversity management, calling on organizations to draw upon diversity as a strength and competitive edge. Diversity management was different from earlier legalistic approaches focused on adhering to anti-discrimination laws in that it was about day-to-day management and the programmes that organizations could implement to best serve diverse employees. Thomas's argument rested on the premise that organizations with strong diversity management programmes would be able to generate better performance via employee diversity, since they would erase the negative performance consequences associated with faulty work processes in diverse workgroups. He did not frame it as such, but he essentially forwarded the argument that the diversity–performance relationship was contingent upon the presence of diversity management programmes.

By 1999, 90 per cent of US federal agencies had adopted diversity management programmes (Kellough and Naff 2004). The USA has been a leader in developing diversity management programmes (Ospina 2001), which is reflected by less frequent adoption in other parts of the world. For example, in 2000, only 45 per cent of UK firms reported that they had a diversity management programme in place (Auluck 2001). In many African countries, emphasis is more likely to be on aggressively hiring employees from underrepresented groups than on diversity management strategy (Rice 2001). While notable for normative purposes, this approach to diversity management is not likely to generate performance gains. If diversity is to benefit organizational performance, strategies for managing differences between employees appear to be key to ensuring that communication and collaboration problems do not result in drawbacks.

For many organizations, diversity management programmes are the latest in a long history of diversity-related initiatives (Table 8.2). Approaches to diversity were primarily legalistic until the late 1970s and early 1980s (and in many countries, remain so), when emphasis started to shift toward more management-oriented approaches (Jackson and Joshi 2001; Pitts and

Table 8.2: Evolution of organizational approaches to diversity

Legalistic approach	Valuing diversity approach	Managing diversity approach
Legally driven emphasis on compliance with anti-discrimination laws	*Ethically driven* emphasis on moral and ethical imperatives related to diversity	*Strategically driven* emphasis on using diversity as a means of boosting performance
Remedial approach that benefits groups that have historically experienced discrimination	*Idealistic* approach that assumes diversity can benefit all	*Pragmatic* approach that understands that diversity has both strengths and limitations
Opens doors by ensuring that discrimination does not keep minority groups from gaining employment	*Opens attitudes, minds, and the culture* by educating employees about the benefits of diversity	*Opens the system* by giving individuals from all backgrounds what they need in order to be successful

Adapted from Henderson (1994).

Wise 2010; Riccucci 2002; Selden and Selden 2001). Researchers began to realize that more progressive employment discrimination protections had made it possible for a wider variety of employees to gain entry into the firm, but the organizational culture often remained the same, preventing non-majority employees from recognizing their full potential. 'Valuing diversity' programmes were created in response to these assimilation issues in order to modify organizational cultures where one perspective seemed to be entrenched, but research soon found that these initiatives rarely achieved their objectives (Bezrukova and Jehn 2001). The more strategic approach to diversity – diversity management – followed in the footsteps of these values-oriented programmes.

While many organizations refer to their initiatives as 'diversity management', the components of their programmes often reflect an evolution that includes earlier focus on compliance. Kellough and Naff (2004) examine what is commonly included in diversity management programmes, identifying seven core components: ensuring management accountability; examining organizational structure, culture, and management systems; paying attention to representation; providing training; developing mentoring programmes; promoting internal advocacy groups; and emphasizing shared values among stakeholders. Some of these components may not be in place to maximize the value of organizational diversity, but rather to ensure that the organization adheres to legal requirements that protect employees from unlawful discrimination. Others, like mentoring programmes and internal advocacy groups, are more strategic and likely to generate performance gains in diverse agencies.

The evolution of empirical research on organizational diversity

The theories discussed above provide an organizing framework for under-standing how diversity affects performance, but data are needed to be confident about the real impact that diversity brings. Public organizations typically collect extensive data on employee demographics – making a straightforward test of diversity effects possible for many public agencies – but the confusion comes in figuring out how to measure outcomes. Performance measurement is a persistent problem in public management that is complicated by the political environment and goal ambiguity that many public agencies face (Boyne *et al.* 2007). Moreover, as diversity research in the for-profit arena identifies contingencies, interactions and non-linearities in relationships between diversity and outcomes, a host of other variables become necessary for empirical tests, and those are typically hard to come by without an original survey (Choi 2009; Pitts and Jarry 2009). Bringing diversity *management* into the equation most certainly requires survey data, archival research and/or content analysis (Kellough and Naff 2004). These concerns are compounded by the problem of organizational access. In order to collect the necessary data, researchers must convince organizations to 'let them in', a proposition that is particularly shaky in an area like diversity that is fraught with such important normative issues. Few organizations want to run the risk of being exposed as having a sub-par diversity management programme or discrim-inatory organizational culture. Finally, the culture of government agencies in many countries is anything but transparent, and the quality of data varies widely.

Only a handful of studies have addressed the diversity–performance link in public agencies (Pitts and Wise 2009). Almost all of these studies are set in the United States, with most using data on federal agencies and public schools. The performance measures used are limited in their scope and number. Despite these challenges, the literature has made substantial pro-gress if evaluated in light of the evolution of empirical research on diversity in public organizations. Public management research has historically been more attentive to the normative and legal issues associated with members of under-represented groups, an approach that is tangential but does not delve into performance-related consequences. The roots of public management research on workforce diversity are in representative bureaucracy, a literature that is tangential but conceptually distinct from work on workforce diver-sity. As scholars began to reject the politics – administration dichotomy in the wake of World War II (Price 1946), worries about the misuse of bureaucratic discretion led to arguments for a public service that was representative of society (Kingsley 1944; Levitan 1946). Early research examined whether the social class origins of bureaucrats were representative of the population as a whole (Kingsley 1944; Long 1952; Van Riper 1958), but by the 1970s, emphasis was much more firmly on racial/ethnic representation (Grabosky and Rosenbloom 1977; Kranz 1974; Meier 1975). In the late 1970s and 1980s, increases in the number of women entering the workforce led to research on representation by gender (Guy 1985; Hale and Kelly 1989; Saltzstein 1979; Riccucci 1986), and representative bureaucracy research continues to demonstrate a strong emphasis on race/ethnicity and gender today (Dolan and Rosenbloom 2003). While these studies did not measure diversity per se, they generated interest in how employees who were different from the mainstream were integrated into public agencies.

Most of this research focused on passive representation, which reflects whether women and people of colour hold positions in government in proportion to their share of the population. This literature typically found that women and people of colour were under-represented in government organizations worldwide, with overall improvements over time despite persistent difficulties at the highest ranks (Cornwell and Kellough 1994; Kellough 1990; Lewis 1992; Lewis and Frank 2002; Riccucci and Saidel 1997, 2001). Some have expanded upon this work to find that passive representation often translates into active representation, where shared social and cultural experiences lead employees to improve services or advocate policies that benefit citizens with the same demographic profile (Hindera 1993; Keiser et al. 2002; Meier 1993; Meier et al. 1999; Selden 1997; Wilkins and Keiser 2006). Other studies have chosen to focus on employee outcomes in lieu of citizen outcomes, finding that advancement and pay gaps tend to exist between men and women (Guy 1993, 1994; Lewis, 1986, 1987, 1992; Naff 1994) and between whites and people of colour (Naff 2001; Naff and Kellough 2003; Page 1994). This area of research paved the way for research on workforce diversity by demonstrating empirically that employee differences could potentially influence work-related outcomes.

Recent studies that explicitly link employee diversity and performance have found limited support for the social categorization and similarity/attraction theories. In their study of Texas public schools, Pitts and Jarry (2007) find that increasing racial/ethnic diversity among teachers corresponds to more students dropping out of school, fewer students passing a standardized graduation exam and fewer students going on to college. In later work using the same dataset, Pitts and Jarry (2009) found that this negative impact lessened over time, reflecting the theory that employees who get to know one another eventually get past the communication and trust issues that diversity creates for them at the outset. Andrews *et al.* (2005) examined racial/ethnic diversity in English local government agencies, finding that agencies with large percentages of nonwhite employees were more likely than others to have low citizen satisfaction score averages. They attribute their finding to the potential for discriminatory attitudes among citizens, which is a slightly different explanation but not inconsistent with social categorization and similarity/attraction theories.

Other research has added diversity management to the equation, finding that organizations with strong diversity management programmes may be able to guard against some of the negative consequences that diversity can create. Using data from US federal government agencies, Choi (2009) finds that diversity management mediates the negative relationships between racial/ethnic diversity, organizational performance and job satisfaction. Using data from the same sample of agencies, Pitts (2009) found that job satisfaction and employee perceptions of performance were lower among people of colour than among whites, a relationship that was mitigated by the extent to which the employee reported diversity management. On the other hand, Naff and Kellough (2003), in a well-designed evaluation of diversity management programmes in US federal agencies, found no relationship between diversity management and employee work outcomes for women and people of colour.

Research on gender and sex has been limited in developing connections to performance. For example, research on emotional labour has demonstrated that men and women tend to segregate into specific types of jobs, leading to a number of management implications that are important but not directly related to performance (Guy *et al.* 2008; Guy and Newman 2004; Meier *et al.* 2006a). More common has been research predicting the representation of women in government, with most of the research set in the United States (see, e.g. Hsieh and Winslow 2006; Llorens *et al.* 2008), and other studies set in Russia (Antonova 2002) and Korea (Kim 2003). Limited research has investigated how men and women manage differently in public organizations, which has indirect implications for performance. For example, DeHart-Davis *et al.* (2006) found that women were likely to score higher on a scale of compassion than men, but differences in public service motivation overall were not statistically significant. Meier *et al.* (2006b) found in their study of Texas superintendents that strategic stance differed by gender, a result expounded in later work finding that these differences in strategies led to higher performance for school districts led by women (Johansen 2007).

Untouched by researchers has been the relationship between the presence of women in public agencies and the *performance* of those organizations. Representative bureaucracy research has demonstrated that female service recipients can benefit from female representation among agency employees (Keiser *et al.* 2002; Wilkins 2007; Wilkins and Keiser 2006), but that does not mean that gender *diversity* among employees will lead to benefits for overall organizational performance. Aside from race and ethnicity, there has been practically no empirical research on the relationship between diversity along *any* other dimension and organizational performance in the public sector. In their analysis of public sector diversity research, Pitts and Wise (2010) identify only eight studies published since 2000 that examine empirical links between diversity and performance. Much work remains to be done in order to understand more fully the impact of workforce diversity on organizational performance.

Future directions for research

Progress in research on diversity and performance will depend on continued efforts to test theoretical propositions empirically. Using new data and innovative methods to test the following three propositions would serve as a crucial first step in this effort:

> *Proposition 1*: Employee diversity leads to faulty work processes, which in turn create communication and coordination difficulties that hinder performance.

Social categorization and similarity/attraction theories suggest that the diversity–performance relationship hinges on process issues. Existing work on diversity in public organizations has shown that racial/ethnic diversity can lead to performance drawbacks (Pitts and Jarry 2007, 2009), but it has not tested the 'black box' of causal forces between diversity and performance. Understanding the specific causal mechanisms and measuring their impacts explicitly will be important to continued theoretical development.

> *Proposition 2*: Employee diversity increases creativity and innovation, which in turn lead to performance benefits in public organizations.

Information and decision-making theories indicate that employee diversity can improve organizational performance via greater innovation and creativity in solving problems. The limited research on diversity in public organizations has shown that this is unlikely to be the case given that the diversity–performance relationship is more often negative than positive, but this research has failed to explicitly examine the causal mechanisms behind the diversity–performance link. It is possible that this is an example of how public organizations differ from for-profit firms, where creativity and innovation may be more valued. It is also possibly the case that the few studies conducted have not operationalized performance to include outcomes related to creativity and innovation.

Proposition 3: The relationship between diversity and performance is contingent upon time and diversity management practices.

Two studies using data from US federal agencies have demonstrated that the diversity–performance link is contingent upon an organization's implementation of diversity management (Choi 2009; Pitts 2009). Research using data from other countries and levels of government is crucial to building a base of evidence that supports this claim. In addition, Pitts and Jarry (2009) show that the diversity–performance relationship is contingent upon time. This makes sense, given that employees who distrust each other and communicate poorly can learn to overcome these obstacles if they work together for an extended period of time. However, their research is limited in that it is based in only one policy setting and it fails to examine the causal mechanisms behind the contingency. More research in this area is needed to ascertain whether diversity management and time are consistently mediators or moderators of the diversity–performance relationship.

In addition to these three explicit propositions, the following four recommendations would move the field forward and improve substantially on the knowledge base that we have created thus far.

First, the field must make greater efforts to engage in empirical research. Whether organizational diversity affects performance is an empirical question on which little evidence has been brought to bear. There are several theoretical explanations for how diversity might influence performance, but they must be tested using original data from public agencies. Those data do not have to be quantitative. Qualitative data would push the field just as far – if not farther – than quantitative data. Well-designed case studies of organizations, both homogeneous and diverse, would assist public management researchers in better understanding the causal mechanisms linking diversity and performance. Those results may not be generalizable to a broad variety of organizations, but neither are the results from a number of large-N quantitative projects. For example, much of the research on diversity uses data from the United States, where racial and ethnic diversity has predominated the literature for some time. Whether, and how, those studies can be generalized to countries where racial/ethnic diversity is minimal is an important question in research. Nonetheless, I argue that the impetus for now is in generating empirical research, *whatever the context*.

Second, public management must consider how organizational diversity is linked to other public management processes. For example, how do diversity management programmes play a role in the larger human resources management context? Do agencies include diversity in their missions and strategic plans, and if they do, what of it? Can diversity competencies be included in performance appraisal systems, such that employees who demonstrate an ability to manage diverse groups effectively are rewarded? Should governments incentivize their agencies to diversify, and if they should, then how would progress be evaluated? There are linkages between organizational diversity and strategy, but they have been underexplored in research (but see Andrews *et al.* 2005; Johansen 2007). If public management is an applied field of study that seeks to provide prescriptions for practising managers, then it must link organizational diversity to processes over which managers have some discretion. It must examine not just how organizational diversity affects performance, but also how management can be used as a means of either buffering the organization from the negative consequences from diversity or exploiting the positive ones.

Third, as we make progress, public management researchers must turn their attention to dimensions of diversity other than race and ethnicity. The impacts of a range of other types of diversity – gender and sex, language, educational background, and sexual orientation – remain underexplored in the public sector context. Public management researchers tend to be more focused on social equity issues than those in the private sector management context, and that is potentially responsible for our emphasis on understanding historically under-represented racial and ethnic minority groups. For example, it is likely that language and cultural diversity is a much more salient dimension in many European workgroups than race and ethnicity, but research in that area is sparse. Data are often unavailable on some of these dimensions – language and sexual orientation, for example – but original data collection may be warranted in order to understand better whether there are performance implications.

Finally, research must sort out whether organizational diversity is likely to affect different performance outcomes in different ways. It seems likely that it would detract from efficiency, but it is possible that it would benefit innovativeness and creativity. If diversity's impact on performance is contingent upon the task at hand, then that means that it is also very likely to be contingent upon the type of performance being measured. Where possible, diversity research should use multiple measures of performance as dependent variables in order to sort out differential impacts. Research should consider how the impacts of employee diversity on performance are contingent upon other internal and external factors, as well as tease out how factors at different levels of analysis – individual, group and organization – affect the impact of diversity on performance.

REFERENCES

Adler, Nancy J. 2003. *International Dimensions of Organizational Behavior*, 4th edn. Cincinnati, OH: South-Western.

Amirkhanyan, Anna A. 2007. 'The smart-seller challenge: exploring the determinants of privatizing public nursing homes', *Journal of Public Administration Research and Theory*, 17, 3, 501.

Ancona, Deborah G., and David F. Caldwell. 1992. 'Bridging the boundary: external activity and performance in organizational teams', *Administrative Science Quarterly*, 37, 4, 634–65.

Andrews, Rhys, George A. Boyne, Kenneth J. Meier, Laurence J. O'Toole, Jr., and Richard M. Walker. 2005. 'Representative bureaucracy, organizational strategy, and public service performance: an empirical analysis of English local government', *Journal of Public Administration Research and Theory*, 15, 4, 489–504.

Antonova, Victoria K. 2002. 'Women in public service in the Russian Federation: equal capability and unequal opportunity', *Review of Public Personnel Administration*, 22, 3, 216.

Auluck, Randhir. 2001. 'The management of diversity: the UK civil service journey continues', in Guido Bertucci (ed.) *Managing Diversity in the Civil Service*. Amsterdam: IOS Press, pp. 59–80.

Balogun, M. Jide. 2001. 'The scope for popular participation in decentralization, community governance, and development: towards a new paradigm of centre-periphery relations', *Regional Development Dialogue*, 21, 1–16.

Bantel, Karen A., and Susan E. Jackson. 1989. 'Top management and innovations in banking: does the composition of the top team make a difference', *Strategic Management Journal*, 10, 1, 107–24.

Barnlund, Dean, and Carroll Harland. 1963. 'Propinquity and prestige as determinants of communication networks', *Sociometry*, 26, 4, 467–79.

Bezrukova, Katerina, and Karen A. Jehn. 2001. 'The effects of diversity training programs', unpublished manuscript, Solomon Asch Center for the Study of Ethnopolitical Conflict, University of Pennsylvania, Philadelphia.

Blau, Peter M. 1977. *Inequality and Heterogeneity*. New York: The Free Press.

Boyne, George A., Kenneth J. Meier, Laurence J. O'Toole, Jr., and Richard M. Walker. 2007. *Public Service Performance: Perspectives on Measurement and Management*. Cambridge University Press.

Brewer, Marilynn B. 1979. 'In-group bias in the minimal intergroup situation: a cognitive-motivational analysis', *Psychological Bulletin*, 86, 2, 307–24.

Burt, Richard, and Robert Regans. 1997. 'Homophily, legitimacy, and competition: bias in manager-peer evaluations', working paper, Graduate School of Business, University of Chicago.

Byrne, Donn, Gerald L. Clore, and Philip Worchel. 1966. 'The effect of economic similarity-dissimilarity on interpersonal attraction', *Journal of Personality and Social Psychology*, 4, 2, 220–4.

Choi, Sungjoo. 2009. 'Diversity in the US federal government: diversity management and employee turnover in federal agencies', *Journal of Public Administration Research and Theory*, 19, 3, 603–30.

Chun, Young Han, and Hal G. Rainey. 2005. 'Goal ambiguity and organizational performance in US federal agencies', *Journal of Public Administration Research and Theory*, 15, 4, 529–57.

Cornwell, Christopher, and J. Edward Kellough. 1994. 'Women and minorities in federal government agencies: examining new evidence from panel data', *Public Administration Review*, 54, 3, 265–76.

Cox, Taylor H., and Stacy Blake. 1991. 'Managing cultural diversity: implications for organizational competitiveness', *The Executive*, 5, 3, 45–56.

Cox, Taylor H., Sharon A. Lobel, and Poppy L. McLeod. 1991. 'Effects of ethnic group cultural differences on cooperative and competitive behavior on a group task', *Academy of Management Journal*, 34, 4, 827–47.

DeHart-Davis, Leisha, Justin Marlowe, and Sanjay K. Pandey. 2006. 'Gender dimensions of public service motivation', *Public Administration Review*, 66, 6, 873–87.

Dobbs, Matti F. 1996. 'Managing diversity: lessons from the private sector', *Public Personnel Management*, 25, 3, 541–54.

Dolan, Julie A., and David H. Rosenbloom. 2003. *Representative Bureaucracy: Classic Readings and Continuing Controversies*. Armonk, NY: ME Sharpe.

Foldy, Erica G. 2004. 'Learning from diversity: a theoretical exploration', *Public Administration Review*, 64, 5, 529–38.

Gardenswartz, L., and A. Rowe. 1998. *Managing Diversity: a Complete Desk Reference and Planning Guide*. New York: McGraw-Hill.

Grabosky, Peter N., and David H. Rosenbloom. 1977. 'Racial and ethnic integration in the federal service', *Social Science Quarterly*, 56, 1, 71–84.

Gruenfeld, Deborah H., Elizabeth A. Mannix, Katherine Y. Williams, and Margaret A. Neale. 1996. 'Group composition and decision making: how member familiarity and information distribution affect process and performance', *Organizational Behavior and Human Decision Processes*, 67, 1, 1–15.

Guy, Mary E. 1985. *Professionals in Organizations: Debunking a Myth*. New York: Praeger.

1993. 'Workplace productivity and gender issues', *Public Administration Review*, 53, 3, 267–82.

1994. 'Organizational architecture, gender and women's careers', *Review of Public Personnel Administration*, 14, 2, 77–90.

Guy, Mary E., and Meredith A. Newman. 2004. 'Women's jobs, men's jobs: sex segregation and emotional labor', *Public Administration Review*, 64, 3, 289–98.

Guy, Mary E., Meredith A. Newman, and Sharon H. Mastracci. 2008. *Emotional Labor: Putting the Service in Public Service*. Armonk, NY: ME Sharpe.

Hale, Mary M., and Rita Mae Kelly. 1989. *Gender, Bureaucracy, and Democracy: Careers and Equal Opportunity in the Public Sector*. New York: Greenwood Press.

Harrison, David A., Kenneth H. Price, and Myrtle P. Bell. 1998. 'Beyond relational demography: time and the effects of surface- and deep-level diversity on work group cohesion', *Academy of Management Journal*, 41, 1, 96–107.

Harrison, David A., Kenneth H. Price, Joanne H. Gavin, and Anna Florey. 2002. 'Time, teams, and task performance: a longitudinal study of the changing effects of diversity on group performance', *Academy of Management Journal*, 45, 5, 1029–45.

Hindera, John J. 1993. 'Representative bureaucracy: further evidence of active representation in the EEOC district offices', *Journal of Public Administration Research and Theory*, 3, 4, 415–29.

Hsieh, Chih-wei, and Elizabeth Winslow. 2006. 'Gender representation in the federal workforce: a comparison among groups', *Review of Public Personnel Administration*, 26, 3, 276–95.

Jackson, Susan E., and Aparna Joshi. 2001. 'Research on domestic and international diversity in organizations: a merger that works?', *Handbook of Industrial, Work, and Organizational Psychology*, 1, 206–31.

Jackson, Susan E., J. F. Brett, V. I. Sessa, D. M. Cooper, J. A. Julin, and K. Peyronnin. 1991. 'Some differences make a difference: individual dissimilarity and group heterogeneity as correlates of recruitment, promotions, and turnover', *Journal of Applied Psychology*, 76, 675–89.

Jehn, Karen A., Clint Chadwick, and Sherry M. B. Thatcher. 1997. 'To agree or not to agree: the effects of value congruence, individual demographic dissimilarity, and conflict on workgroup outcomes', *International Journal of Conflict Management*, 8, 4, 287–305.

Johansen, Morgen S. 2007. 'The effect of female strategic managers on organizational performance', *Public Organization Review*, 7, 3, 269–79.

Keiser, Lael R., Vicky M. Wilkins, Kenneth J. Meier, and Catherine A. Holland. 2002. 'Lipstick and logarithms: gender, institutional context, and representative bureaucracy', *American Political Science Review*, 96, 3, 553–64.

Kellough, J. Edward. 1990. 'Integration in the public workplace: determinants of minority and female employment in federal agencies', *Public Administration Review*, 50, 5, 557–66.

Kellough, J. Edward, and Katherine C. Naff. 2004. 'Responding to a wake-up call: an examination of federal agency diversity management programs', *Administration and Society*, 36, 1, 62–77.

Kettl, Donald F. 2000. 'The transformation of governance: globalization, devolution, and the role of government', *Public Administration Review*, 60, 6, 488–97.

Kim, Chon Kyun. 2003. 'Representation and policy outputs: examining the linkage between passive and active representation', *Public Personnel Management*, 32, 4, 549–60.

Kingsley, J. Donald. 1944. *Representative Bureaucracy: an Interpretation of the British Civil Service*. Yellow Springs, Ohio: Antioch Press.

Kochan, T., K. Bezrukova, R. Ely, S. Jackson, A. Joshi, and K. Jehn. 2003. 'The effects of diversity on business performance: report of the diversity research network', *Human Resource Management*, 42, 1, 3–21.

Konrad, Alison M. 2003. 'Special issue introduction: defining the domain of workplace diversity scholarship', *Group and Organization Management*, 28, 1, 4–21.

Kranz, Harry. 1974. 'Are merit and equity compatible?', *Public Administration Review*, 34, 5, 434–40.

Levitan, David M. 1946. 'The responsibility of administrative officials in a democratic society', *Political Science Quarterly*, 61, 4, 462–598.

Lewis, Gregory B. 1986. 'Gender and promotions: promotion chances of white men and women in federal white-collar employment', *Journal of Human Resources*, 21, 3, 406–19.

1987. 'Changing patterns of sexual discrimination in federal employment', *Review of Public Personnel Administration*, 7, 2, 1–18.

1992. 'Men and women toward the top: backgrounds, careers, and potential of federal middle managers', *Public Personnel Management*, 21, 4, 473–91.

Lewis, Gregory B., and Sue A. Frank. 2002. 'Who wants to work for the government?', *Public Administration Review*, 62, 4, 395–404.

Lincoln, James R., and John Miller. 1979. 'Work and friendship ties in organizations: a comparative analysis of relational networks', *Administrative Science Quarterly*, 24, 2, 181–99.

Llorens, Jared J., Jeffrey B. Wenger, and J. Edward Kellough. 2008. 'Choosing public sector employment: the impact of wages on the representation of women and minorities in state bureaucracies', *Journal of Public Administration Research and Theory*, 18, 3, 397–411.

Loden, Marilyn, and Judy B. Rosener. 1991. *Workforce America! Managing Employee Diversity as a Vital Resource*. Homewood, IL: McGraw-Hill.

Long, Norton. 1952. 'Bureaucracy and constitutionalism', *American Political Science Review*, 46, 3, 808–18.

McGrath, Joseph E., Jennifer L. Berdahl, and Holly Arrow. 1995. 'Traits, expectations, culture, and clout: the dynamics of diversity in work groups', in Susan Jackson and Marian N. Ruderman (eds.) *Diversity in Work Teams: Research Paradigms for a Changing Workplace*. Washington, DC: American Psychological Association, pp. 17–45.

McLeod, Poppy L., and Sharon A. Lobel. 1992. 'The effects of ethnic diversity on idea generation in small groups', *Academy of Management Best Paper Proceedings*, 22, 227–31.

Meier, Kenneth J. 1975. 'Representative bureaucracy: an empirical analysis', *American Political Science Review*, 69, 2, 526–42.

1993. 'Latinos and representative bureaucracy testing the Thompson and Henderson hypotheses', *Journal of Public Administration Research and Theory*, 3, 4, 393–414.

Meier, Kenneth J., and John Bohte. 2007. *Politics and the Bureaucracy*. Belmont, CA: Thomson Wadsworth Publishing.

Meier, Kenneth J., Sharon H. Mastracci, and Kristin Wilson. 2006a. 'Gender and emotional labor in public organizations: an empirical examination of the link to performance', *Public Administration Review*, 66, 6, 899–909.

Meier, Kenneth J., Laurence J. O'Toole, Jr., and Holly T. Goerdel. 2006b. 'Management activity and program performance: gender as management capital', *Public Administration Review*, 66, 1, 24–36.

Meier, Kenneth J., Robert D. Wrinkle, and J. L. Polinard. 1999. 'Representative bureaucracy and distributional equity: addressing the hard question', *Journal of Politics*, 61, 4, 1025–39.

Messick, D., and D. Massie. 1989. 'Intergroup relations', *Annual Review of Psychology*, 40, 45–81.

Mohammed, Susan, and Linda C. Angell. 2004. 'Examining the moderating effects of team orientation and team process on relationship conflict', *Journal of Organizational Behavior*, 25, 8, 1015–39.

Naff, Katherine C. 1994. 'Through the glass ceiling: prospects for the advancement of women in the federal civil service', *Public Administration Review*, 54, 6, 507–14.

2001. *To Look Like America: Dismantling Barriers for Women and Minorities in Government*. Boulder, CO: Westview Press.

Naff, Katherine C., and J. Edward Kellough. 2003. 'Ensuring employment equity: are federal diversity programs making a difference?', *International Journal of Public Administration*, 26, 12, 1307–36.

OECD. 2003. *The Economic and Social Aspects of Migration*. OECD Working Paper Series.

Osborne, David, and Ted Gaebler. 1992. *Reinventing Government: How the Entrepreneurial Spirit is Transforming Government*. Reading, PA: Addison-Wesley.

Ospina, Sonia. 2001. 'Managing diversity in civil service: a framework for public organizations', in Guido Bertucci (ed.) *Managing Diversity in the Civil Service*. Amsterdam: IOS Press, pp. 11–30.

Page, Paul. 1994. 'African-Americans in executive branch agencies', *Review of Public Personnel Administration*, 14, 1, 24–37.

Pelled, Lisa H., Kathleen M. Eisenhardt, and Katherine R. Xin. 1999. 'Exploring the black box: an analysis of work group diversity, conflict, and performance', *Administrative Science Quarterly*, 44, 1, 1–28.

Perry, James L. 1997. 'Antecedents of public service motivation', *Journal of Public Administration Research and Theory*, 72, 2, 181–97.

Pitts, David W. 2005. 'Diversity, representation, and performance: evidence about race and ethnicity in public organizations', *Journal of Public Administration Research and Theory*, 15, 4, 615–31.

2006. 'Modeling the impact of diversity management', *Review of Public Personnel Administration*, 26, 3, 245–64.

2007. 'Implementation of diversity management programs in public organizations: lessons from policy implementation research', *International Journal of Public Administration*, 30, 12, 1573–90.

2009. 'Diversity management, job satisfaction, and organizational performance: evidence from US federal agencies', *Public Administration Review*, 69, 2, 328–38.

Pitts, David W., and Elizabeth M. Jarry. 2007. 'Ethnic diversity and organizational performance: assessing diversity effects at the managerial and street levels', *International Public Management Journal*, 10, 2, 233–54.

2009. 'Getting to know you: time, ethnicity, and performance in public organizations', *Public Administration*, 87, 3, 503–18.

Pitts, David W., and Lois R. Wise. 2010. 'Workforce diversity in the new millennium: prospects for research', *Review of Public Personnel Administration*, 30, 1, 44–69.

Price, Donald K. 1946. 'Staffing the Presidency', *American Political Science Review*, 40, 6, 1154–68.

Radin, Beryl. 2006. *Challenging the Performance Movement: Accountability, Complexity, and Democratic Values*. Washington, DC: Georgetown University Press.

Rainey, Hal G. 1993. 'Toward a theory of goal ambiguity in public organizations', *Research in Public Administration*, 2, 121–66.

2003. *Understanding and Managing Public Organizations*. San Francisco, CA: Jossey-Bass.

Riccucci, Norma M. 1986. 'Female and minority employment in city government: the role of unions', *Policy Studies Journal*, 15, 1, 3–15.

2002. *Managing Diversity in Public Sector Workforces*. Boulder, CO: Westview Press.

Riccucci, Norma M., and Judith R. Saidel. 1997. 'The representativeness of state-level bureaucratic leaders: a missing piece of the representative bureaucracy puzzle', *Public Administration Review*, 57, 5, 423–30.

2001. 'The demographics of gubernatorial appointees: toward an explanation of variation', *Policy Studies Journal*, 29, 1, 11–22.

Rice, Mitchell F. 2001. 'The need for teaching diversity and representativeness in university public administration education and professional public service training programmes in Sub-Saharan Africa', in Guido Bertucci (ed.) *Managing Diversity in the Civil Service*. Amsterdam: IOS Press, pp. 99–110.

Richard, Orlando C. 2000. 'Racial diversity, business strategy, and firm performance: a resource-based view', *Academy of Management Journal*, 43, 2, 164–77.

Robinson, Gail, and Kathleen Dechant. 1997. 'Building a business case for diversity', *Academy of Management Executive*, 11, 3, 21–31.

Rubaii-Barrett, Nadia, and Lois R. Wise. 2007. 'From want ads to websites: what diversity messages are state governments projecting?', *Review of Public Personnel Administration*, 27, 1, 21–38.

Rushton, Michael. 2008. 'A note on the use and misuse of the racial diversity index', *Policy Studies Journal*, 36, 3, 445–59.

Saltzstein, Grace H. 1979. 'Representative bureaucracy and bureaucratic responsibility: problems and prospects', *Administration and Society*, 10, 4, 465–79.

Selden, Sally C. 1997. *The Promise of Representative Bureaucracy: Diversity and Responsiveness in a Government Agency*. Armonk, NY: ME Sharpe.

Selden, Sally C., and Frank Selden. 2001. 'Rethinking diversity in public organizations for the 21st century: moving toward a multicultural model', *Administration and Society*, 33, 3, 303–22.

Stephan, Walter G., and Cookie W. Stephan. 1985. 'Intergroup anxiety', *Journal of Social Issues*, 41, 3, 157–75.

Tajfel, Henri. 1981. *Human Groups and Social Categories: Studies in Social Psychology.* Cambridge University Press.

1982. 'Social psychology of intergroup relations', *Annual Reviews in Psychology*, 33, 1, 1–39.

Thomas, R. Roosevelt. 1990. 'From affirmative action to affirming diversity', *Harvard Business Review*, 68, 2, 107–17.

Triandis, Harry C. 1960. 'Cognitive similarity and communication in a dyad', *Human Relations*, 13, 2, 175–91.

Triandis, Harry C., Lois L. Kurowski, and Michele J. Gelfand. 1994. 'Workplace diversity', *Handbook of Industrial and Organizational Psychology*, 4, 2, 769–827.

Turner, John C. 1982. 'Towards a cognitive redefinition of the social group', *Social Identity and Intergroup Relations*, 15, 2, 40–54.

1987. *Rediscovering the Social Group: A Social Categorization Theory.* Oxford, UK: Blackwell.

Tziner, Aharon, and Dov Eden. 1985. 'Effects of crew composition on crew performance: does the whole equal the sum of its parts?', *Journal of Applied Psychology*, 70, 1, 85–93.

Van Riper, Paul P. 1958. *History of the United States Civil Service.* New York: Row, Peterson.

Watson, Warren E., Kamalesh Kumar, and Larry K. Michaelsen. 1993. 'Cultural diversity's impact on interaction process and performance: comparing homogeneous and diverse task groups', *Academy of Management Journal*, 36, 3, 590–602.

Wilkins, Vicky M. 2007. 'Exploring the causal story: gender, active representation, and bureaucratic priorities', *Journal of Public Administration Research and Theory*, 17, 1, 77–89.

Wilkins, Vicky M., and Lael R. Keiser. 2006. 'Linking passive and active representation by gender: the case of child support agencies', *Journal of Public Administration Research and Theory*, 16, 1, 87–102.

Williams, Katherine Y., and Charles A. O'Reilly. 1998. 'Demography and diversity in organizations: a review of 40 years of research', *Research in Organizational Behavior*, 20, 77–140.

Wise, Lois R., and Mary Tschirhart. 2000. 'Examining empirical evidence on diversity effects: how useful is diversity research for public-sector managers?', *Public Administration Review*, 60, 5, 386–94.

Wittenbaum, Gwen M., and Garold Stasser. 1996. 'Management of information in small groups', in Judith L. Nye and Aaron M. Brower (eds.) *What's Social about Social Cognition.* Thousand Oaks, CA: Sage Publications, pp. 3–28.

Zenger, Todd R., and Barbara S. Lawrence. 1989. 'Organizational demography: the differential effects of age and tenure distributions on technical communication', *Academy of Management Journal*, 32, 2, 353–76.

9

Performance management: does it work?

George A. Boyne

Introduction

The idea that organizations should measure and actively manage their performance is a core element of recent public sector reforms in many nations, and is strongly encouraged by international bodies such as the OECD and World Bank. This doctrine of 'performance management' has taken root not only in US federal (Milakovich 2006), state (Moynihan 2006) and local governments (Krane 2008) but also in national government agencies in China (Chan and Gao 2009), New Zealand (Norman 2002) and Western Europe (Pollitt 2005), in local governments in the UK (Boyne *et al.* 2004), and in former Soviet states (Verheijen and Dobrolyubova 2007). Thus it can be argued that performance management appears to be viewed positively by governments across the globe, and is believed by senior policy-makers to lead to better public service performance.

Like many aspects of New Public management (NPM), performance management has roots in public choice theory (Boyne *et al.* 2003). In the era before the deluge of performance indicators in the public sector, writers such as Niskanen (1971) argued that public organizations were less efficient than their private sector counterparts, partly because their performance was opaque to citizens and politicians. Only the bureaucrats knew the true cost of services, and so were able to 'budget-maximize', thereby pursuing their own interests rather than the public interest and reducing the efficiency and cost-effectiveness of service delivery. One policy response to this problem was to expose public agencies to competition, which was intended to reveal the price and performance of alternative providers and so pressurize the bureaucracy to deliver better results. Another response was to encourage or force public organizations to collect and publish data on their performance. Such data can, in principle, be used by politicians to hold the bureaucracy accountable, by citizens to make informed choices between different public and private service providers, and by managers themselves to check their own performance and to inform strategies for service improvement. Thus performance measurement and management may alleviate principal-agent problems in the public sector, and help public organizations to achieve better results.

The aims of this chapter are to explore the theoretical arguments for and against performance management as a way of running public organizations, assess the empirical evidence on its costs and benefits, and delineate a research agenda for further work on this topic. Why is performance management expected to have positive (or negative) consequences for organizational achievements? What do we know about the effects of performance management in practice? And which major theoretical issues remain to be resolved? In the first part of the chapter the meaning of performance management is discussed, arguments on its effects are summarized and synthesized, and testable propositions on the consequences of this style of management are developed and specified. In the second part, the methods and findings of empirical studies that have sought to identify the impact of performance management are critically reviewed. The conclusion contains recommendations for research that will provide a more complete and more accurate picture of the connections between performance management and organizational outputs and outcomes.

It should be noted at the outset that the focus of the chapter is on processes for managing *organizational* rather than *individual* performance (otherwise known as human resource management – see Hartog *et al.* 2004). The term organizational performance covers achievements on criteria such as efficiency, equity, effectiveness and citizen satisfaction. It can, of course, be argued that the performance management of organizations cannot work without the performance management of individuals, and aspects of this are explored in Chapters 3 and 7 of this book. It should also be noted that the concept of performance management has become somewhat elastic in the academic literature, and has stretched to cover many different parts of management, including organizational missions, strategies, goals and formulation and implementation (see, for example, Bouckaert and Halligan 2008). Although performance management overlaps with, and may contribute to, activities such as setting organizational goals (see Chapter 2 of this book) and strategies (see Chapter 10), it seems essential to treat it as conceptually and empirically separable from other management functions, otherwise it would be impossible to identify its distinct contribution to public service performance. This is not to argue that performance management has effects that are entirely separate from other environmental and organizational variables. As will be argued below, the impact of performance management is likely to interact with organizational characteristics such as public service motivation and the propensity for managerial gaming.

Theoretical effects of performance management

Performance management differs from the conventional focus in public organizations on 'input management' (concerned mostly with controlling budgets and staffing) or 'process management' (which emphasizes consistency with rules and precedents). By contrast, performance management is intended to direct the attention of public officials towards organizational achievements rather than inputs or procedures. Thus in the contemporary literature it is also known as 'managing for results' (Moynihan 2006) or 'managing for outcomes' (Heinrich 2002), although critics argue that it is more accurately described as 'managing by (dubious) numbers' (Hood 2007). Although performance management is closely associated with the 'new public management' reform agenda of the last twenty years, it also resonates strongly with previous 'rationalist' regimes in the public sector such as management by objectives (Rodgers and Hunter 1992) and corporate planning (Boyne 2001). Despite the change in the labels, as Heinrich (2002: 712) notes the 'central purpose of these initiatives has been unchanging: to improve public management and program outcomes'.

Performance management can be divided into three distinct elements that are linked to each other both conceptually and practically: selecting indicators, setting targets, and taking action to influence scores on the indicators and the extent of target achievement. The first element in itself is simply performance measurement; it is the addition of explicit expectations and the use of indicators in organizational decisions that convert performance measurement into performance management. In turn the third element of performance management, taking action, has implications for traditional public management concerns such as inputs and procedures, because information on current or projected performance may lead to new budget allocations and organizational routines.

In this section of the chapter the theoretical links between the three elements of performance management and organizational success (or failure) are explored. The 'meta-proposition' implicit in NPM reforms – that performance management leads to better performance – is unpacked, and a set of more precise propositions is developed from arguments in the literature that critique this approach to the management of public organizations. This literature contains an implicit alternative meta-proposition: that performance management leads to worse performance. The first meta-proposition implies that each element of performance management taken in isolation, and all three in combination, will lead to better performance. Thus,

> Meta-Proposition 1: Performance management has a positive effect on organizational performance in the public sector.

On the other hand, the extensive criticisms of performance management and its elements suggest the opposite proposition, that

> Meta-Proposition 2: Performance management has a negative effect on organizational performance in the public sector.

One of the purposes of this chapter is to navigate between these extreme positions of 'performance management is good/bad' and to develop a more balanced and nuanced agenda for theoretical and empirical research.

Selecting indicators

Performance indicators provide a quantitative scale against which current and subsequent achievements can be assessed and tracked. A huge public management literature has critically reviewed the indicators that are typically used by public organizations (see, for example, Kravchuck and Schack 1996; Norman 2007; Smith 1993). In brief, these criticisms are that organizational goals that are not easily measurable are neglected by managers, that the indicators are either too few (thereby providing an incomplete picture of performance) or too many (reflecting a lack of clear priorities), and that the indicators may reflect the external circumstances of an organization rather than the talents or efforts of its managers (in other words, that measured performance is not truly attributable to the organization).

Such criticisms raise a number of theoretical questions about the impact of performance management on organizational results. First, are stronger positive effects produced by indicators that track public service outcomes (e.g. better health, lower unemployment, less crime) rather than organizational workloads or outputs? This seems likely because the 'things that really matter' are being measured (as opposed to intermediate steps in the production process), so effort will not be displaced towards organizational activities rather than service results (Kerr 1975). However, such outcomes are often beyond the control of a single organization or even all public agencies taken together.

For example, a global financial crisis makes it very difficult for government officials to shape economic outcomes such as employment levels. In these circumstances, movement on the outcome indicators may not be attributable to the managers being held accountable against them. In this case public officials may be demotivated, withdraw discretionary effort, and sit back and see if they win or lose a performance indicators game that resembles a lottery. This leads to the following propositions:

Proposition 1: Performance indicators are more likely to lead to better service results if they focus on outcomes rather than outputs or activities.

Proposition 2: The positive relationship between indicators that focus on outcomes and service results will be weaker when such outcomes are viewed by managers as 'uncontrollable'.

A second theoretical issue in indicator selection is whether it is better to have few or many indicators. A small number of indicators is usually thought to focus efforts and bring clarity of operational goals. On the other hand, a large number of indicators should ensure that no important organizational objectives are overlooked, and make it easier to take account of trade-offs between attempts to achieve better scores on different indicators (Ridgeway 1956). This suggests that the relationship between the number of indicators and service performance is likely to be non-linear: a small set may leave important organizational goals out of the mix, but a large set may leave managers confused about what they are supposed to achieve. Thus a position somewhere in the middle may be 'just right', in which case:

Proposition 3: The relationship between the number of indicators and service performance resembles an 'inverted u'.

A final theoretical puzzle in indicator selection is how different approaches to the attribution problem are likely to affect the link between performance management and organizational success. Put simply, a reliance on 'raw' performance indicators may give a misleading impression of the achievements of organizations that face different circumstances. In this case, both managers themselves and external stakeholders are likely to get a false impression of the extent of organizational success, and a performance management regime is likely to have perverse results (e.g. skewing rewards and recognition towards organizations that have benefited from favourable circumstances rather than effective management). One way of dealing with this problem is to select indicators for areas of activity that are largely within the direct control of organizations (e.g. quantity of output, efficiency) rather than those that are strongly affected by external conditions (quantity of outcomes, cost-effectiveness). As noted above, however, this is likely to lead to goal displacement and effort substitution towards activities that may be linked only weakly to the ultimate purposes of the organization. An alternative approach is to design indicators that are 'better than raw' because they take external constraints into account (Andrews *et al.* 2005; Rubinstein *et al.* 2003). This raises the possibility, however, of endless wrangles about what the relevant external circumstances are, how they should be weighted, and displacement of managerial effort into statistical politics rather than service delivery. Such adjusted performance scores may also be less easy for internal (e.g. staff) and external (e.g. service consumers) stakeholders to interpret, and thereby weaken the employee focus and accountability that performance management is supposed to bring. These arguments lead to two propositions:

> *Proposition 4*: Performance indicators that are adjusted for 'degree of difficulty' will have stronger positive effects than raw performance indicators.
>
> *Proposition 5*: The positive effect of performance indicators that are adjusted for 'degree of difficulty' will be stronger if they can be easily interpreted by internal and external stakeholders.

Setting targets

This second element of performance management involves setting precise expectations for future achievements on the indicators that have been selected. What score on the indicator does the organization expect to attain by some specific date? (A target without a time period for its achievement is not actually a target.) Many of the theoretical arguments on target effects, both for and against, are similar to arguments on the effects of performance indicators. The extra theoretical twist is that targets add 'bite' to performance indicators and reinforce their positive or negative effects on organizational results.

The benefits of targets are argued to be greater focus and clarity of organizational goals. Many goals of public organizations are ambiguous, not least because this facilitates the building of coalitions and the political support that is required for goals to be adopted in the first place. However, such ambiguity can have negative effects on organizational performance, because managers and other stakeholders may be confused about what an organization is trying to achieve (Chun and Rainey 2005). Targets can alleviate this problem by clarifying the purpose of organizational efforts, and thereby motivating staff and mobilizing resources towards the precise goal that has been set. However, as with the arguments on performance indicators, setting a target is likely to lead to the neglect of other organizational objectives, because managerial attention and organizational resources are likely to be directed towards a narrow set of objectives. This is especially likely to be the case if the target has rewards or sanctions attached to it (see below). Thus the first two propositions on targets are:

Proposition 6: A target boosts performance on the indicator that is targeted.

Proposition 7: A target cuts performance on indicators that are not targeted.

Taken together, these two propositions imply that the net effect of a target is indeterminate: it will depend on the relative impact on targeted and non-targeted indicators, and the relative weights that are attached to performance on these indicators. The consequence may be that organizations that deliver public services 'hit the target but miss the point' (because high performance requires that a range of objectives are achieved simultaneously, some of which may be not only outside the set of targets but, as noted above, outside the suite of performance indicators altogether).

The impact of targets may be partly contingent on how many are set. If the purpose of targets is to improve goal clarity and channel efforts towards improving scores on the relevant indicators, then more and more targets reintroduce the very ambiguity and 'mission creep' that a target regime is meant to remove. Thus, a higher number of targets will be counterproductive and lead to lower performance after a point of diminishing returns is reached. The optimal number of targets may vary with the range of services and sub-services that an organization provides, the number of dimensions of performance against which it is judged, and the variety of stakeholders that need to be satisfied. Nevertheless, controlling for these organizational characteristics, it seems likely that the positive effects of targets will eventually turn negative. This suggests that:

Proposition 8: The relationship between the number of targets and service performance resembles an 'inverted U'.

Critics of targets argue that they lead to a displacement of political and managerial effort from providing services to managerial gaming or 'playing the indicators' (Courty and Marschke 2007). Early research on performance management found evidence of such behaviour in industrial enterprises in the former Soviet Union (Berliner 1956), and recent cases of fraudulent behaviour in the pursuit of targets has been uncovered by various bodies responsible for auditing and inspecting government agencies in the UK. For example, data on ambulance response times seem to have been altered by officials so that cases within the period 8–9 minutes were 'reclassified' by officials as within the target time of 8 minutes (Bevan and Hood 2006). In a more systematic study, Bohte and Meier (2000) show that Texas school districts exempt students from exams in order to raise scores on performance indicators, thereby giving an inflated impression of their actual success. Such evidence suggests that improvements in *measured* performance exceed improvements in actual performance because managers distort the data in order to give the appearance that targets have been hit. This leads to the proposition that:

> *Proposition 9*: The relationship between targets and performance is moderated by managerial gaming.

Many writers suggest that organizational goals should be set in consultation with those responsible for achieving them (see Locke and Latham 2002). In the absence of such consultation, managers and front-line workers may be resistant to the goals and withdraw support from (or even deliberately sabotage) their accomplishment. By contrast, participation in the goal-setting process is believed to result in higher commitment and effort and thereby better performance. A counter-argument, however, is that handing control over the setting of targets to those that are responsible for achieving them is likely to lead to another form of gaming: the selection of targets that are too soft and not sufficiently challenging. Such easy targets are more likely to be reached, but with little real boost to performance. Putting these arguments together implies that the relationship between participation in target setting and performance improvement is non-linear:

> *Proposition 10*: Consultation with staff responsible for achieving a target is likely to moderate the link between target setting and performance; in particular, the relationship between the extent of consultation and service performance will resemble an inverted-U.

Taking action

The final major element of performance management is to take action that will influence scores on indicators and the extent of target achievement. Such action implies that performance information enters the decision-making process of the organization (rather than being collected and then ignored), which in turn converts performance measurement into performance management. The most widely debated form of managerial action in relation to performance indicators and targets is the provision of *incentives* to organizations and their sub-units: either rewards for good performance, or sanctions for failure to meet expectations (Swiss 2005). Such incentives are usually theorized as budgetary (thereby boosting or cutting the revenue of organizations) or pecuniary (raising or reducing the pay of individuals or groups). Indicators or targets that have incentives attached to them have been referred to as 'high stakes' performance management regimes, because they promise significant extra rewards or, more rarely, threaten to impose penalties.

Arguments about incentives invariably raise questions about the motives of public officials. Two basic models of motives in the public sector can be identified. The first, associated with public choice theory, is that bureaucrats promote their own careers and are keen to secure an easy life, with little regard for the welfare of society (Downs 1967; Niskanen 1971). This leads to the fundamental public choice proposition of budget maximization, which in turn implies that managers will be keen to hit targets that have extra revenue attached to them. An alternative set of assumptions about bureaucratic behaviour is found in the literature on public service motivation (see Chapter 7). Here the idea is that public officials' primary goal is to promote public welfare and to meet the needs of service recipients rather than their own personal needs. In this case a larger budget will be appealing in order to raise the quantity and/or improve the quality of public services, so managers with this set of motives will also be keen to hit targets that bring extra spending for their organization. Thus, regardless of whether bureaucrats are assumed to be self-interested or public spirited, targets with budgetary rewards should lead to higher scores on performance indicators:

> *Proposition 11*: The positive effect of a target is strengthened by budgetary incentives for organizations.

In contrast to budgetary rewards for organizations, the performance effects of monetary rewards for individuals are less clear-cut. Several studies have shown that managers in the public sector are less motivated by material rewards than are their private sector counterparts (Boyne 2002). Thus, direct monetary incentives for staff are unlikely to have strong effects on target achievement. Nevertheless, even public managers are likely, other things being equal, to be attracted by higher pay, so financial incentives should lead to higher target achievement *if rewards are seen as being allocated fairly*. As Swiss (2005: 594) argues, 'if the incentives violate the workers' sense of procedural and distributive justice, the incentives will cause resentment rather than the desired behaviour'. Public services are typically provided by teams rather than individuals, so an important issue becomes the distribution of extra money between the members of the team. If the allocation criteria, and the actual distribution, of the monetary rewards is viewed positively by staff responsible for achieving a target, then the promise of extra pay should lead to higher service achievements (or, at least, higher scores on performance indicators). If the distribution of monetary payments is seen as unfair then members of the team may be demotivated, and the attachment of higher pay to a target is likely to lead to group conflict and lower performance. Thus,

> *Proposition 12*: The impact of a target is moderated by perceptions of the fairness of the distribution of pecuniary rewards.

A further complication with offering a monetary reward to groups or individuals is that this might conflict with the views of managers and service professionals about how public organizations should be run. If people are attracted to public service primarily for idealistic reasons (or if they become socialized into this way of thinking after they join), then the introduction of a form of performance-related pay that is linked to target achievement could 'crowd out' their intrinsic motivation. Such intrinsic motivation to serve the public rather than serve for pay is likely to vary across services (perhaps higher in social care or in special-needs education than in garbage collection) and contexts (perhaps higher in organizations that are staffed by career civil servants than by a mix of these and managers recently recruited from the private sector). Thus,

> *Proposition 13*: The impact of monetary rewards is moderated by service motivation.

It has been argued widely that performance measurement per se has negative effects on the equity of public service provision (Boyne *et al.* 2003; Cutler and Waine 1997). The assumption is that, in order to achieve better scores on performance indicators and to hit targets, organizations will focus on 'easy customers' and neglect 'difficult customers'. For example, schools that are placed in league tables will seek to admit pupils who are likely to get good exam grades, and exclude those who are less likely to do well; similarly, hospitals that get judged on patient mortality may avoid treating 'high risk' patients. This would clearly be inequitable because those in highest need are denied public service provision, which can be regarded as a perverse outcome if the role of the state is to match resources to need (Le Grand 1982). If this effect of performance measurement is present, then the provision of incentives could exacerbate the inequity. In other words, existing resources may be unfairly allocated in the quest to get more resources by achieving better performance scores and meeting targets:

> *Proposition 14*: The provision of incentives for meeting targets is negatively related to performance on the criterion of equity.

Evidence on the effects of performance management

In this section of the chapter the available evidence on the effects of performance management on public services is reviewed in order to assess the validity of the theoretical arguments that were discussed above. Does setting performance indicators and targets, and providing incentives to get better scores and hit targets, make a difference to organizational achievements? As Ammons and Rivenbark (2008: 305) note, 'hard evidence documenting performance measurement's impact on management decisions and service improvement is rare'. Despite the vast literature that has emerged on performance indicators and performance management, few researchers have sought to test the links between these activities and organizational performance. Yet, there are fragments of quantitative and qualitative evidence that can allow initial judgements to be made on whether the three elements of performance management have positive or negative consequences for organizational results.

Selecting indicators

An evaluation of the effects of the presence of performance indicators per se faces a conundrum: ideally, the achievements of organizations with performance indicators would be compared with the achievements of organizations without them, but in the absence of performance indicators in one of the groups how would their relative success be judged? Empirical studies have used two research designs to deal with this issue and make assessments of the effects of performance indicators. One method is to compare early and late adopters of performance indicators, and the other is to examine the extent of adoption (e.g. by counting the number of indicators).

A study in the first category is Hanushek and Raymond's (2005) analysis of the introduction of 'accountability systems' for US schools. An accountability system is 'defined as publishing outcome information on standardized tests for each school along with providing a way to aggregate and interpret the school performance' (Hanushek and Raymond 2005: 306). During the 1990s all US states introduced such performance indicators that allowed the success or failure of different schools to be compared and tracked over time, but different states introduced the indicators in different years. Hanushek and Raymond (2005) evaluate the impact of this accountability regime on the growth in student performance between the fifth and eighth grade for the years 1992 to 2002. In order to assess the impact of performance indicators, they measure the number of years during this period that an accountability system was in place in each state, and expect that this will be positively related to the growth in student achievement. However, the statistical results show that these variables are unrelated, which suggests that the introduction of a mandatory and uniform regime of performance measurement makes no difference to pupil achievement.

Yang and Hsieh (2007) evaluate the impact of the extent of adoption of performance measurement on 'managerial effectiveness' in city governments in Taiwan. The extent of adoption was measured by managers' perceptions of the use of indicators of inputs, outputs, outcomes, efficiency and satisfaction. In a set of structural equation models, this measure has a consistent positive relationship with a factor that measures managerial effectiveness. However, it would be risky to infer that the adoption of performance measures is associated with organizational success. The managerial effectiveness factor contains items that relate to the performance measures themselves (e.g. 'the organization's performance indicators are reliable') as well as their effects (e.g. 'the organization's performance measurement improves productivity'). It would have been helpful to have a separate measure of perceptions of effects, and to examine the link between this variable and the extent of adoption of performance indicators. Moreover, measures of performance based on 'hard' indicators of organizational achievements would provide more confidence that the adoption of performance measurement actually matters. In addition, the cross-sectional research design in this study leaves open the possibility of reverse causality: it seems plausible that organizations with high scores on managerial effectiveness are more likely to adopt performance measurement.

These two studies, then, provide little clear evidence on the validity of meta-propositions M-P1 and M-P2. In addition, the more specific propositions

P1–P5 on selecting indicators remain to be tested. Further research therefore needs to investigate the performance consequences of different types of indicators (outputs or outcomes, raw or adjusted), different numbers of indicators, and their susceptibility to managerial control. For the present, the safest inference from the very limited empirical evidence is that simply adopting performance indicators makes no difference to organizational performance. The next sections consider whether the addition of targets or incentives leads to different results.

Setting targets

Four empirical studies have examined the impact of various aspects of targets on public service performance. These studies investigate the relative performance of organizations with and without a target on an indicator, the number of targets, and the extent of consultation in setting a target.

Boyne and Chen (2007) examine the impact of targets in 147 English local authorities between 1998 and 2003. The target regime they analyse was known as 'Local Public Service Agreements' (LPSAs). Under an LPSA each local authority attempted to hit twelve targets negotiated with central government, in exchange for a maximum financial reward of 2.5 per cent of its revenue budget. The targets could be spread across many services, or concentrated on a few services. Each authority selected from a long menu of performance indicators provided by central government, so the question 'do targets make a difference?' can be answered directly by comparing the achievements of local authorities with and without an LPSA target on each indicator. Boyne and Chen (2007) assess target effects on four measures of pupils' exam performance in secondary schools, using a panel dataset that covers the periods before and after the introduction of the LPSA regime. This analytical method allows a simultaneous 'before and after' and cross-sectional comparison of target effects. The results show that authorities with a target on an indicator performed better than authorities without a target, and performed better than themselves in the pre-target period. As Boyne and Chen (2007) note, this need not imply that the net effect of targets on educational performance is as positive as the results suggest, because non-targeted aspects of education provision may have been neglected during this period. Thus the results support target proposition P5, but do not provide evidence on P6 (that targets cut performance on non-targeted services). Furthermore, the nature of LPSAs makes it impossible to disentangle the impact of targets per se from the impact of the financial rewards associated with the targets.

Whether targets alone would have the same positive effect remains an open question.

Hyndman and Eden (2001) undertake a qualitative study of performance management, including targets, in nine executive agencies in the Northern Ireland civil service. Their data and conclusions are based on interviews with the chief executives of these agencies. This group of interviewees was 'chosen because of its seniority, assumed detailed knowledge of the issues and its ability to provide an overview of the entire operations of the agency' (Hyndman and Eden, 2001: 584). The rationale for the creation of such executive agencies was to provide a clearer framework for reporting and improving performance, partly through the use of indicators and targets, and for holding top managers to account. Perhaps unsurprisingly then, 'all of the respondents perceived that focusing on mission, objectives, targets and performance measures had improved the performance of the agency for all stakeholders' (Hyndman and Eden 2001: 592). This evidence supports not only P6 (that targets boost performance) but also M-P1. Whether other stakeholders (such as middle managers, front-line staff and service users) agreed with the views of their chief executives is unknown. It is important to note, however, that perceptions of performance management tend to be significantly more positive amongst senior than middle managers (Frazier and Swiss 2008).

Evidence on whether the number of targets makes a difference to service performance is provided by Boyne and Chen's (2007) study of LPSAs in England. Boyne and Chen's statistical evidence suggests that more LPSA targets for education are associated with better exam results. The range of this variable is, however, quite restricted (1–6), so perhaps, as proposition P8 suggests, the impact eventually becomes negative at a higher number of targets. Boyne and Gould-Williams (2003) also examine the impact of the number of targets (from 0 to 9) on the achievements of local authority service departments in Wales. The measures of targets and performance are based on survey responses from managers in May and December 1999 respectively. They find that a higher number of targets was associated with lower managerial perceptions of performance on two measures of service quality and one measure of efficiency, but was unrelated to the other four performance measures in their dataset. A final test of the link between the number of targets and organization performance is contained in Heinrich's (2002) analysis of the Job Training Partnership Act in the USA. The target measure in this study is the number of minimum targets that job placement agencies need to meet to qualify for performance bonuses. This turns out to have no significant effect on the key measure of the performance of job placement agencies: the earnings of individuals once they leave the job training programme.

Thus the three studies of the number of targets provide contradictory results: one finds a positive effect, one a negative effect, and one no significant effect. However, none of these studies tests for a non-linear effect of the number of targets, and so do not bear directly on P8 which suggests that a larger number of targets at first produces better results but at some point becomes counterproductive. It is possible that the apparently conflicting results of the empirical studies would be reconciled through testing for this non-linear effect of the number of targets.

One study has examined the consequences of the extent of consultation in setting targets. Walker and Boyne (2006) examine the influence of 'target ownership' on the performance of 117 upper-tier local authorities in England. The target measures were derived from a large survey of managers in 2001. The target ownership variable is taken from survey questions on (a) whether targets were agreed by those responsible for meeting them, and (b) whether the targets were viewed as achievable. These variables were tested against four measures of organizational success: the 'core service performance' element of the 2002 Comprehensive Performance Assessment, and local authority officers' perceptions of service efficiency, responsiveness and effectiveness. The latter variables were also derived from the survey of local authorities in 2001. The statistical results show that the target ownership variable had a significant positive relationship with all four measures of service achievements. In other words, whether service performance is measured objectively or subjectively, a target regime is more likely to work if it is accompanied by consultation with the staff responsible for service delivery and if the targets are viewed as realistic. This evidence does not, however, directly address P10, which implies a non-linear relationship between participation in target setting and organizational performance.

In sum, the available evidence suggests that targets and consultation on setting targets are associated with higher performance, but is very mixed on the impact of the number of targets. Thus the balance of the findings from these studies is consistent with MP-1 that targets have a positive effect, whereas little of the evidence supports the contradictory meta-proposition MP-2 that targets make public service performance worse. Again, however, it is important to note that the evidence is sparse, and that tests of propositions P7–P10 are either indirect or absent. Consequently, we have no knowledge from systematic empirical studies that reveals whether targets are bad for non-targeted indicators and services, whether the effects of the number of targets and the extent of consultation in target setting are non-linear, and whether any positive effects of targets are moderated by managerial gaming.

Taking action

Despite widespread criticisms of targets and the incentives attached to them, very little empirical evidence is available on the consequences of rewards and sanctions. As noted above, some studies (e.g. Boyne and Chen 2007) examine target regimes that contain incentives, but have been unable to identify the separate effects of the incentives element. A comprehensive and rigorous study that examines this issue is Hanushek and Raymond's (2005) analysis of variations in pupil performance across the US states (see above). All states introduced accountability requirements for their school systems, but some required only the reporting of performance information whereas others also added rewards for good results and sanctions for poor results. The measure of incentives is broad, and includes budgetary rewards for schools, extra pay for teachers, threats of school closure and vouchers for pupils to attend alternative schools. The statistical evidence shows that 'just reporting results has minimal impact on student performance and that the force of accountability comes from attaching consequences such as monetary awards or takeover threats to school performance' (Hanushek and Raymond 2005: 298). Thus incentives matter, but the measure of incentives is too broad-brush to provide direct evidence on the consequences of budgetary rewards (P11) or the moderation of pecuniary rewards by perceptions of fairness (P12) and the level of public service motivation (P13). Nevertheless, the statistical results in this study support M-P1: performance management (and, in particular, targets with incentives) is associated with higher public service performance.

Finally, Hanushek and Raymond's (2005) study also provides evidence on P14 (that incentives will reduce the equity of public service provision). They examine the impact of school accountability systems on the gap in performance between white and Hispanic pupils, and the gap between white and black pupils. The former narrowed while the latter grew, so a straightforward interpretation of the implications for the validity of P14 is impossible. Nevertheless, if equity has not uniformly improved or deteriorated, the evidence supports neither M-P1 nor M-P2.

Conclusion

Policies that have encouraged or enforced performance management have their roots in arguments that public bureaucracies are inefficient and unresponsive to the demands of political principals and the needs of service recipients. Performance management is intended to address these problems by measuring and comparing the standards achieved by different organizations, setting targets for future achievements and providing incentives to hit these targets. However, critics of performance management argue that it creates or exacerbates the very problems that it is supposed to solve: it wastes resources on measuring and tracking a partial picture of service performance, encourages managerial gaming, and reduces equity in the allocation of service outputs and outcomes.

This chapter has sought to shed light on these competing theoretical views by going beyond their contradictory meta-propositions on performance management, and developing a more specific set of propositions on the consequences of the three elements of performance management: selecting indicators, setting targets and taking action. It then attempted to evaluate the validity of these propositions by synthesizing the evidence from empirical studies of the effects of performance management on organizational achievements. This evidence turned out to be sparse and limited in a variety of ways. The institutional context of the empirical studies is mostly subnational governments in the USA and UK; little is known about the consequences of performance management in other nations and other types of public organizations. Most studies consider only one of the three elements of performance management (most frequently that of target setting), and include only one dimension of public service performance. Whether gains in any one dimension are bought at the expense of losses in others is therefore unknown.

Nevertheless, it can be concluded that the balance of the empirical evidence is consistent with the meta-proposition that performance management is associated with better public services. Although some of the evidence is neutral, very little of it fits the competing meta-proposition that performance management makes public services worse. Indeed, only one of the eight empirical studies that have systematically investigated the effects of performance management finds any evidence of negative effects (Boyne and Gould-William's (2003) analysis of the impact of the number of targets on managerial perceptions of service performance).

Although most of the available evidence is consistent with the view that performance management works, the quantity and quality of the studies is clearly too low to draw firm conclusions. Moreover, of the fourteen propositions specified in this chapter, only two have been tested directly: P6 (that targets are associated with better performance on the indicators that are targeted) and P14 (that incentives for target achievement reduce service equity). This leaves a large research agenda for future studies to establish whether different types of performance indicators have different effects, whether the net impact of targets is positive or negative (and is moderated by variables such as managerial gaming), and whether budgetary or pecuniary incentives work better.

Perhaps research on performance management could itself benefit from some performance management (albeit very 'light touch', of course, as befits scientific endeavour). If so, the performance indicators would cover the number of hypotheses tested rigorously and comprehensively, the target would be a shift from conceptual critiques of performance management to systematic evaluations, and the incentive would be evidence to refine our theories and provide better advice to governments about when performance management works best.

REFERENCES

Ammons, David, and William Rivenbark. 2008. 'Factors influencing the use of performance data to provide municipal services: evidence from the North Carolina Benchmarking Project', *Public Administration Review*, 68, 3, 304–18.

Andrews, Rhys, George A. Boyne, Jennifer Law, and Richard M. Walker. 2005. 'External constraints on local service standards: the case of comprehensive performance assessment in English local government', *Public Administration* 83, 4, 639–56.

Berliner, Joseph. 1956. 'A problem in Soviet business administration', *Administrative Science Quarterly*, 1, 1, 86–101.

Bevan, Gwyn, and Christopher Hood. 2006. 'What's measured is what matters: targets and gaming in the English national health care system', *Public Administration* 84, 4, 517–38.

Bohte, John, and Kenneth Meier. 2000. 'The motivation for organizational cheating', *Public Administration Review*, 60, 2, 173–82.

Bouckaert, Geert, and John Halligan. 2008. *Managing Performance: International Comparisons*. London: Routledge.

Boyne, George A. 2001. 'Planning, performance and public services', *Public Administration* 79, 1, 73–88.

Boyne, George. A. 2002. 'Public and private management: what's the difference?', *Journal of Management Studies*, 39, 1, 97–122.

Boyne, George A., and Alex Chen. 2007. 'Performance targets and public service improvement', *Journal of Public Administration Research and Theory*, 17, 3, 455–77.

Boyne, George A., and Julian Gould-Williams. 2003. 'Planning and performance in public organizations', *Public Management Review*, 5, 1, 115–32.

Boyne, George A., Catherine Farrell, Jennifer Law, Martin Powell, and Richard Walker. 2003. *Evaluating Public Management Reforms: Principles and Practice*. Philadelphia and Buckingham: Open University Press.

Boyne, George A., Jennifer Law, Julian Gould-Williams, and Richard M. Walker. 2004. 'Problems of rational planning in public organizations: an empirical assessment of the conventional wisdom', *Administration and Society*, 36, 3, 328–50.

Chan, Hon, and Jie Gao. 2009. 'Putting the cart before the horse? Accountability of performance', *Australian Journal of Public Administration*, 68, S51–S68.

Chun, Yung Han, and Hal G. Rainey. 2005. 'Goal ambiguity and organizational performance in US Federal Agencies', *Journal of Public Administration Research and Theory*, 15, 3, 529–57.

Courty, Pascal, and Gerald Marschke. 2007. 'Making government accountable: lessons from a federal job training program', *Public Administration Review*, 67, 6, 904–16.

Cutler, Ivor, and Barbara Waine. 1997. *Managing the Welfare State*. Oxford: Berg.

Downs, Anthony. 1967. *Inside Bureaucracy*. Boston: Little Brown.

Frazier, Andrew, and James Swiss. 2008. 'Contrasting views of results-based management tools from different organizational levels', *International Public Management Journal*, 11, 2, 214–34.

Hanushek, Eric, and Margaret Raymond. 2005. 'Does school accountability lead to improved student performance?', *Journal of Policy Analysis and Management*, 24, 2, 297–327.

Hartog, Deane, Paul Boselie, and Jaap Paauwe. 2004. 'Performance management: a model and research agenda', *Applied Psychology*, 53, 5, 556–69.

Heinrich, Carolyn. 2002. 'Outcomes-based performance management in the public sector: Implications for government accountability and effectiveness', *Public Administration Review*, 62, 6, 712–25.

Hood, Christopher. 2007. 'Public service management by numbers: Why does it vary? Where has it come from? What are the gaps and the puzzles?', *Public Money and Management*, 27, 2, 95–102.

Hyndman, Noel, and Ron Eden. 2001. 'Rational management, performance targets and executive agencies: views from agency chief executives in Northern Ireland', *Public Administration*, 79, 4, 579–98.

Kerr, Stephen. 1975. 'On the folly of rewarding A while hoping for B', *Academy of Management Journal*, 18, 5, 769–83.

Krane, Dale. 2008. 'Can the 'Courthouse Gang' go modern? Lessons from the adoption of performance-based management by county governments', *Public Performance and Management Review*, 31, 3, 387–406.

Kravchuk, Robert, and Ronald Schack. 1996. 'Designing effective performance–measurement systems under the Government Performance and Results Act of 1993', *Public Administration Review*, 56, 4, 348–58.

Le Grand, Julian. 1982. *The Strategy of Equality*. London: Allen and Unwin.

Locke, Edwin, and Gary Latham. 2002. 'Building a practically useful theory of goal setting and task motivation: a 35 year odyssey', *American Psychologist*, 57, 9, 705–17.

Milakovich, Michael. 2006. 'Comparing Bush-Chaney and Clinton-Gore performance management strategies: are they more alike than different?', *Public Administration*, 84, 3, 461–78.

Moynihan, Donald. 2006. 'Managing for results in State Government: evaluating a decade of reform', *Public Administration Review*, 66, 1, 77–89.

Niskanen, William. 1971. *Bureaucracy and Representative Government*. Chicago: Aldine-Atherton.

Norman, Richard. 2002. 'Management through measurement or meaning? Lessons from experience with New Zealand's public sector performance management systems', *International Review of Administrative Sciences*, 68, 4, 619–28.

2007. 'Managing for outcomes while accounting for outputs', *Public Performance and Management Review*, 30, 4, 536–49.

Pollitt, Christopher. 2005. 'Performance management in practice: a comparative study of executive agencies', *Journal of Public Administration Research and Theory*, 16, 1, 25–44.

Ridgeway, V. F. 1956. 'Dysfunctional consequences of performance measurements', *Administrative Science Quarterly* 1, 2, 240–7.

Rodgers, Robert, and John Hunter. 1992. 'A foundation of good management practice in government: management by objectives', *Public Administration Review*, 52, 1, 27–39.

Rubinstein, Ross, Amy Schwartz, and Leanna Stiefel. 2003. 'Better than raw: a guide to measuring organizational performance with adjusted measures', *Public Administration Review*, 63, 5, 607–15.

Smith, Peter. 1993. 'Outcome-related performance indicators and organizational control in the public sector', *British Journal of Management*, 4, 1, 135–51.

Swiss, James. 2005. 'A framework for assessing incentives in results-based management', *Public Administration Review*, 65, 5, 592–602.

Verheijen, Tony, and Yelena Dobrolyubova. 2007. 'Performance management in the Baltic States and Russia', *International Review of Administrative Sciences*, 73, 2, 205–15.

Walker, Richard M., and George A. Boyne. 2006. 'Public management reform and organizational performance: an empirical assessment of the UK Labour Government's public service improvement strategy', *Journal of Policy Analysis and Management*, 25, 2, 371–93.

Yang, Kaifeng, and Jun Hsieh. 2007. 'Managerial effectiveness of government performance measurement', *Public Administration Review*, 67, 6, 861–79.

10

Strategy: which strategic stances matter?

Richard M. Walker

Introduction

Strategy, or strategic management, is concerned with the means and ends of service delivery – organizational behaviour, organizational action and performance. In public agencies strategic management focuses on mission and organizational purpose, sometimes referred to as the creation of public value, sources of support and legitimacy together with operational matters to ensure that purposes are achieved (Moore 1995). Put another way, it is about 'maximiz[ing] value, given a number of choice constraints' (Lane and Wallis 2009: 105). Strategy has been described as managing outwards to stakeholders and citizens, upwards to political authority and downwards or inwards to the 'organization's current performance' (Moore 1995: 73). Haass's (1999) analogy of a compass similarly notes the holistic nature of strategic management: a public service manager is at the centre and manages north up the hierarchy to superior officers and politicians, south to employees, east to other colleagues in the organization and west to those outside the organization who may affect the work of the manager and public agency. Common to these three brief definitions of strategic management are: organizational process and practices that focus on weighing up and balancing opportunities and constraints from the environment with internal capabilities, with the aim of enhancing public value and to achieve higher levels of organizational performance.

This discussion of strategy alludes to two distinctive aspects: strategy formulation or processes and strategy content. The literature on strategy processes (or means) examines behaviour in organizations and the ways in which actors organize and plan strategy. In short, strategy process or strategy making is about how objectives and actions are selected or formulated (Hart 1992). The dominant approaches to strategy making in public organizations have been associated with logical incrementalism and rational planning (Dror 1973; Elbanna 2006; Mintzberg 1994; Quinn 1980). The majority of the effort in the public management literature has been addressed towards questions of process (see Bryson 2004; Hickson *et al.* 1986; Ring 1988; Ring and Perry 1985). Rational planning, and its impact on performance, as viewed from the perspective of performance management, has been reviewed in Chapter 4. The focus in this chapter is upon ends, or strategy content: 'a pattern of action through which [organizations] propose to achieve desired goals, modify current circumstances and/or realize latent opportunities' (Rubin 1988: 88) or 'the services to be offered, the ways they are provided, and the kinds of resources need' (Joldersma and Winter 2002: 87). The focus is upon how an organization selects its strategy content, how it interacts with its environment, and the way it seeks to improve performance and enhance public value.

Research on public sector strategy and performance is in its infancy – as we note below, there are only a handful of empirical studies that examine these relationships. The relatively small number of studies can be attributed to three factors. First, the historical or traditional view of public organizations cast them as inert agencies controlled by higher levels of political authority with little room for manoeuvre by public managers. They were simply responsible for the implementation of the policies developed by politicians (Ring and Perry 1985). Second, public organizations have ambitious goals, multiple stakeholders to satisfy and decisions are rule bounded (Bozeman 2000; Chun and Rainey 2005). Strategic management developed as an arena of research and practice for private organizations that are seen to have higher levels of managerial autonomy, clear goals and key identifiable stakeholders. Strategic management was seen as an anathema to public service organizations. Third, there has not been, and still largely is not, comprehensive and readily available data on the performance of public organizations. Without such data it is not possible to examine the effectiveness of alternative strategic management approaches.

Management is now, however, omnipresent – reforms over the last two decades have sought to increase managerial autonomy by separating policy from implementation and have decentralized organizations to an arm's length from government (Pollitt and Bouckaert 2004). While goals remain ambiguous (see Chapter 2 by Rainey and Jung), greater emphasis has been placed upon missions and goals through techniques such as performance management (see Boyne in Chapter 9). Changes in the environment have also freed up the capacity for managerial discretion, notable here are changes in technology which offer alternative ways to garner information on the organizational environment and to improve performance and thereby offer managers additional discretion (Lane and Wallis 2009). Performance has also become a major concern of the stakeholders of public organizations. Users and citizens want information on the performance of the services they receive and fund through fees and taxation. Higher levels of government use this information for the purposes of accountability and to drive up performance, sometimes for political ends. The agencies whose performance is under scrutiny are also interested in this performance information, and Behn (2003) suggests that they may use this data for controlling the organization, budgeting and cost control, motivating, promoting, celebrating and learning. It may also extend to purposes of legitimization (Ashworth *et al.* 2009). Changing public institutions and their management, together with increased availability of performance information means that in the early part of the twenty-first century strategy is an important topic in public administration and management research (see, for example, Andrews *et al.* 2009c; Boyne and Walker 2004; Joyce 1999; Lane and Wallis 2009; Meier *et al.* 2007; Moore 1995; Williams and Lewis 2008).

The balance of this chapter pans out thus: models of strategy content are reviewed in the following section. While a number of models of strategy content have been developed in the public sector, those with stronger propositions on performance, and where we see empirical tests thereof on public organizations were originally developed for private firms and we touch on this burgeoning literature. Following this the empirical evidence on public organizations is reviewed prior to presenting still unexplored research questions and propositions on strategy content and performance.

Models of strategy content in public organizations

Public management models of strategy content

Although the majority of effort has been directed towards uncovering and explaining strategy processes (see, for example, Bryson 2004; Joyce 1999) a number of scholars have attempted to develop models of strategy content. Here we briefly review those efforts.

Stevens and McGowan (1983) developed six generic approaches to strategy content: seeking external revenue, compromising existing authority and financial position (e.g. by defaulting on debt), increasing internal revenue, seeking additional state aid and authority, the state paying high-cost items and cutting safety and human services. These were developed in a largely inductive manner by asking managers and mayors in ninety US local governments to respond to twenty-five measures of fiscal stress. Consequently, the items in the typology are highly specific to one organizational problem and the authors conclude that it would be valuable to develop measures of performance to juxtapose with these strategies.

Based upon case studies of four agencies in Ohio, Wechsler and Backoff (1986) derive four models of strategy content: developmental, transformational, protective and political. Each strategy is derived from a combination of eight variables that include measures of goals (whether control over strategic direction is external or internal and the balance between external and internal targets), stances (the objectives of strategy, whether strategy anticipates events or reacts to them and the orientation towards change and the status quo) and actions (whether the scope of strategy covers a broad or narrow set of issues). Three of these variables describe organizational processes (the extent to which external actors attempt to influence the strategy of an agency, whether control over strategic direction is external or internal and the level of management attention given to strategic issues). While goals, stances and actions have a concern with strategy content, a focus on processes conflates strategy making and content.

This tendency of the early efforts of public management scholars to examine strategy content developed from case studies and can be seen in the work of Rubin (1988). Rubin posits four typologies: first, the 'saga' is 'a strategy configured to regain or protect a position or set of values perceived to be threatened by major internal or external change'. The 'quest' 'derives from a desire to make fundamental change in the current operations, priorities, or values of the organization'. Third, the 'venture' is 'a pattern of action that focuses on either perceived opportunities or emergent problems' and finally, the 'parlay' 'evolves in situations of extreme turbulence ... where no clear trends or historic patterns can be discerned with any degree of confidence' (1988, 90–3). Here we find examples of goals (saga), and a description of the environmental circumstances an organization may face (parlay). The quest clearly captures aspects of strategy content discussing actions and values, but is only one of the four typologies proposed.

Nutt and Backoff's (1993) discussion of strategy comes closest of those in the public sector to a consideration of performance, but does not quite engage with the debate. They argue that the strategy of an agency can by judged on two variables: 'the need for action' and 'the level of responsiveness to such needs'. Based upon these two variables they proceed to define eight types of strategy: dominators ('produce a strategy that takes action with little responsiveness to legitimate authority or stakeholders'), directors ('accept some modest formal accountability'), posturers ('adopt a strategy minimal action'), accommodators (have 'some commitment to action in the agenda of issues'), drifters ('make work programmes and routines ... to create the aura of action'), bureaucrats ('demonstrate moderate responsiveness by using programmed routines and standardised responses'), compromisers (prioritize 'needs and the actions each implies by playing one constituency against another'), and mutualists (respond 'to a diverse and ever-changing set of needs through strategy developments to meet those needs') (Nutt and Backoff 1993: 197–205). These categories conflate a number of issues – strategy and accountability – and draw on the wider generic literature (see below).

All of these typologies of strategy content overlook one of the key concepts of strategic management and the focus of this edited volume – performance. None makes a direct link to performance, i.e. they do not claim that any one approach is likely to lead to success, or that performance may vary depending on the framework adopted. And as we have noted in our discussion, all suffer in some way, notably collating strategy formulation with strategy content (Boyne and Walker 2004).

The application of generic models of strategy content to public organizations

Public management scholars have published more widely on models of strategy content adopted from the generic management literature than those that have been developed within the discipline. Predominantly, attention has been focused on two models: firstly Miles and Snow's (1978) strategic framework and to a lesser extent Porter's (1980) generic strategies – both of these frameworks make comment on the link between strategy content and performance.

Miles and Snow's (1978) typology of four stances was derived from detailed case studies. The framework was argued to be generic, that is, it would apply to any type of organization and their empirical work included hospitals in the USA, organizations with a public purpose. They derived four typologies. *Prospectors* are organizations that 'almost continually search for market opportunities, and ... regularly experiment with potential responses to emerging environmental trends' (Miles and Snow 1978: 29). In public organizations a prospector is likely to be a leader in their field, a 'first mover', or winner of innovation awards. A prospecting public agency may be seeking to expand its budget, may invade the 'policy space' of other agencies (Downs 1967), or may be innovative within its pre-existing budget where organizational slack permits (Bourgeois 1981). Strategic priorities in a public sector prospector would revolve around being more proactive than other agencies, innovating and risk taking (Boschken 1988).

Defenders are organizations that take a conservative view of innovation, and are not leaders in the field but instead are late adopters of innovations once they have been tried and tested. They typically compete on price and quality rather than on new products or markets and 'devote primary attention to improving the efficiency of their existing operations' (Miles and Snow 1978: 29); in short, they seek better performance focusing on core services to retain their existing activities and protect their share of the public budget. *Analysers* represent an intermediate category, sharing elements of both prospector and defender. Analysers are rarely 'first movers' but, instead, 'watch their competitors closely for new ideas, and ... rapidly adopt those which appear to be most promising' (Miles and Snow 1978: 29). *Reactors* are organizations in which top managers frequently perceive change and uncertainty in their organizational environments but lack a consistent and stable strategy. A reactor 'seldom makes adjustment of any sort until forced to do so by environmental pressures' (Miles and Snow 1978: 29). A reactor stance is equivalent to strategy absence, because an organization largely responds to external forces, and has no consistent or coherent strategy of its own (Inkpen and Chaudhury 1995).

Theoretical argument and empirical evidence have been presented for the applicability of the Miles and Snow framework to public organizations. Some evidence on the likelihood of public agencies adopting a reactor stance was provided by Royston Greenwood (1987). Greenwood's concern was not, however, with performance, rather he examined the relationship between strategy and structure and showed from a survey of English local government, and interviews with chief executive officers, how the choice of strategy led to an alignment with structure as predicted in the wider framework developed by Miles and Snow. A longitudinal study of six seaports on the US Pacific Coast also demonstrated the veracity of the Miles and Snow framework for public organizations. Over two decades and more Boschken (1988) notes how prospectors shifted their strategic stance towards that of an analyser and achieved compatibility with industry maturity, whereas the defenders and reactors remained unchanged which harmed their fit with changes in seaports during this period. Boyne and Walker (2004) argued for the adoption of the Miles and Snow framework as a model of strategy content for public organizations because it captures the main responses organizations are likely to make in response to changes in the organizational environment: innovate, maintain the current focus or await instructions.

Second, Porter (1980) developed a model of three distinct generic strategies. Like those of Miles and Snow they have explicit links to performance. First, 'cost leaders' sell their products at prices below those of their competitors. Second, creating and selling products to customers that are perceived as unique is a strategy of 'differentiation'. Companies may adopt a 'focused' strategy, which involves competing in a narrow segment of the market, through either cost leadership or differentiation. These strategies are all associated with higher levels of performance. The final strategy is referred to as 'stuck in the middle', and refers to a situation where a firm does not choose one of these three approaches – in this case performance is poor.

Joldersma and Winter (2002) apply a combined Miles and Snow and Porter model to hybrid organizations, i.e. public task organizations exposed to market processes, in dynamic environments. They argue that these organizations are likely to pursue strategies of differentiation and focus and correspond with Miles and Snow's analyser category. However, like the majority of the public management literature this study does not explore the relationship between strategy content and performance.

The majority of attention in the public management literature has been focused upon the work of Miles and Snow. This is probably because of the presumption of a competitive strategy in the work of Porter (1980). The remainder of this chapter is directed towards the Miles and Snow framework.

Propositions in the literature on strategy content and performance

The central contention of Miles and Snow's (1978) model of strategy is that prospectors, analysers and defenders perform better than reactors, which is supported by studies of private firms (Conant *et al.* 1990; Hawes and Crittenden 1984; Shortell and Zajac 1990; Slater and Olson 2001). However, a reactor stance is not always associated with poor performance. Snow and Hrebiniak's (1980) study of four industries confirmed Miles and Snow's primary hypothesis, except in the case of highly regulated industries where reactors outperformed prospectors and defenders. This finding may have implications for the relative effectiveness of different strategies in the public sector. A reactor stance may be a deliberate and positive choice in a public sector environment that values responsiveness to the shifting demands of external stakeholders, especially if strategy content is routinely imposed by regulatory agencies (Bozeman and Straussman 1990; Nutt and Backoff 1993; Rainey 1997). Prospectors may be perceived as excessively eager to take risks, and defenders may be seen as reluctant to respond to pressures for change.

Reactors, unconstrained by a fixed strategic posture, may be more pliable and more ready to please their political superiors (Boyne and Walker 2004). Thus, in principle, a reactor stance can be seen as the best fit with the political circumstances that shape perceptions of organizational performance in the public sector (Rainey and Steinbauer 1999).

Miles and Snow (1978) maintain that there are no performance differences between prospectors, analysers and defenders, a view supported by the findings of Slater and Olson (2001). However, the evidence on the relative performance of prospectors and defenders is neither comprehensive nor conclusive. Evans and Green's (2000) study of Chapter 11 bankruptcy notes that business turnaround is more likely to be achieved by prospectors than defenders. Hambrick (1983) concludes that prospectors outperform defenders on market share changes, but that this pattern is reversed for return on investment. Zajac and Shortell's (1989) analysis of US hospitals found that the performance of defenders fell behind other generic strategy types when the environment called for a more proactive approach. Woodside *et al.*'s (1999) analysis concludes that prospectors outperform defenders, who in turn outperform reactors.

Private sector evidence on the proposition from the writings of Miles and Snow that the performance of prospectors, defenders and analysers is higher than that of reactors receives broad but mixed support. The application of the Miles and Snow framework to the public sector has led to a slight variation on these propositions, which was initially derived from the private sector evidence. The propositions are that a prospector stance is positively related to organizational performance, and prospectors and defenders outperform reactors. While prospectors and defenders are argued to be positively related to performance, a reactor stance is negatively related to organizational achievements (Andrews, Boyne and Walker 2006).

The central proposition of the strategic management literature goes beyond a consideration only of strategy content, and argues that an organization needs to align its strategy with the organization's internal characteristics and the external environment. Only when this is achieved will organizational effectiveness be enhanced. This framework of multiple contingencies is central to Miles and Snow's (1978) characterization of strategy, and from this perspective research that primarily examines strategy content deals with misspecified relationships. Organizations have to find appropriate relationships between the 'entrepreneurial' problem (which strategy to adopt), the 'engineering' problem (which technologies to use) and the 'administrative' problem (which processes and structures to select). By their nature, prospectors are more focused on entrepreneurial questions and examine the services they deliver with a view towards innovation, defenders place emphasis on core services and efficiency and focus upon engineering problems and questions, while analysers focus on both of these questions and problems. Each typology is concerned with the questions and solutions to the administrative problem. Reactors respond to these issues in uncertain and inconsistent ways and are more likely to be influenced by the environment (Miles and Snow 1978, and also see Conant *et al.* 1990).

While Miles and Snow argue that performance is contingent on internal characteristics and environmental circumstances they are largely quiet on the latter. However, it is possible to trace out relationships across these variables from their work – I do this for prospectors and defenders (and below I argue that analysers are a redundant category and reactors have no predicted relationship because they lack a stable and coherent strategy). Defenders align themselves with centralized organizational structures because they need to both control operations centrally and vest power in top-level managers who can take an overview of the organization as a whole (Miles and Snow 1978: 41–4). Defenders adopt high levels of planning in their organizational processes because they need to undertake detailed analysis on how to achieve their goals. This emphasis on mechanistic structures and processes suggests that defenders are more likely to achieve optimal levels of performance in predictable and stable environments (see Andrews *et al.* 2008).

The achievement of high levels of performance in prospectors is proposed to be dependent upon an alignment of decentralized structures and decision making to permit staff at multiple levels to apply their expertise and implement fluid planning processes because they are in a state of flux, engaging in new opportunities prior to the completion of planning (Miles and Snow 1978: 59–62). Their propensity towards innovation with organic structures indicates that they are associated with an uncertain organizational environment.

Questions of measurement

Strategy content frameworks have typically been developed by way of inductive methods, and typically have used case studies as the basis of generalization to a wider population of organizations. From the prior discussion, it is clear that some of these approaches to measuring and operationalizing strategy content have been more successful than others. Here the purpose is to outline some of the measurement issues within the public management strategy content typologies, and then to examine the use of categorical and continuous scales in the operationalization of Miles and Snow's framework.

The models of strategy content developed from public management evidence were predominantly based on case studies. For example, Stevens and McGowan (1983) asked managers and mayors in ninety US local governments to identify whether they were using any of twenty-five strategic responses to fiscal stress. Factor analysis was used to group these into six generic approaches: seek external revenue, compromise existing authority and financial position, increase internal revenue, seek additional state aid and authority, state pays high-cost items, and cut safety and human services. These categories reveal the weakness in this typology alluded to above: it is specific to a certain set of environmental circumstances and focuses upon specific actions rather than an orientation to service delivery and performance. Wechsler and Backoff (1986) undertook four case studies in Ohio state agencies (Department of Natural Resources, Department of Mental Retardation and Developmental Disabilities, Department of Public Welfare and the Public Utilities Commission of Ohio). The study was longitudinal, spanning eighteen months and drawing upon interviews with civil servants and agency stakeholders and secondary sources of data, typically reports. Agencies were rated in relation to eight strategic dimensions: strength of external influence, locus of strategic control, impetus for strategic action, strategic orientation, orientation towards change, scope of strategic management, strategic management activity level, direction of strategic movement.

Miles and Snow's framework was developed from case-study research in a number of industries. Measurement of the typology has moved from unidimensional classification to multi-item scales. The dominant approach to the operationalization of the typology assumed that an organization can be placed into one of the strategic types, i.e. a prospector, a defender, an analyser or a reactor. Managers, when completing questionnaires on this typology, were asked to read a series of competing paragraphs that categorized an organization and to indicate which approximated to their organization. This approach, referred to as self-typing, was widely adopted (for private sector studies see Hambrick 1983; Segev 1987; Snow and Hrebiniak 1980; Zahra 1987). Figure 10.1 provides an illustration of this approach and shows the survey items used in Greenwood's (1987) study of English local authorities. Boyne and Walker (2004: 237) note that this approach does not result in the complete, mutually exclusive and internally homogeneous categories necessary to achieve a

The style of the local authority

Which one of the following descriptions most closely fits your local authority compared to other local authorities? There may be elements of each description in the authority – in fact, there probably are - but we would like you to indicate which description is more typical of your local authority. Please tick the appropriate box.

- TYPE A. This type of local authority prefers stability to experimentation and innovation. It concentrates resources upon statutorily prescribed services and makes a deliberate effort to provide stability in their provision. Established and understood ways of working are preferred. A central concern is to make the local authority more efficient.

- TYPE B. This type of local authority consciously and systematically seeks to learn how other local authorities and other types of organizations perform similar functions. There is a desire to know what new services are being developed, and what new ways of delivering services are to be found elsewhere. But there is a preference not to try out unproven ideas or develop new, untested services. Nevertheless new patterns of services and new ways of working are systematically identified and appraised, and adopted quickly when their efficacy has been demonstrated.

- TYPE C. This type of local authority actively seeks new opportunities and challenges. New kinds of services and new ways of working are vigorously sought and implemented. The local authority values being 'first in' on service developments and ways of working, even though some experiments will be unsuccessful. Continual innovation and experimentation are preferred to stability.

- TYPE D. This type of local authority values stability but introduces change as circumstances require. Knowledge of new ideas and practices is not systematically sought but acquired through the informal local government grapevine. Existing practices are made as effective as possible and change occurs largely in response to external events.

Figure 10.1: The Paragraphing Approach to Strategy Content: Defenders, Analysers, Prospectors and Reactors
Source: Greenwood 1987: 310–11.

good typology, and conclude that this work takes the 'form of asking private managers to identify whether their company is, for example, a "cat", "dog", or "fish"'. To overcome these difficulties they proposed that organizations are not likely to display a single dominant strategy, but rather vary across the strategic stances in relation to different spheres of their activities. Given this, strategy variables should be treated as continuous, not categorical.

Scholars in the management community have also engaged in debate about the best way to operationalize the framework (see for example Snow and Hambrick 1980). The major change came when Conant *et al.* (1990) criticized prior research for adopting the paragraphing or self-typing approach because it only captures one or two aspects of the contingent relationships between strategy, process, structure and environment. To this end they developed eleven multi-item scales to measure the overall Miles and Snow framework, that is, both the strategic types and the adaptive cycle of components: entrepreneurial (organizational goals and which strategy to adopt), engineering (technological goals and approach), and administration (the selection of structures and process). Figure 10.2 provides an illustration of the types of questions posed, in this example they are associated with the entrepreneurial problem or product and market domain. However, their analysis moves

Entrepreneurial—product market domain

In comparison to other HMOs, the services which we provide to our members are best characterize as:

(a) Services which are more innovative, continually changing and broader in nature throughout the organization and marketplace. (P)
(b) Services which are fairly stable in certain units/departments and markets while innovative in other units/departments and markets. (A)
(c) Services which are well focused, relatively stable and consistently defined throughout the marketplace. (D)
(d) Services which are in a state of transition, and largely based on responding to opportunities or threats from the marketplace or environment. (R).

(P) = prospector, (D) = defender, (A) = analyzer, (R) = reactor

Figure 10.2: Illustration of Conant *et al.*'s Multi-item Scale to Operationalize Miles and Snow
Source: Conant et al. (1990: 381)

back from allowing organizations to vary by strategic stance, as argued by Boyne and Walker (2004), and they categorize organizations on a majority-rule decision structure: 'organizations were classified as defenders, prospectors, analysers, or reactors, depending on the archetypal response option that was selected most often' (Conant *et al.* 1990, 373). Desarbo and colleagues (2005: 56), in an extensive exploration of the Miles and Snow framework, implement the Conant *et al.* questionnaire and adopt more stringent decision rules requiring 'at least seven "correct" answers out of the 11 items' to be classified as a prospector or defender. These two examples premise their argument on the effect of strategy on performance based on categorical variables.

Research operationalizing the Miles and Snow framework in public organizations has predominantly focused on strategy content, allowing for strategy to vary within agencies, and has thus recorded strategy content as a continuous variable (Andrews *et al.* 2009c; Meier *et al.* 2007). Strategy has been operationalized using single-item measures (see, for example, Andrews, Boyne and Walker 2006) and multi-item indexes (see, for example, Andrews *et al.* 2009a). Studies have also operationalized other aspects of the entrepreneurial, engineering and administrative problems central to the adaptive cycle (Andrews *et al.* 2008; Andrews *et al.* 2009a, 2009b). Table 10.1 illustrates the measures used in studies of Welsh local government, and the factor-derived solutions with measurement drawn from prior work on the framework (Miles and Snow 1978; Miller 1986; Snow and Hrebiniak 1980).

Two competing propositions emerge from this discussion. From the generic management literature a view that strategy is a categorical variable, and from the public management literature that it is a continuous variable.

Table 10.1: Descriptive measures and factor-analytic results of Miles and Snow's strategy archetypes

Measures	Factor 1	Factor 2	Factor 3
Prospector			
We continually redefine our service priorities	−.31	**.71**	.07
We seek to be first to identify new modes of delivery	−.20	**.86**	.01
Searching for new opportunities is a major part of our overall strategy	−.38	**.74**	.20
We often change our focus to new areas of service provision	.11	**.82**	−.16
Defender			
We seek to maintain stable service priorities	−.09	.07	**.79**
The service emphasises efficiency of provision	−.34	.31	**.62**
We focus on our core activities	.00	−.19	**.79**
Reactor			
We have no definite service priorities	**.77**	−.21	−.07
We change provision only when under pressure from external agencies	**.89**	−.04	−.12
We give little attention to new opportunities for service delivery	**.70**	−.41	−.10
The service explores new opportunities only when under pressure from external agencies	**.90**	−.05	−.07
We have no consistent response to external pressure	**.47**	−.35	−.23
Eigenvalues	3.31	2.95	1.79
Cumulative variance	27.60	52.21	67.10

Source: Andrews *et al.* (2009b: 9)

If the debate on the measurement of strategy is divergent then the debate on how to operationalize and measure performance can only be described as rampant. Details on this topic were outlined in the Introduction to this book and will not be repeated here. Needless to say that there is, as yet, no clear agreement on how best to measure organizational performance – the dependent variable in these studies – and that availability of data varies by study. In the studies reported on below different measures of performance are used. Two are composite measures of overall organizational performance, but differently constructed (Andrews, Boyne and Walker 2006; Andrews *et al.* 2009a), while the other studies use outcome measures from education programmes.

Empirical evidence

Data sources

Tests of the Miles and Snow strategy content propositions on the performance of public agencies has been predominantly undertaken on three datasets; two from the UK and one from the USA. The UK datasets include a study of Welsh local government and a large-scale study of English local government. The English study draws upon a panel of data collected between 2000 and 2008 and reports on a survey of just under 140 major local governments, providing data on managers' perceptions and behaviours in relation to a variety of measures of management and organization. This is supplemented with measures of organizational performance taken from the Audit Commission (2002) and background variables, typically based on UK 2001 Census data. The Welsh study takes departments within local government as the unit of analysis and reports on around sixty of these. It similarly draws upon the UK census and includes measures of performance derived from departmental level performance indicators. In the USA context work has been undertaken on Texas school districts. This is a large-scale dataset pooling data from 2000–2005 and includes performance data and a variety of socioeconomic controls from the Texas Education Authority and has been supplemented by a bi-annual survey of school district superintendents. In total just over 3,000 cases from this dataset have been applied to this research question.

Studies from these datasets examine the relationship between strategy and performance as either an independent effect, typically controlling for a number of other explanatory and confounding variables, or undertake joint tests. In these contingent models other variables of interest include centralization, red tape and regulation. Two studies offer a departure from these by undertaking tests of the full Miles and Snow framework (Andrews, Boyne, Meier *et al.* 2008; Meier *et al.* 2010). I commence with a review of the independent effect studies.

Independent effect studies

A number of studies have demonstrated that prospectors are high performing organizations, and that they do outperform defenders and reactors. However, these findings are not consistent and vary by other variables controlled for, and context. The first public sector test was undertaken by Andrews, Boyne and Walker (2006), and examined strategy content amongst 119 English local authorities, with lags between the measurement of strategy and performance. Their results revealed a hierarchy of effects on performance: prospecting is positively related to service achievements, defending is neutral and reacting, negative. The conclusion of this study is that when controlling for the presence of other strategic stances in an organization, prospecting is the best option and reacting the worst.

Similar findings are presented in a study of sustainable management and organizational strategy (Enticott and Walker 2008). Drawing on a sub-sample of the English panel, these authors primarily focus on the effect of sustainable management on organizational performance and sustainable performance, and note that sustainable management only has an effect on sustainable performance. In their models they control for prospecting, defending and reacting. They also find that prospecting out-trumps other strategy stances, but do not find that reacting has a detrimental effect on sustainable performance. Thus, controlling for a range of other variables leads to further subtle changes away from the hierarchical set of propositions developed and supported by Andrews, Boyne and Walker (2006). Boschken's (1988) case study of six ports also noted a hierarchy of achievement, with prospectors the highest performers, followed by defenders and reactors. However, Boschken was more circumspect about the achievements of defenders, often casting them as considerably poorer performers than prospectors.

Controlling for strategy formulation, and shifting the context of the study from England to Wales, offers a further twist to the story. The approaches of rational planning, logical incrementalism and strategy absence result in an ongoing positive association for the relationship between prospecting and performance. However, the inclusion of additional controls also leads to defending becoming a force for good in the battle to enhance organizational effectiveness. Reacting remains stubbornly statistically insignificant in the models presented by Andrews *et al.* (2008). These findings for strategy content and performance are more akin to the relationship proposed by Miles and Snow: that there are no differences between prospectors and defenders, and that both outperform reactors.

Defending is shown to be the strategy most likely to result in higher levels of organizational performance in Texan school districts when the dependent variable is measured as the student exam pass rate. In these models Meier *et al.* (2007) control for a number of facets of management (networking, school board contact, quality, experience and personnel stability) and a variety of socioeconomic and school-based external constraints. By examining differing aspects of organizational performance, Meier *et al.* uncover an interesting set of relationships, suggesting that strategic stance is contingent upon the organizational goal being measured. For example, exam pass rates for different ethnic groups suggest that prospecting can harm the achievements of black students while reacting can assist white students. Reacting similarly has positive effects on high-end performance measures (for university-bound students) as has prospecting – interestingly defending no longer matters. For low-achieving students, strategy content is shown not to matter, rather other facets of management are more important.

This brief review, of an admittedly small number of studies, points towards the contingent nature of public management. As we moved through these four studies the range of additional variables included in the models increased. While controlling for other variables is an important aspect of model specification, what matters in the context of this chapter is that strategy content remains an important variable that helps explain the performance of public agencies. Clearly there are questions of external validity in stating this: the theories are tested in three different contexts. The English context placed emphasis on new approaches to management and service delivery during the period of the research (Walker and Boyne 2006). Alternatively, the UK-based studies drew on measures of overall organizational effectiveness and were limited in the extent to which they could examine different aspects of performance: in Texas a number of dimensions of performance could be tapped, and therefore offered more tantalizing results. However, the dimension of performance of greatest importance to school superintendents was basic examination passes.

Moderated models

We now turn to the important question of the impact of moderating variables in the strategy content–performance relationship. As noted above, these models move closer to tests of the proposed relationships by Miles and Snow.

Public management researchers have identified three important variables when examining the moderated relationship between strategy content and performance: regulation, red tape and representative bureaucracy. Regulation is an important aspect of public service delivery, and forms of regulation are found in most political systems. While the purpose of regulation is to place checks and balances within a system of service delivery, the questions posed about regulation are concerned with the extent to which it assists with or damages attempts to maintain and raise the standards of public service performance. Andrews *et al.* (2008) hypothesize that the process of inspecting services (measured by the number of annual inspection interventions over two years) weakens the relationship between organizational strategy and performance and that supportive regulation (as perceived by local government civil servants) has a positive impact on the already beneficial relationship between strategy and performance. Prior to testing these moderating hypotheses Andrews *et al.* (2008) include independent effect models of the relationship between strategy content and performance; these show a positive effect from prospecting. The inclusion of environmental constraint variables and controls for inspection and regulation do not, however, lead to any statistically significant effects from defending or reacting. In the interactive models the propositions are partly upheld – inspection damages performance for prospectors and reactors, while regulatory support enhances performance. Neither interaction is significant for defending.

In a similar vein, Walker and Brewer (2009) examine the relationship between strategy content, red tape and organizational performance in English local governments drawing upon a segment of the panel data. They demonstrate that a strategy of prospecting can offset the detrimental impacts of red tape, but that in organizations with a reacting stance the presence of red tape worsens performance. The interaction between red tape and defending neither assists nor detracts from performance outcomes. In their study of representative bureaucracy Andrews *et al.* (2005) note in their independent effects model that prospecting increases performance while reacting has a harmful effect, reflecting the findings of Andrews *et al.* (2006). Their modelling shows that local authorities with high percentages of senior managers from ethnic minorities are viewed to have lower performance, when performance is measured by citizens' satisfaction with their local government. This negative, and damaging finding is not, however, uncovered in organizations that have a high propensity towards prospecting. While these studies do not address the central propositions of the strategy literature, they show that a strategy of prospecting can have a number of beneficial effects on variables of particular importance to public management.

The above studies test the effect of strategy content on performance, often within moderated models, and always controlling for spurious relationships. A few studies have sought to test more explicitly the notion that strategy's impact on performance will be greatest when external and internal factors are in alignment. One facet of the nature of the relationship between organizational success, strategy and organizational characteristics is tested by Andrews *et al.* (2009b). In the Welsh local government dataset they examine the effects of centralization, as measured by the hierachy of authority and participation in decision making. The findings point towards the veracity of the Miles and Snow framework: centralization in decision making works best in conjunction with defending, while organizations that emphasize prospecting are high performance when their structures allow for decentralized decision making. This article examines only one of the possible contingent relationships that are advanced by Miles and Snow as a mechanism of higher levels of performance.

Two studies have sought to test in a more comprehensive manner the contingent nature of the strategy–performance hypothesis as advanced by Miles and Snow. Andrews, Boyne and Meier *et al.* (2008), working with the English local government dataset, tested the fully specified Miles and Snow model using four years of data across 396 local governments. In the base model they again note the hierarchical relationship between organizational performance and strategy content: prospecting is positively associated with performance, defending is statistically insignificant and reacting is negative when controlling for structure (decentralization), processes (incremental) and environmental uncertainty and environmental constraints. To model the complex relationships between these variables the authors examine multiple interactions between the sets of variables. They commence with two-way interactions (for example prospecting × decentralization, prospecting × incremental processes and prospecting × uncertainty) and then move to three- and finally four-way interactions (for example prospecting × decentralization × incremental processes × uncertainty). Only the inclusion of the two-way interactions offer additional explanatory power to the model, but this only isolates three statistically significant relationships. Overall these are lacklustre results, and result in dissipation of the effects of strategy content. In a second study these authors (Meier *et al.* 2010) examine the interactive relationships between strategy, structure and the environment amongst school districts in Texas and again demonstrate that the anticipated contingencies are not uncovered.

The authors of these two studies speculate that this may be because of poor theory (strategic fit has no effect on organizational effectiveness) or because the theory does not operate on public organizations as it does on private ones. They speculate that it could arise because organizational adaptation to achieve fit may be less in the public than private sectors, given the frequent external pressures to adopt new structures and processes. Success and alignment across internal and external characteristics could also be linked to goals, and the multiple objectives of public organizations may work to cloud these relationships – facets of public organizations that are often suggested to differentiate them from private organizations. It is also possible that the methodological challenges posed by the statistical estimates influence the results, or that the ways in which strategy content is operationalized has an effect: in all the models reported it is allowed to vary, whereas in the original conceptualization these were categorical variables. This latter point once again raises questions about the most appropriate way to measure strategy.

Summary

Overall this stream of research on the Miles and Snow model of strategy content indicates that strategy content is clearly an important variable that influences the performance of public agencies. Typically, a strategy of prospecting will be associated with higher levels of organizational performance, and in many cases this approach will out-trump defending and reacting. These findings do not hold up in all contexts and prospecting does not always surpass defending (Andrews *et al.* 2009a). A reactor is very infrequently associated with higher levels of performance (Meier *et al.* 2007), but is rather viewed as the 'lemon' of strategic management and harmful to performance. These findings are broadly supported in moderated models, and in the cases of regulation, red tape and representative bureaucracy prospecting is the stance best able to overcome obstacles and achieve higher levels of organizational performance. However, tests of the proposed more fully contingent relationships between internal and external organizational characteristics offer lacklustre results.

An agenda for research

Research on strategy content has been growing in the public management literature since the 1980s. This literature has shifted from the generic management journals (Ring 1988; Ring and Perry 1985; Stevens and McGowan 1983) to public administration and management outlets (Andrews *et al.* 2006, 2009b; Nutt and Backoff 1993; Boyne and Walker 2004; Meier *et al.* 2007). Research that sought to develop models of strategy content for public service organizations was fraught with difficulties, typically conflating issues of strategy process and content. They also failed to include specifications about likely performance impacts and ways in which public value might be built, a central requirement for any model of strategic management. Consequently, these models have not been subjected to empirical scrutiny.

More recently scholars have turned to existing models of strategy content from the generic management literature. Two models have been examined in some detail, those of Miles and Snow (1978) and Porter (1980). The work of Porter has not been subjected to extended empirical scrutiny, partly because of its focus on competitive strategy which does not sit too comfortably within the context of public organizations, even after decades of marketization reforms. The Miles and Snow framework has received much more attention and would appear to offer some capacity to explain the performance of public agencies. The analysis of the Miles and Snow framework leads to a number of propositions for public management researchers to examine. A number of these propositions are grounded in the empirical research reviewed in this chapter. However, a number are more speculative and directed towards thinking about future studies of strategy in public organizations:

Proposition 1: Additional models of strategy content for public organizations are required.

What is noticeable from this review is the lack of competing models of strategy content. More effort needs to be focused on developing models of strategy content that clearly operationalize the plan of action to achieve desired goals and the ways that this links to organizational performance. This may include adapting existing models. For example, while Porter's model of competitive strategy is often argued to be inappropriate in public settings, public agencies are involved in a variety of competitive processes, be these competing for customers, engaging in turf battles or competing for budget dollars. Conceptual development is, therefore, the first area where more effort needs to be invested by public management scholars.

Proposition 2: Strategy content varies within organizations.

The discussion on the nature of strategy content and the best way to operationalize it is not complete: the generic management literature favours a categorical approach, while public management scholars have a preference for continuous measures that allow strategy content to vary across an organization. This perspective is predicated on a view that organizations are complex and that this is likely to result in the adoption of multiple strategies. This is likely to be a particularly fruitful area of enquiry, and should lead to wider contributions to the strategic management literature.

Proposition 3: Public organizations need to adopt proactive strategies to achieve higher levels of performance.

Proposition 4: Reacting is the 'lemon' of strategy content.

Proposition 5: Alternative strategies are likely to be associated with different dimensions of organizational performance.

Proactive strategies associated with prospecting and defending are more regularly associated with higher levels of performance in the studies reviewed. This proposition, as with the view that reacting is the least helpful strategy in public organizations, is in keeping with the original tenets of Miles and Snow. There are also clear links to the work of Porter. Porter argued that organizations have to make choices about which market they are in, and as such have to be proactive. For Porter 'stuck in the middle' is similar to Miles and Snow's reactor – an organization without clear purpose. The studies that adopted continuous measures of strategy and different dimensions of performance uncovered different relationships between different aspects of the production of public services. For example, it is likely that a strategy of defending will more strongly associated with efficiency and value for money. It is likely that both prospectors and defenders will make strong achievements against effectiveness, meeting core organizational goals. Prospectors may make achievements across a number of dimensions of performance. A prospector's outward orientation and propensity for innovation means that they may be adopting new practices to meet goals and needs and thereby enhance equity and effectiveness. Alternatively, new processes may be implemented that have a positive effect on efficiency. The evidence in the studies reviewed here strengthens the argument that organizations display different organizational strategies and indicates ways in which they may assist with different organizational tasks.

Proposition 6: The relationship between strategy content and performance is contingent on other internal characteristics and the organizational environment.

Proposition 7: The relationship between strategy content and performance is likely to be contingent on organizational goals in public organizations.

Evidence from studies examined in this chapter using two-way interactions between strategy and structure indicated that positive effects were uncovered between particular stances and decentralization/centralization (Andrews *et al.* 2009b). However, once more complex relationships are introduced these relationships dissipate (see Meier *et al.* 2010). The growing body of evidence on the public management–performance hypothesis points toward its contingent nature. While it is possible that the alignment that Miles and Snow offered does not hold, it is very likely that the effect of strategy is moderated by other internal and external organizational characteristics, and additional research is required to offer greater insights into these relationships. This research should include key organizational variables, such as structure and process, as discussed here, but also leadership, culture, networking and perturbations in the organizational environment. One area where evidence and knowledge can fruitfully be developed is in relation to organizational goals in public organizations. In this book Rainey and Jung have reviewed the work on goal ambiguity to show that organizations with less clear goals have a hard time achieving high levels of performance. If this is the case, relationships between strategy and performance might more readily be noted in organizations with less complex and ambiguous goals.

Proposition 8: Proactive strategies can combat the negative effects of some public sector maladies.

Reforms in the public sector have focused on attempting to remove some of the more entrenched problems in public organizations. Evidence on the effectiveness of proactive strategies (those reviewed in this chapter were largely prospecting) clearly points towards ways in which it can address red tape and how it can alleviate some of the complications associated with accountability processes. Thus, the adoption of proactive strategy content approaches by public agencies may offer valuable tools in the battle against public sector maladies, including redundancy, corruption and bureaucratic imperialism.

Concluding comment

All organizations have to make decisions about the strategies they wish to adopt, their internal characteristics and the external environment. The decisions made on these important variables by organizational actors have been shown in empirical studies to have consequences for public service performance and public values. It is possible to draw some conclusions on the value of proactive strategies and their relationship to some other variables of importance. As we noted earlier in the chapter, the evidence base is currently rather thin, particularly in relation to questions of external validity, and much needs to be done to move toward a normative theory on strategy content in public service organizations.

REFERENCES

Andrews, Rhys, George A. Boyne, Jennifer Law, and Richard M. Walker. 2008. 'Organizational strategy, external regulation and public service performance', *Public Administration*, 86, 1, 185–203.

2009a. 'Strategy formulation, strategy content and performance: an empirical analysis', *Public Management Review*, 11, 1, 1–22.

2009b. 'Centralization, organizational strategy and public service performance', *Journal of Public Administration Research and Theory*, 19, 1, 57–80.

2009c. 'Strategy, structure and process in the public sector. A test of the Miles and Snow model', *Public Administration*, 87, 4, 732–49.

Andrews, Rhys, George A. Boyne, Kenneth J. Meier, Laurence J. O'Toole, Jr., and Richard M. Walker. 2005. 'Representative bureaucracy, organizational strategy and public service performance: an empirical analysis of English local government', *Journal of Public Administration Research and Theory*, 15, 3, 489–504.

2008. 'Strategic fit and performance: a test of the Miles and Snow model', paper presented at the Proceedings of *Organizational Strategy, Structure, and Process: A Reflection on the Research Perspective of Miles and Snow* conference, Cardiff University, December 2008. Downloaded from www.cf.ac.uk/carbs/research/groups/clrgr/research/public/how_public.html 28 April 2009.

Andrews, Rhys, George A. Boyne, and Richard M. Walker. 2006. 'Strategy content and organizational performance: an empirical analysis', *Public Administration Review*, 66, 1, 52–63.

Ashworth, Rachel, George A. Boyne, and Rick Delbridge. 2009. 'Escape from the iron cage? Organizational change and isomorphic pressures in the public sector', *Journal of Public Administration Research and Theory*, 19, 1, 165–87.

Audit Commission. 2002. *Comprehensive Performance Assessment*. London: Audit Commission.

Behn, Robert. 2003. 'Why measure performance? Different purposes require different measures', *Public Administration Review*, 63, 5, 586–606.

Boschken, Herman L. 1988. *Strategic Design and Organizational Change*. Tuscaloosa: University of Alabama Press.

Bourgeois, Lynton J. III. 1981. 'On the measurement of organizational slack', *Academy of Management Review*, 6, 1, 29–39.

Boyne, George A., and Richard M. Walker. 2004. 'Strategy content and public service organizations', *Journal of Public Administration Research and Theory*, 14, 2, 231–52.

Bozeman, Barry. 2000. *Bureaucracy and Red Tape*. Upper Saddle River, NJ: Prentice Hall.

Bozeman, Barry, and Jeffery D. Straussman. 1990. *Public Management Strategies*. San Francisco: Jossey-Bass.

Bryson, John, M. 2004. *Strategic Planning for Public and Nonprofit Organizations*, 3rd edn. San Francisco: Jossey-Bass.

Chun, Young Han, and Hal G. Rainey. 2005. 'Goal ambiguity and organizational performance in US federal agencies', *Journal of Public Administration Research and Theory*, 15, 1, 1–30.

Conant, Jeffrey. S., Michael. P. Mokwa, and P. Rajan Varadarajan. 1990. 'Strategic types, distinctive marketing competencies and organizational performance: a multiple measures-based study', *Strategic Management Journal*, 11, 5, 365–83.

Desarbo, Wayne S., C. Anthony Di Benedetto, Michael Song, and Indrajit Sinha. 2005. 'Revisiting the Miles and Snow strategic framework: uncovering interrelationships between strategic types, capabilities, environmental uncertainty, and firm performance', *Strategic Management Journal*, 26, 1, 47–74.

Downs, Anthony. 1967. *Inside Bureaucracy*. Boston, MA: Little, Brown.

Dror, Yehexkel. 1973. *Public Policy Making Re-examined*. Bedfordshire: Leonard Hill.

Elbanna, Said. 2006. 'Strategic decision-making: process perspectives', *International Journal of Management Reviews*, 8, 1, 1–20.

Enticott, Gareth, and Richard M. Walker. 2008. 'Sustainability, performance and organizational strategy: an empirical analysis of public organizations', *Business Strategy and the Environment*, 17, 1, 79–92.

Evans, Jocelyn D., and Corliss L. Green. 2000. 'Marketing strategy, constituent influence, and resource allocation: an application of the Miles and Snow typology to closely held firms in Chapter 11 Bankruptcy', *Journal of Business Research*, 50, 2, 225–31.

Greenwood, Royston. 1987. 'Managerial strategies in local government', *Public Administration*, 65, 3, 295–312.

Haass, Richard N. 1999. *The Bureaucratic Entrepreneur: How to be Effective in any Unruly Organization*. Washington, DC: Brookings Institution.

Hambrick, Donald C. 1983. 'Some tests of the effectiveness and functional attributes of Miles and Snow's strategic types', *Academy of Management Journal*, 26, 1, 5–26.

Hart, Stuart. 1992. 'An integrated framework for strategy-making processes', *Academy of Management Review*, 17, 2, 327–51.

Hawes, John M., and William. F. Crittenden. 1984. 'A taxonomy of competitive retailing strategies', *Strategic Management Journal*, 5, 3, 275–87.

Hickson, David, Richard Butler, David Cray, Geoffrey Mallory, and David Wilson. 1986. *Top Decisions*. Oxford: Blackwell.

Inkpen, Andrew, and Nandan Chaudhury. 1995. 'The seeking of strategy where it is not: towards a theory of strategy absence', *Strategic Management Journal*, 16, 4, 313–23.

Joldersma, Cisca, and Vijco Winter. 2002. 'Strategic management in hybrid organizations', *Public Management Review*, 4, 1, 83–99.

Joyce, Paul. 1999. *Strategic Management for the Public Services*. Buckingham: Open University Press.

Lane, Jan-Erik, and Joseph Wallis. 2009. 'Strategic management and public leadership', *Public Management Review*, 11, 1, 101–20.

Meier, Kenneth, J., Laurence J. O'Toole, Jr., George A. Boyne, and Richard M. Walker. 2007. 'Strategic management and the performance of public organizations: testing venerable ideas again recent theories', *Journal of Public Administration Research and Theory*, 17, 3, 357–77.

Meier, Kenneth J., Laurence J. O'Toole, Jr., George A. Boyne, Richard M. Walker, and Rhys Andrews. In press. 'Alignment and results. Testing the interaction effects of strategy, structure, and environment from Miles and Snow', *Administration & Society*.

Miles, Raymond E., and Charles C. Snow. 1978. *Organizational Strategy, Structure and Process*. New York: McGraw-Hill.

Miller, Danny. 1986. 'Configurations of strategy and structure: towards a synthesis', *Strategic Management Journal*, 7, 3, 233–49.

Mintzberg, Henry. 1994. *The Rise and Fall of Strategic Planning*. New York: Prentice-Hall.

Moore, Mark H. 1995. *Creating Public Value. Strategic Management in Government*. Cambridge, MA: Harvard University Press.

Nutt, Paul, and Robert Backoff. 1993. 'Organizational publicness and its implications for strategic management', *Journal of Public Administration Research and Theory*, 3, 2, 209–31.

Pollitt, Christopher, and Geret Bouckaert. 2004. *Public Management Reform*, 2nd edn. Oxford University Press.

Porter, M. 1980. *Competitive Strategy*. New York: Free Press.

Quinn, James. 1980. *Logical Incrementalism*. Homewood, IL: Richard D. Irwin.

Rainey, Hal. G. 1997. *Understanding and Managing Public Organizations*. San Francisco: Jossey-Bass.

Rainey, Hal. G., and Paula Steinbauer. 1999. 'Galloping elephants: developing elements of a theory of effective government organizations', *Journal of Public Administration Research and Theory*, 9, 1, 1–32.

Ring, Peter. 1988. 'Strategic issues: what are they and where do they come from?', in John Bryson and Robert C. Einsweiler (eds.) *Strategic Planning*. Chicago: Planners Press, pp. 121–43.

Ring, Peter, and James Perry. 1985. 'Strategic management in public and private organizations: implications of distinctive contexts and constraints', *Academy of Management Review*, 10, 2, 276–86.

Rubin, Michael. 1988. 'Sagas, ventures, quests and parlays: a typology of strategies in the public sector', in John M. Bryson and Robert C. Einsweiler (eds.) *Strategic Planning*. Chicago: Planners Press, pp. 84–105.

Segev, E. 1987. 'Strategy, strategy making, and performance – An empirical investigation', *Management Science*, 33, 2, 285–69.

Shortell, Stephen M., and Edward J. Zajac. 1990. 'Perceptual and archival measures of Miles and Snow's strategic types: a comprehensive assessment of reliability and validity', *Academy of Management Journal*, 33, 4, 817–32.

Slater, Stanley F., and Eric. M. Olson. 2001. 'Marketing's contribution to the implementation of business strategy: an empirical analysis', *Strategic Management Journal*, 22, 11, 1055–67.

Snow, Charles C., and Donald Hambrick. 1980. 'Measuring organizational strategies: some theoretical and methodological problems', *Academy of Management Review*, 5, 4, 527–38.

Snow, Charles C., and Lawrence G. Hrebiniak. 1980. 'Strategy, distinctive competence, and organizational performance', *Administrative Science Quarterly*, 25, 2, 317–36.

Stevens, John M., and Robert P. McGowan. 1983. 'Managerial strategies in municipal government organizations', *Academy of Management Journal*, 26, 3, 527–34.

Walker, Richard M., and George A. Boyne. 2006. 'Public management reform and organizational performance: an empirical assessment of the UK Labour government's public service improvement strategy', *Journal of Policy Analysis and Management*, 25, 2, 371–94.

Walker, Richard M., and Gene A. Brewer. 2009. 'Can management strategy minimize the impact of red tape on organizational performance?', *Administration & Society*, 41, 4, 423–48.

Wechsler, Barton, and Robert W. Backoff. 1986. 'Policy making and administration in state agencies: strategic management approaches', *Public Administration Review*, 46, 4, 321–7.

Williams, Wil, and Duncan Lewis. 2008. 'Strategic management tools and public sector management. The challenge of context and specificity', *Public Management Review*, 10, 5, 653–71.

Woodside, Arch G., Daniel P. Sullivan, and Randolph J. Trappey. 1999. 'Assessing relationships among strategic types, distinctive marketing competencies, and organizational performance', *Journal of Business Research*, 45, 2, 135–46.

Zahra, Shaker A. 1987. 'Corporate strategic types, environmental perceptions, managerial philosophies and goals: an empirical study', *Akron Business and Economic Review*, 18, 2, 64–77.

Zajac, Edward J., and Stephen M. Shortell. 1989. 'Changing generic strategies: likelihood, direction and performance implications', *Strategic Management Journal*, 10, 5, 413–30.

Introduction

The preceding chapters have identified many ways that the study of public management and performance has grown both in scope and complexity, opening doors for continued theoretical advancement. Our knowledge of how the behaviour of public managers can affect organizational outcomes has grown substantially, and as a field, public management continues to develop. We have seen the ways in which questions of networks and governance have altered how we think about and study public management, and these lines of inquiry have offered incredible opportunities to ask new and interesting questions. These theoretical advancements have also led us to pursue new and better data on the behaviour of public managers and the outcomes they seek to affect. This increase in the availability of data has led to a diversification of methodological techniques employed in public management research, many of which have greatly expanded our ability to explore the multifaceted relationship between management and performance.

This chapter offers a discussion of the ways in which different methodological approaches could push our thinking into new areas of research – a discussion that will begin with two important caveats. First, I am not a methodologist, and this discussion is not written for methodologists. This chapter is simply an effort to encourage management researchers to consider different approaches and how those approaches can steer our thinking into new areas. This is not an attempt to be comprehensive, but it is a simple effort to spark conversation and creativity in thinking about future directions for research. Second, I realize that some may view this discussion as committing the unforgivable sin of encouraging scholars to learn a new trick and look for places to show it off. It is not. I, too, chide students for abandoning good social science methods by choosing a research question solely because of their fascination with their recently learned methodological approach, but

I also believe that we can benefit from considering the ways in which 'new'[1] (or underutilized) methodologies open doors for empirical work.

This chapter will begin with a brief discussion of a few hurdles that are often faced by researchers in public management, and some of the few relatively common, but often underutilized, techniques that could aid in our investigations of the link between management and performance. I then move to an overview of two rarely employed methodologies in the management literature, hierarchical modelling and experimental methods, and how they can improve our work on existing questions and encourage us to think about different approaches to issues that are fundamental to the study of public management and performance. These two are chosen because they are both methodologies that have been used widely in other fields but have received little attention in public administration and public management. For each method, I will offer a brief description of the approach, outline the ways in which researchers can improve upon current methodological approaches, and move to a discussion of theory building. This chapter then moves to a discussion of the use of qualitative research in public management and how quantitative scholars could incorporate qualitative methodologies into their work.

Methodological issues in public management research

The use of linear regression techniques (ordinary least square (OLS), logit) has dominated work in public management, but in recent years, research on public management has expanded well beyond basic regression. Scholars now employ a wide range of new techniques, some of which are small adjustments to basic regression, but many are quite different. The expansion is probably attributable to the increasing availability of data on public managers and the increasing range of statistical methodologies developed by researchers and taught in graduate programmes. These new techniques allow us to deal with many of the common methodological problems that are often found in research on public management and performance.

Endogeneity

Some of the problems we face are simply due to the fact that our data rarely conform to the assumptions of linear regression. For example, many

---

[1] I use the term 'new' with some reservation, as none of these methodologies are really new at all. By 'new', I mostly mean underutilized by scholars of management and performance.

scholars seek to understand how variations in the activities of public managers affect performance outcomes. Yet, we know that these public managers are almost always subject to accountability policies, oversight, or 'performance management' programmes that are designed to influence the ways in which managers behave. These systems are set up so that if an organization's performance fails to meet a certain standard, the manager will bear some responsibility and will be expected to take actions that will improve outcomes. As such, we may speculate that an organization's performance will affect the behaviour of managers as much as the behaviour of managers will affect performance.

We have a number of options for dealing with endogeneity, many of which have been used regularly in public administration research. Some scholars utilize two-stage least squares (or three-stage least squares) analysis (for an example, see Moon and Bretschneider 2002). Two-stage least squares has been very useful in many situations, but it requires the incorporation of instrumental variables – variables that have a relationship with the endogenous independent variable but not the dependent variable – which may not exist. When data exist for multiple time points, scholars often incorporate lagged dependent variables (LDV) to deal with endogeneity. The reasoning for doing so is quite straightforward: if we want to isolate the effect of management on performance, but we have concerns that past performance affects management, then we can control for past performance through the inclusion of the lagged dependent variable.

Non-linearity

As we advance our understanding of how management affects organizations, we should consider the functional form of those relationships. We have a large body of evidence on how collaboration improves performance in public agencies, but there are many reasons to believe that this may not be a linear relationship. Instead, we might find that collaboration will lead to performance gains up to a point, but at some point, increased collaboration no longer yields positive results (Hicklin *et al.* 2008). Conversely, some of the research on collaboration argues that collaboration is a process of identifying partners and establishing common goals before the actual work can take place (McGuire 2006). In these situations, we may find that managers must invest a substantial amount of time in building collaborative relationships before those partnerships will pay off. Exploring functional forms may open up new avenues for theory building.

Independence of observations

Lastly, much of the quantitative work in public management must deal with the fact that most data on public managers violates the assumption that our observations are independent. We often analyse data that is drawn from multiple public managers, many of whom are clustered within agencies, states, divisions, or even offices. As such, their behaviour, perceptions and work can all be affected by the behaviour, perceptions and work of others in the organization. Additionally, public managers operating in the same jurisdiction, agency or policy area may be influenced by informal norms, culture, oversight efforts, agency mission, economic fluctuations and a host of other influences. Scholars may deal with these issues by making small additions to their models, such as clustering the standard errors. However, others may find it more appropriate to move to hierarchical linear modelling.

Hierarchical linear modelling

Hierarchical linear modelling (HLM or multilevel modelling) is designed to allow researchers to combine data collected at multiple levels of aggregation more appropriately (Raudenbush and Bryk 2002). HLM has been used for quite some time in the field of education research, to identify how individual- and organizational-level factors influence student learning. In these studies, the dependent variable is usually some measure of individual student performance – for example, a student's score on a standardized exam. The independent variables used to predict student performance are a combination of individual-level measures that capture the student's background and classroom-level variables that are often the focus of the research. The individual-level variables are likely to include socioeconomic measures, race, gender, parental involvement, native intelligence, or some other set of predictors. At the classroom level, we would likely see teacher characteristics, class size, class demographics and measures of teaching practices. In a three-level model, we may see school-level characteristics included as well. Through this analysis, scholars seek to isolate the effect of variations in teaching techniques or classroom interventions.

So what advantages does HLM offer over linear regression? If we were to use OLS in the previous example, we would have two options. Option one is to conduct our analysis at the individual level and include all classroom-level measures as independent variables. However, in doing so, we are assuming that each student's learning is independent of every other student. Although this may be true for students who attend different schools, it is not true for students in the same class. These students are working closely within the same environment, receiving the same instruction, which means that their learning will not be fully independent of the other students' learning. Option two is to calculate a class average and conduct our study at the class level. This decision would result in throwing away considerable variation at the individual level, and we lose a considerable amount of valuable data.

We often make very similar decisions when analysing data on public management. Our data on managers and performance often include multiple managers who are grouped within organizations, agencies, local authorities, states or other important institutional arrangements. Much like students in a classroom, these managers co-exist in the same environment and are subject to the same political principals, agency heads or other authorities. We cannot assume that the observations are independent (a fundamental assumption in linear regression techniques), and as such, HLM is more appropriate for specifying these models.

Using HLM in our work on management and performance

Although HLM can improve our specification, there may be an additional advantage. Incorporating a multilevel approach in our work can also encourage us to think more systematically about how management and performance are influenced by politics, structures and environmental shifts. Our field has benefited from very thoughtful discussions of how public managers operate in a complex environment, with calls to consider how 'layers of government' affect managers and their organizations (Lynn, Heinrich and Hill 2001). The empirical work that has been paired with the theoretical arguments has utilized multilevel modelling and highlighted the ways in which it offers a better test of our theories (for example, see Lynn, Heinrich and Hill 2000).

Yet, few scholars have incorporated hierarchical modelling into their research, despite our interest in performance management, accountability systems or the role of political principals. As with most methodologies, we want to avoid the trap in which our having a 'hierarchical hammer' makes every question look like a 'hierarchical nail', but in the case of management and performance, the vast majority of our questions are already 'hierarchical nails'.

Management at multiple levels

Even if we limit our focus to factors within public agencies, we still have incredible opportunities to use a multilevel frame to ask different questions.

Too often, our findings treat managers as a monolithic group, and for many studies, the data are drawn from the top manager in the agency. How do we know if these findings are generalizable to middle managers? Could the strength of the relationship between management and performance be affected by where these managers exist within the organization?

HLM not only allows us to better specify our models that include managers at multiple levels, but it encourages us to think about the interactive effect of management at multiple levels. Consider the work on collaborative management. Most studies have found that increased efforts to build and strengthen relationships outside of one's organization – regardless of whether we talk about collaboration (Andrews *et al.* 2006; Bardach 1998; O'Leary and Bingham 2009), activation (Agranoff and McGuire 2001), networking (Meier and O'Toole 2003), or increasing network integration through coordination and joint programmes (Milward and Provan 1998) – often lead to improved outcomes for an organization. How does this apply to middle managers? Do they have the authority to build relationships outside of their home organization? Or would collaboration, in this context, involve other sub-units within the larger agency? We lack a strong body of evidence that speaks to whether increased collaboration is simply 'good management' or if these activities should be limited to only those managers with the authority and resources to speak on behalf of the entire organization.

On one hand, we may find that this outward-looking, relationship-building management style is more effective throughout the organization, such that all managers would be better off spending their time interacting with stakeholders outside their agency. If the findings from much of the existing literature are generalizable, this would be a reasonable hypothesis. Yet, it is just as likely that these findings are limited to certain types of managers. Instead, we may find that, from an organizational perspective, an optimal management strategy would involve a division of labour, in which certain managers do most of the work involving inter-organizational relationships, while other managers focus more on those issues that are internal to the organization.

Further still, we may not only find that the relationship between management and performance varies by levels within the organizational hierarchy, but we may also find that the effectiveness of particular managerial strategies depends on the managerial strategies of others in the organization. For the sake of clarity, let's consider an example.

Assume we are studying a particular group of state-level bureaucratic agencies in the United States. Each agency has an agency head (AH) and a team of regional directors (RD) that oversee individual offices. Given the established work on collaboration and performance, we construct a one-dimensional measure of collaboration for each manager. If we start at the top of the organization, we could test whether collaboration on the part of the agency head affects agency performance (AP), measured as the average performance of all offices in the state.

$$AP = AH$$

Assuming we find a positive relationship, what does this mean for regional directors? So, we decide to add them into the study. We could average their collaboration scores and include them, but then we obscure any opportunity to consider variations among offices within the state. Instead, we choose to look at the managerial activities of both agency heads and regional directors, and how their activities affect office performance (OP).

$$OP = AH + RD$$

If we continue in OLS, we ignore the fact the many of these regional directors work for the same agency head and operate in the same state. Not only does this violate the assumption of independence in OLS, it also ignores the (very likely) possibility that the agency heads can affect the ways in which regional directors are able to affect performance. Some may argue that the benefits of using hierarchical modelling are strictly limited to improving our analysis of data drawn at different levels of aggregation. Although this is true from a purely methodological standpoint, I believe that the use of HLM also encourages us to consider new questions. In this case, is the effectiveness of middle manager collaboration dependent on levels of collaboration of managers at the top of the hierarchy? Stated differently, is the most effective management strategy for the regional director contingent on the actions of the manager at the top of the hierarchy? Whether we have interest in exploring the effectiveness of managers who are often constrained by the multiple levels of governance (Lynn *et al.* 2001), or we want to understand management at multiple levels in an organization better, multilevel modelling may help guide our ability to do so.

Experimental methods

Experimental methodology is probably the area that is most ripe for development in public management. Although I often hear scholars discuss an interest in using experimental methods in their work, we have yet to see much work using this approach. This is unfortunate, as there are many questions that are central to public management that could be addressed through this type of research. Additionally, the use of experimental methods has a long history in other fields – most notably psychology, international relations and political behaviour. As such, many public management scholars have access to colleagues on their campus that are well-trained in designing and conducting experiments, along with the lab space necessary to carry out this work.

Granted, many scholars in public administration have used quasi-experimental designs, but few have moved to 'pure' experiments. All methodological approaches have their strengths and weaknesses, but the advantage offered by the use of laboratory experiments is a powerful one: an increase in interval validity. Scholars often point to the use of large-N, quantitative studies of management as a way to control for key differences among organizations, environments and individuals, but we still face limitations. Additionally, we face a number of difficulties when we are trying to collect data on managerial preferences, strategies, goals and decision making. Whether we collect these data through surveys or interviews, we regularly must consider problems with social desirability, inaccurate recall, purposeful deception and attitudes that do not link to actual behaviours. Moving to a laboratory context, with the use of randomly assigned control and experimental groups, can give us greater leverage in isolating the effects of certain interventions.

Over fifteen years ago, the *Journal of Public Administration Research and Theory* published a special issue on the use of experimental methods in public management research. In this issue, Bozeman and Scott (1992) discussed the usefulness of laboratory experiments in research on public management and pointed to a number of reasons explaining why the use of experimental methods has been rare in public management research. Some of these complaints include our interest in practical application (which can be difficult when we move to a laboratory setting), a preference for field experiments, a lack of experimental methods training in the doctoral curriculum, concerns over the credibility of findings generated through experiments, and few research questions in which the level of analysis is the individual. Although many of these explanations are still true, the literature on public management has moved in directions that have raised more questions in which individuals are the focus.

Consider a few of the questions that we have asked in recent work. What factors influence a manager's choice to engage in more collaborative management? How do accountability pressures influence the behaviour of managers?

If we subject managers (and their organizations) to greater levels of competition, will they become more efficient? Do street-level bureaucrats behave differently based on the race of the client? Do managers of public organizations manage differently from managers of private organizations? Each of these questions has some dimension that we could begin to tap with the use of well-designed experiments.

Recent work by Brewer and Brewer (forthcoming) highlights the utility of pure experiments. Their work tested for the existence of public service motivation by randomly assigning subjects to two groups. One group was told they were performing an exercise for a corporation, while the other group was told that the exercise was conducted for a government agency. Both groups performed the same task, but in their analysis, Brewer and Brewer found that the government group actually performed at higher levels than the group who believed they were working for a corporate organization.

Maybe our interest is in accountability policies or performance management. We have a number of studies that examine how increased pressures from political principals affect the behaviour and preferences of public managers. How do we know if these accountability policies are what is affecting public managers, versus a host of other possible influences? Obviously, we do our best to control for competing influences, but we are always limited in our ability to do so. In a laboratory setting, we can design experiments in which the only difference between the control group and the experimental group is the level of governmental oversight. With this design, any differences among the groups can be appropriately attributed to the varying levels of governmental oversight.

As a field, a move to experimental methods would also require continuous attention to concerns over ethical issues faced when conducting experiments. Whether we are using deception in the experiment or choosing to withhold an intervention that we expect to be beneficial to a population, experimental research may introduce increased levels of risk related to human subjects that most scholars in public management have not faced before. Increasing levels of risk in our research would also require that both scholars and graduate students receive better training on ethics in research and guidance on how to design research projects in ways that will not prevent these projects from getting through the institutional review boards at the researcher's home institution.

Additionally, management scholars face concerns over practical application and policy learning that are often not as important for scholars in other fields. The concerns we already face in connecting theory to practice could become even greater as we move our work away from the complex environments in which managers operate to a more controlled environment. As such, we must consider how, over time, we could connect the experimental work to the non-experimental body of literature, while also considering the ways in which this research can inform practitioners and policy-makers.

Obviously, there are limitations to the knowledge that can be generated through laboratory experiments (which are reviewed in depth by Bozeman and Scott (1992)), but as a field, we are passing up an opportunity to add another dimension to our body of research – an addition that would complement our existing work. Since the 1992 symposium, a search of *Journal of Public Administration Research and Theory* yields only a few articles using 'pure' experiments (Nutt 2006; Landsbergen *et al.* 1997; Scott 1997; Knott *et al.* 2003). Searches of other journals also yield very few uses of experimental methods (and often none at all). Regardless of whether one believes that experiments will uncover important truths or provide nothing more than theoretical exercise, some work using experimental methods in public management is warranted.

Developing new datasets

As mentioned earlier, our field continues to benefit from increased availability of data on management and performance, but there are still areas that need improvement. A number of scholars have discussed concerns over measurement of these concepts, concerns that are often difficult to address. One of the chief concerns involves measuring managerial activity, especially in a way that is applicable in dissimilar organizations and across different levels of managers. This issue is most clear in evaluating the research on networking and collaboration.

Consider a few of the ways in which networking and collaboration have been measured: tracking formal communication across organizations (Milward and Provan 1998), individual self-reports of frequency of interaction with various actors/organizations (Daley 2009; Meier and O'Toole 2003), aggregations of individual self-reports in an organization (Andrews *et al.* 2006), content analysis of secondary sources (Moynihan 2009), and many others. Not only do our measures of networking and collaboration differ in how they are collected, but they capture very different things. Despite the continued discussions of networking, networks and collaboration as a monolithic body of work, there are stark differences among measuring perceptions of behaviour, measuring the flow of information across offices, and measuring structural characteristics of an organization. Yet, few scholars are meticulous about differentiating among dissimilar measures and discussing the implications of moving from one type of measure to another.

One of the most common differences seen in the literature on management and performance is the units of analysis. Both management and performance can be measured at the individual level, the organizational level, at some level in between (i.e. programme level), or even at the network level (Talbot 2005). We also see some studies that pair management data collected at one level (such as the individual) with management data collected at another level (often the organization). Given the diversity of possibilities, it is difficult to know how to combine these data in the most methodologically appropriate way.

Enticott *et al.* (2009) offer an excellent discussion of the issues that are faced when scholars utilize survey data to construct management measures, both at the individual and organizational level. In their analysis, Enticott *et al.* compare the various ways in which scholars utilize managerial surveys, finding important differences between using elite surveys and using multiple informants. They then go on to discuss the differences in the ways in which multiple informants are aggregated (echelon versus simple mean). Their careful discussion of measurement and research design offers an example of the importance of fully considering how our measures match our concepts and how alternative specifications can provide valuable information. Clearly, what could seem as a small decision about measurement can substantially affect our research findings. As we push to develop new datasets, we must also consider the importance of measurement.

Old dogs, new tricks and little baby puppies

We often see scholars advocate the adoption of underutilized methodologies. Sometimes these calls come from reviewers, discussions (much like this one), or a lone methodologist in the back of the room during conference Q&A. But much like the 1992 symposium on experimental methods, we rarely see much progress. Who has the time? And where would we start? For many researchers, their methodological skills are mostly limited to what they learned in graduate school. These skills can often be developed by learning from colleagues within the researcher's department, but many scholars may not have access to those people.

Maybe the key to moving our field forward in broadening our use of different methodologies is through training our graduate students. Other disciplines have overcome many of these same obstacles through the use of summer methodological institutes. In the USA, many faculty members and graduate students attend the Summer Program in Quantitative Methods of Social Research, hosted by the Inter-University Consortium for Political and Social Research (ICPSR 2009) in Ann Arbor, Michigan. Participants attend courses that are offered in two different sessions, each lasting four weeks. These courses range from introductory courses to very advanced work, and many of the topics are focused on more specialized methodologies. These condensed-format classes offer the opportunity to receive expert training and build relationships with other scholars using similar techniques in a (relatively) low-cost way.

A very similar programme is offered in the UK through the Essex Summer School in Social Science Data Analysis and Collection (Essex 2009). This programme offers three sessions, each lasting two weeks. Much like the ICPSR programme, these courses offer a wide range of methodological skills and vary from very introductory courses for scholars who are new to quantitative work to very advanced for those who already have a strong foundation in quantitative work. These programmes have been well attended by scholars in other disciplines, and they may be the right place to start for public management scholars seeking to add to their expertise. This would require a serious effort on the part of our schools and departments to encourage faculty members and graduate students to attend these workshops, to aid in offsetting the cost of these endeavours, and considering ways in which participation in these sessions would contribute to progress in the degree programme or to promotion and tenure.

Qualitative methods

Although this essay has focused exclusively on quantitative methods, we should also consider the ways in which our work – and the work of the students we train – would benefit from mixed-methods research designs that incorporate qualitative methods. There is a great deal of high-quality qualitative work in our field (for an example, see Golden 2000), but too often, scholars self-segregate into quantitative and qualitative camps, rarely giving serious consideration to the other side. Yet, in doing so we miss the opportunity to exploit the advantages of other techniques and do high-quality, mixed-methods research. Although they may choose to study only those questions that are best examined through one methodological approach, our field will benefit by producing scholars who are more broadly trained. Obviously, this means more than telling our students to take four advanced quantitative courses and 'throw in a few interviews'.

Quantitative scholars could move to a more mixed-methods approach by adopting methodologies that incorporate both quantitative and qualitative techniques. Our field already has a number of scholars engaged in elite interviewing, detailed case studies or action research. Additionally, scholars have often engaged in archival research to study the development and management of government agencies, yet we rarely see these methods paired with quantitative work to offer a more complete investigation of the link between management and performance. Each of these techniques allows the researcher to take advantage of the breadth and depth of information that can be gathered through interviews, analyses of legislation, historical agency documents, while still retaining the ability to conduct more generalizable, 'large-N' analyses.

Certain methodologies lend themselves to the intersection of quantitative and qualitative methods. Content analysis allows scholars to analyse text – often drawn from interviews, agency documents, media coverage and various other sources – to track the inclusion of certain concepts, phrases or characterization of particular programmes, policies or decisions, and these data can be converted into quantitative data. A number of scholars in public administration have been utilizing content analysis (Moynihan and Ingraham 2003; May *et al.* 2008; Moynihan 2009; Wilkins 2007), but relatively few of these studies address the link between management and performance. Moving to a more mixed-methods approach – whether that be through coupling dissimilar methodologies or utilizing those methodologies that bridge the quantitative/qualitative divide – will offer new opportunities to build a strong body of literature on the ways in which managers can affect organizational performance.

This is a great time to be a scholar of public management. The research conducted on management and performance enjoys the attention of many talented scholars and substantial practical relevance in this age of increased accountability pressures. We benefit from new and improved data sources that provide us with the opportunity to study our questions using better measures of management and performance. As we take advantage of theoretical and empirical developments, we must continually revisit our choice of methodology and be open-minded about moving to new approaches, without chasing fads.

It is exciting to think about where the scholarship on management and research will go from here. We can only hope that we will continue to move forward, broadening our scope, advancing our understanding and uncovering the ways in which public managers can move their agencies forward to promote better outcomes for the citizens they serve. As we continue down this path, our ability to develop new theories will depend, in part, on our ability to employ methodologies that can appropriately account for the multifaceted relationships that we have identified as important in linking public management to organizational performance.

REFERENCES

Agranoff, Robert, and Michael McGuire. 2001. 'Big questions in public network management research', *Journal of Public Administration Research and Theory*, 11, 3, 295–326.

Andrews, Rhys, George A. Boyne, and Richard M. Walker. 2006. 'Strategy content and organizational performance: an empirical analysis', *Public Administration Review*, 66, 1, 52–63.

Bardach, Eugene. 1998. *Getting Agencies to Work Together: The Practice and Theory of Managerial Craftsmanship*. Washington, DC: Brookings Institution.

Bozeman, Barry, and Patrick Scott. 1992. 'Laboratory experiments in public policy and management', *Journal of Public Administration Research and Theory*, 2, 3, 293–313.

Brewer, Gene A., and Gene A. Brewer, Jr. Forthcoming. 'Experimental methods in public management research: a demonstration parsing public/private differences', *Journal of Public Administration Research and Theory*.

Daley, Dorothy M. 2009. 'Interdisciplinary problems and agency boundaries: exploring effective cross-agency collaboration', *Journal of Public Administration Research and Theory*, 19, 3, 477–93.

Enticott, Gareth, George A. Boyne, and Richard M. Walker. 2008. 'The use of multiple informants in public administration research: data aggregation using organizational echelons', *Journal of Public Administration Research and Theory*, 19, 2, 229–53.

Essex. 2009. Essex Summer School in Social Science Data Analysis and Collection. University of Essex. www.essex.ac.uk/methods/.

Golden, Marissa Martino. 2000. *What Motivates Bureaucrats? Politics and Administration During the Reagan Years*. New York: Columbia University Press.

Hicklin, Alisa, Laurence J. O'Toole, Jr., and Kenneth J. Meier. 2008. 'Serpents in the sand: managerial networking and nonlinear influences on organizational performance', *Journal of Public Administration Research and Theory*, 18, 2, 253–73.

ICPSR. 2009. 'Summer program in quantitative methods of social research', *Inter-University Consortium for Political and Social Research*. www.icpsr.umich.edu/sumprog/index.html

Knott, Jack H., Gary J. Miller, and Jay Verkuilen. 2003. 'Adaptive incrementalism and complexity: experiments with two-person cooperative signaling games', *Journal of Public Administration Research and Theory*, 13, 3, 341–65.

Landsbergen, David, David H. Coursey, Stephen Loveless, and R. F. Shangraw, Jr. 1997. 'Decision quality, confidence, and commitment with expert systems: an experimental study', *Journal of Public Administration Research and Theory*, 7, 1, 131–58.

Lynn, Laurence E., Carolyn Heinrich, and Carolyn Hill. 2000. 'Studying governance and public management: challenges and prospects', *Journal of Public Administration Research and Theory*, 10, 2, 233–61.

2001. *Improving Governance: a New Logic for Empirical Research*. Washington, DC: Georgetown University Press.

May, Peter J., Samuel Workman, and Bryan D. Jones. 2008. 'Organizing attention: responses of the bureaucracy to agenda disruption', *Journal of Public Administration Research and Theory*, 18, 4, 517–41.

McGuire, Michael. 2006. 'Collaborative public management: assessing what we know and how we know it', *Public Administration Review*. Special Issue (December), 33–43.

Meier, Kenneth J., and Laurence J. O'Toole, Jr. 2003. 'Public management and educational performance: the impact of managerial networking', *Public Administration Review*, 63, 6, 689–99.

Milward, H. Brinton, and Keith G. Provan. 1998. 'Principles for controlling agents: the political economy of network structure', *Journal of Public Administration Research and Theory*, 8, 2, 203–21.

Moon, M. Jae, and Stuart Bretschneider. 2002. 'Does the perception of red tape constrain IT innovativeness in organizations? Unexpected results from a simultaneous equation model and implications', *Journal of Public Administration Research and Theory*, 12, 2, 273–92.

Moynihan, Donald P. 2009. 'The network governance of crisis response: case studies of incident command systems', *Journal of Public Administration Research and Theory*, 19, 4, 895–915.

Moynihan, Donald P., and Patricia W. Ingraham. 2003. 'Look for the silver lining: when performance-based accountability systems work.' *Journal of Public Administration Research and Theory*, 13, 4, 469–90.

Nutt, Paul C. 2006. 'Comparing public and private sector decision-making practices', *Journal of Public Administration Research and Theory*, 16, 2, 289–318.

O'Leary, Rosemary, and Lisa Blomgren Bingham. 2009. *The Collaborative Public Manager: New Ideas for the Twenty-First Century*. Washington, DC: Georgetown University Press.

Raudenbush, Stephen W., and Anthony S. Bryk. 2002. *Hierarchical Linear Models: Application and Data Analysis Methods*, 2nd edn. Thousand Oaks, CA: Sage Publications.

Scott, Patrick G. 1997. 'Assessing determinants of bureaucratic discretion: an experiment in street-level decision making', *Journal of Public Administration Research and Theory*, 7, 1, 35–58.

Talbot, Colin. 2005. 'Performance management', in Ewan Ferlie, Laurence E. Lynn and Christopher Pollitt (eds.) *The Oxford Handbook of Public Management*. Oxford University Press.

Wilkins, Vicky M. 2007. 'Exploring the causal story: gender, active representation, and bureaucratic priorities', *Journal of Public Administration Research and Theory*, 17, 1, 77–94.

Conclusion: enriching the field

George A. Boyne, Gene A. Brewer and Richard M. Walker

Introduction

The impact of management on the performance of public organizations has become a major question for researchers in the last two decades. Although this issue has been debated extensively in the past, it is only more recently that it has been addressed through rigorous empirical studies that draw upon theories of organizational and managerial behaviour. In addition, only since the late 1980s have concepts and measures of performance been prominent on the academic agenda; somewhat belatedly, policy-makers and managers might argue, because these are the issues that dominate their working lives. This interest in performance has coincided with, and been reinforced by, the widespread availability of data on the efficiency and effectiveness of public organizations as a consequence of the adoption of New Public Management (NPM) reforms. The coalescence of theoretical interest in management and performance with the availability of data that allow propositions to be tested has led to a surge of projects and papers on the topic. In our view this focus on performance is entirely appropriate, because traditional research on public management has concentrated too much on inputs, activities, structures and processes, and neglected what public organizations actually achieve and the determinants of success or failure. In sum, research on management and performance is not simply an academic fad, but is increasingly the topic that defines public management as an applied social science that seeks to contribute to both theory and practice (Andrews and Boyne 2010).

In this book we have sought to draw together what is known about the impact of public management on performance, and to set out methodological and theoretical agendas for the next phase of work in the field. The effects of organizational goals, structures, finance, red tape, networking, public service motivation, employee diversity, performance management, and strategy have been reviewed in this book. For each of these topics the contributing authors have clarified the theoretical basis for links with performance, discussed definitions and measures of the key concepts, reviewed the empirical studies that have been conducted and their methodological strengths and weaknesses, summarized the main patterns in the evidence and highlighted propositions that draw out the main research directions in the field. Thus we have clarified the state of the art (and state of the emerging science), and provided a foundation for additional theoretical and empirical research on each of the topics that have been covered in the book.

In this final chapter we address two issues that go beyond incremental improvements to the 'normal science' of public management and performance. First, we argue for a set of theoretical assumptions, and a related range of parallel shifts in measures and methods, that reflect the complexity of the links between management and performance. In doing so, we draw out some of the main theoretical assumptions that have been implicit in traditional work in the field, and build on the more nuanced and sophisticated models that underlie the propositions in the preceding chapters. Second, we identify theoretical perspectives on management and performance that have received little explicit attention in previous work, but seem to offer much promise for further progress in understanding why some organizations perform better than others, and we highlight some generic methodological issues that need to be resolved in future empirical studies.

Public management and performance: from simplicity to sophistication

The work in this field that has been published in the last twenty years can be seen as the beginnings and foundations of a research programme that will endure for as long as governments provide services and seek ways to achieve better results. These initial studies have many strengths, and have already provided insights into some of the links between management and performance in the public sector. For example, the available evidence suggests that performance is generally higher in organizations that have clear goals, low levels of red tape and employees with strong public service motivation. Yet, as with any new field of scientific inquiry, the first wave of studies is limited in a variety of ways. It is, therefore, important to reflect on some of the implicit assumptions in previous work that may constrain further development of the field. In particular, studies to date have often:

1. Treated each aspect of management (e.g. goal ambiguity, red tape) as a 'compound' variable, and not disaggregated it into constituent elements that may have different performance effects;

2. Examined only one dimension of performance, and neglected potential trade-offs between different dimensions;
3. Assumed that the impact of management is linear and is not, for example, subject to diminishing returns; and,
4. Tested for the separate effect of management, and not taken into account that it may moderate the impact of other variables, be moderated by them, or have an impact on other determinants of performance that are further along the 'chain of causation'.

We now discuss each issue in turn, and illustrate our arguments with propositions from the preceding chapters.

Disaggregating the dimensions of management

Many of the studies that we have reviewed in this book use aggregate measures of specific dimensions of management; for example, the performance effects of red tape, organizational diversity or financial management might be explored, treating each of these as a 'composite' variable. However, more recent work is beginning to unpack these variables into sub-dimensions, which in turn allows their detailed, and possibly contradictory or reinforcing, effects to be evaluated. For example, in Chapter 5, Brewer and Walker argue that different aspects of red tape (e.g. internally selected by an organization or externally imposed upon it) are likely to have different effects on performance; and in Chapter 2 Rainey and Jung point out that goal ambiguity can be decomposed into at least four elements, some of which have effects that work against each other. Similarly, Brewer proposes in Chapter 7 that the public service motivation sub-dimension of 'compassion' will have positive effects on equity and consumer satisfaction, while 'concern for the public interest' is more likely to make a difference to service quality and effectiveness. Rhys Andrews' arguments on organizational structure in Chapter 3 add a further twist: not only will different sub-dimensions of management have different effects, but they are likely to have mutually reinforcing effects that would be missed by an aggregate measure or by taking each of them separately. Thus Andrews proposes that combinations of formalization, centralization and specialization will have especially strong consequences for performance.

Such propositions imply that significant progress could be made through further conceptual clarification of the major aspects of management that we have reviewed in this book, and by theorizing how the sub-dimensions of each concept are linked to each other and to performance, both separately and in combination. This would need to be accompanied by better datasets and more nuanced survey questions that tease out the elements of each dimension of management, which in turn would raise practical questions about the balance between survey length and precision on the one hand, and the rate and representativeness of survey responses on the other.

The performance kaleidoscope

Most studies of the determinants of performance focus on only one aspect of the concept – for example, effectiveness, consumer satisfaction, efficiency and (very rarely) equity. This narrow approach implicitly assumes that a single dimension of performance can stand for the achievements of an organization taken on the whole (on the mistaken assumption that all of the different elements of performance are positively correlated), or that the sole dimension that has been measured is somehow the one that merits the closest attention. This latter perspective suggests that performance should be looked at through a telescope, when in fact it resembles a kaleidoscope, with many parts that shift as they bump into each other. In other words, a focus on a single dimension of performance may be misleading because a management variable that is positively related to one may be negatively related to others, and because an improvement in one area may cause deterioration elsewhere.

These ideas are reflected in some of the propositions in earlier chapters. For example, in Chapter 6, Meier and O'Toole argue that although managerial networking with external stakeholders has positive effects on organizational effectiveness (the percentage of school pupils who pass standardized tests), it has negative effects on equity (the level of pupil attainment in different ethnic groups). Similarly, Boyne argues in Chapter 9 that targets are likely to raise achievement on the performance indicators that are targeted, but to lead to worse results on other indicators. Such propositions on networking and targets clearly cannot be tested without taking account of a variety of dimensions of performance.

A significant theoretical advance would be to explore the causal logic of the link between different dimensions (and sub-dimensions) of management and a range of performance criteria. At present, some of these are being mapped inductively in the minority of studies that use measures of several criteria of performance. This could usefully be complemented by a theoretical exercise that seeks to think through the mixed effects of management on different aspects of public service success or failure. Empirical tests of the propositions from such theory building would, of course, require datasets that capture many dimensions of performance, including both 'archival' measures of concepts such as efficiency and effectiveness, and 'perceptual' measures of the views of different stakeholders such as citizens, consumers and professional regulators. Although there has been much debate on the relative merits of archival and perceptual measures, a consensus is emerging that both are required to provide a comprehensive picture of performance (Andrews *et al.* 2010; Brewer 2006; Kelly and Swindell 2002). Moreover, propositions on the contradictory effects of management variables, and the trade-offs between different dimensions of performance, cannot be tested without taking both types of measures into account.

The impact of management: curves and tipping points

The first wave of studies on management and performance has been dominated by tests of linear effects. In other words, the impact of a management variable is assumed to be uniformly positive or negative and on a consistent trajectory throughout its range. Little account is usually taken of the possibility that management may be subject to increasing or decreasing returns (and thereby resemble a curve), or that relationships that start out positive or negative may eventually turn in the opposite direction (and therefore be characterized by a tipping or turning point).

A number of propositions in earlier chapters take up the theme of non-linear management effects. For example, Meier and O'Toole conjecture that managerial networking is subject to diminishing returns. Initially, networking has a strong positive effect because organizations that have little engagement with the outside world are unlikely to have good relationships with funders, political principals or citizen groups. Shifting from no networking to some networking is, therefore, likely to reap substantial rewards. However, as managers spend more and more time networking, the benefits from this activity are likely to become smaller, because fewer and fewer nuggets of useful information and political support remain untapped. Thus the impact of networking will remain positive, but will resemble a curve that 'flattens out' near the top end. Beyond this point, the impact of networking may even turn negative, as too little attention is devoted to internal operations and service delivery, and performance is thereby undermined by managers whose attention is disproportionately devoted to the external environment. Another set of propositions on non-linear effects is put forward in Boyne's chapter on performance management. In Chapter 9 he argues that the impact of performance indicators and targets is at first positive, because they help to direct attention to what is important to the organization, and the level of success that is expected. However, a proliferation of indicators and targets is counter-productive, and eventually the effects turn negative as confusion rather than clarity is produced (see also Rainey and Jung's arguments on goal ambiguity in Chapter 2).

These propositions on the non-linear (inverted u-shaped) relationship between management and performance raise a more general theoretical issue. Put simply, all of the positive effects that have so far been uncovered might eventually become 'too much of a good thing'. Any single manage-ment activity, if pushed too far, may produce diminishing or even negative returns. This is all the more likely because managers face constraints that mean more time and energy devoted to one activity (e.g. external network-ing) must come at the price of the neglect of others (e.g. internal perform-ance management). Economists refer to this as 'opportunity costs': that is, the time and energy expended on one activity necessarily precludes the pur-suit of other activities which might be even more beneficial in the long term. Once again, recent empirical work provides some clues on the curves and tipping points that may exist, but solid theoretical work on this issue would help to provide structure and coherence to the emerging findings. All that can be said for now is that in a world of multiple management activities that are performed simultaneously, the logic of testing for only linear perform-ance effects is tenuous.

Management: working alone or working on the chain gang?

Tests of the impact of management have conventionally assumed that it has a separate or additive effect on performance. In other words, when other influ-ences on performance are held constant, management independently pro-duces better or worse results. By contrast, some recent empirical studies, and many of the propositions in the preceding chapters, assume that the impact of management is contingent on other variables, and that its effects are part of a complex causal chain. Three main ways in which management works in combination with other explanatory variables can be distinguished. First, it moderates (either reinforces or suppresses) the impact of other determin-ants of performance. For example, in Chapter 6, Meier and O'Toole argue that managerial networking can mitigate the negative impact of an exter-nal crisis. Similarly, in Chapter 10 Walker argues that an abundant resource environment might be best exploited by a strategy of prospecting. In these ways, management can turn the effects of external circumstances in a more favourable direction. Different aspects of management may also be related to each other in this way. For example, in Chapter 4 Andrews puts forward the proposition that organizational structure mitigates the positive performance effects of innovation and organizational commitment. Thus management does not work alone; rather it bends and shapes the impact of other external and internal (exogenous or endogenous) variables.

Second, the impact of management is itself moderated (reinforced or suppressed) by other influences on performance. The moderators in this case may be other organizational or managerial characteristics. For example, in Chapter 3 Moynihan and Andrews argue that the impact of financial management is contingent on leadership and culture, and that the positive effect of financial management is strengthened by managerial autonomy over resource allocation. Similarly, in Chapter 5, Brewer and Walker argue that the negative impact of red tape is mitigated by organizational strategy, and in Chapter 6 Meier and O'Toole propose that networking and management capacity have mutually reinforcing positive effects on performance. A final illustration of how the impact of management is moderated by other variables is provided by Boyne's propositions on target effects in Chapter 9: he argues that the positive effect of targets is reinforced by budgetary incentives, but suppressed by managerial gaming and public service motivation.

Finally, the first two ways that management works in combination with other variables, by moderating or being moderated, imply that it *interacts* with them. A third way that management combines with other variables is that its relationship with them is *causal*. In other words, the impact of management is indirect: it has an effect on other variables which in turn influence performance. Pitts in Chapter 8 best illustrates this point in his propositions on the impact of organizational diversity. One of these propositions is that diversity exacerbates coordination and communication problems, and these lead to lower organizational performance. Note here that diversity does not simply interact with whatever problems already exist; it has a causal effect which makes them worse. Similarly, Pitts proposes that diversity leads to greater creativity and innovation in organizations, and these characteristics in turn produce better results. Again, the argument is that diversity causes changes in other variables that subsequently improve performance.

In sum, many of the propositions that have been developed in this book suggest that the impact of management should not be considered in isolation. These propositions need to be tested through interaction terms in multivariate models (to examine whether management moderates or is moderated by other explanatory variables), or in structural equation models (see Chapter 11) that examine the direct and indirect effects of management in the causal chains that lead to higher or lower performance.

Public management and performance: towards theoretical and methodological enrichment

In this final section of the book we build on the preceding chapters by discussing theoretical issues that have received little attention in the field to date, and highlighting methodological issues that need to be resolved in the next phase of empirical research on management and performance.

Broadening the theoretical base

Many theoretical topics remain to be explored in studies of organizational success and failure in the public sector. Indeed, public management research has only begun to grapple with the vast array of perspectives that have been explored in studies of the performance of private organizations. Here we limit our attention to three issues that have already received some attention in the broad public management literature, and which could usefully be applied to the understanding of variations in the performance of public organizations.

The first of these is leadership, an important concept in public management which many scholars and practitioners link with performance. Yet we have not systematically included leadership in this volume because there are so few tests of its impact on performance (a rare and excellent exception is Fernandez 2005). Case studies to date suggest that leadership is not a primary factor impacting organizational performance; rather, leadership appears to exert much of its impact in combination with other variables (which, as noted above, may be tested via interactive terms that show mediating and moderating effects). This suggests that researchers should rethink the leadership concept in the public sector, as they are doing in the management field at large, with greater emphasis being placed on networks, horizontal interactions and team building. It does not seem to be so much about heroic or charismatic figures barking out orders and leading change in public organizations; rather, effective leaders may do a lot of angling and hedging, working behind the scenes, inducing cooperation and collaboration, and attempting to influence performance in subtle, indirect ways. This does not necessarily reduce the importance of leadership in public organizations; it merely suggests that leadership requires a higher degree of skill and acumen, as well as knowledge of the actors and context, than we have hitherto recognized. A related leadership topic that deserves much more attention is executive succession: what is the impact of a change in leadership on the performance of public organizations? When is a 'change of the guard' adaptive for organizations, and when is it disruptive? This can be regarded as the acid test of whether leadership matters: if replacing the top manager (or the top management team) in a public organization has significant effects, then all the effort that has gone into conceptualizing public leadership and speculating on its effects will begin to look worthwhile.

Another somewhat neglected topic in 'explaining performance' is the Meier–O'Toole contention that public organizations (and probably all organizations) are auto-regressive systems. Certainly past performance explains the lion's share of current performance in almost every empirical analysis that has included the auto-regressive term. So perhaps there are implications of this finding that have not been fleshed out. For example, this 'carry-over effect' seems to ratchet up the importance of small, incremental performance improvements, in part because public organizations not only benefit from them in the present, but they have cumulative effects over time. When framed as public service outcomes, such as job placements, number of high school dropouts prevented, or a reduction in automobile fatalities, it is easy to see how small improvements can have a mounting effect in subsequent periods, and can interact or combine with other variables (i.e. a dropout prevented or a life saved on the highways can lead to a job placement in future periods) to synergistically produce markedly greater outcomes for society. In other words, a small increase in performance can arguably produce a large yield over a ten-year period. There may, in addition, be other implications of the auto-regressive term that should be explored.

One topic that is receiving increased attention in the public administration literature is bureaucratic autonomy (for example, see Carpenter 2001). The concept of autonomy is referred to in many different ways (for example, it has been called discretion, flexibility, risk taking, entrepreneurship, and other terms), and it resonates with many different theoretical perspectives. Yet the common denominator is that bureaucratic agencies may perform better if they can carve out a somewhat autonomous existence – or at least some wiggle room for innovation and risk taking. (The relationship is probably curvilinear – performance probably suffers when there is too little or too much autonomy.) In any case, the public service performance literature needs to pay more attention to the concept of bureaucratic autonomy.

In addition, Rainey and Steinbauer (1999) contended that overhead political support is an important prerequisite for organizational performance and effectiveness in the public sector (also see Rourke 1984; Wilson 1989). This raises the bar for public organizations: they may need to cultivate a degree of overhead political support while simultaneously etching out a measure of bureaucratic autonomy – concepts that may not travel well together. Nonetheless, public management scholars need to investigate the performance-related effects of overhead political support and bureaucratic autonomy more carefully.

Strengthening methodology

Some streams of the performance literature look across policy or service areas (English local government studies; US federal agency studies), while other streams of work bore down into particular policy or service areas (Texas school district analyses; NASP-2 state health and human service information technology managers). But no one is paying careful attention to variation across policy or service areas – at least not consistently and over the long term. It may simply be harder to manage social welfare programmes than sanitation or transportation programmes, and performance researchers should be the first to trumpet this finding if it is true. Such a finding would actually comport with several other literatures on service delivery and contracting, for example, and provide cover for public agencies and managers that are tasked with what Hargrove and Glidewell (1990) refer to as 'impossible jobs'. Such evidence would inject a degree of realism into the political process by informing policy-makers and the public that certain public services are more problematic to implement than others; they may require more investment and patience along the way; and they may ultimately produce incomplete or less than stellar results. There may be other important things that we could divine from looking more carefully at variation across policy or service types (Ripley and Franklin 1991).

A similar point is made by Heinrich and Lynn (2000) and Hill and Hupe (2009) in their expanded frameworks of governance. These scholars contend that public management and public service performance are embedded in a thick web of hierarchical and horizontal relationships. Chapter 11 suggests that hierarchical linear modelling and other innovative methodological techniques are required to capture this complexity. The need to do so is driven by the same argument outlined above. Researchers commit the sin of model specification error unless they include all of the major drivers of performance in their theoretical and empirical models. There is every reason to believe that some of these drivers may subsume or negate others, since in the real world they co-exist in a dense space and time. For example, how can researchers untangle the impact of hierarchy from service type unless the variables are examined together? Many institutions of governance lie on the periphery of public management – such as the UK Audit Commission and overhead political authorities in the USA. Many other actors are involved in the policy process in democratic countries – such as the media, interest groups, nonprofit organizations and private contractors who are delivering public services. Researchers must, therefore, cast a wide net to ensure that all relevant actors and organizations are included.

Researchers need to start planning studies that are broad enough to examine all of the major factors known to impact performance together. In other words, these studies need to include all relevant drivers of performance and let variables such as managerial quality and networking compete in the same equations with strategy content, red tape, public service motivation and other variables to determine which of these variables may subsume others, and which may exert the most powerful independent effects on performance. We are now pressing toward middle-range theories of public service performance, but it is not too soon to envision more robust and complete models.

Another matter of great concern in survey research is how to structure the sample properly. Some studies have used elite surveys (for example, Texas school district studies), while others have composed broader samples consisting of managers (English local government studies) or all employees (US federal agency studies). Another type of variation is in the unit of analysis. Some studies define the relevant unit as central governments (for example, cross-country studies) while others compose samples of corporate-like multiplex governments (English local governments) or organizations that are more service specific (US federal agencies, US state health and human service agencies, and Texas school districts). Clearly the path chosen is likely to affect the results. For example, management and performance is likely to be more problematic in large, complex, multitasking forms of government than in smaller, simpler, and more policy-specific forms. Perhaps more important, such differences in the unit of analysis raise questions about the generalizability of findings. Are researchers comparing apples to oranges when they try to synthesize findings across studies utilizing different units of analysis? This is a methodological issue that needs to be addressed straightforwardly: what are the biases inherent in each type of sample and unit of analysis? What is the best unit of analysis for the purpose of generalizability (if there is one)? And how should samples be structured optimally to study public service performance on the whole? (And is the answer different if we are prying into governmental, organizational or policy performance?)

Concluding comment: prospects for progressing to 'normal science'

This book has demonstrated that public management scholars are now taking the management–performance hypothesis seriously. As was shown in Chapter 1, and subject to systematic review through the book, the number of studies addressing aspects of this debate is growing apace. Research on public management and performance can now be conceivably cast as a paradigm: there are an increasing number of scholars who share a set of beliefs, comprehend a set of common problems and possess an understanding of how they should be investigated (Kuhn 1962). While a paradigm has perhaps been developed over the last two decades, an underlying theoretical framework shared by many social scientists working on this question is not yet completely in hand. In Chapter 1 we point towards frameworks such as the work conducted by the Government Performance Project (Ingraham *et al.* 2003) and Rainey and Steinbauer's (1999) galloping elephants. The more comprehensive performance and governance frameworks developed by O'Toole and Meier (1999) and Lynn and colleagues (Lynn *et al.* 2001) clearly move towards more far-reaching theory, but considering the limited amount of empirical verification that has occurred, we remain at the level of mid-range theory. What offers the editors of this book optimism that we might move toward a 'theory of public service performance' is that major theoretical breakthroughs have been witnessed in recent years, and rigorous empirical tests of the public management–performance hypothesis are regularly conducted to drive knowledge in this important area of applied social science scholarship forward. If the public management academic community continues to address these questions, some of which are discussed above, and can crystallize the paradigm, the next major review of studies in this field may be able to talk about normal science – that is, bringing together accepted theory and empirical evidence on the topic – and be optimistic that a paradigm shift or a scientific revolution might be witnessed. Perhaps more important is the possibility that governments everywhere could become more productive and effective if they had a sufficient knowledge base on how to do so. To this larger cause we dedicate this work.

REFERENCES

Andrews, Rhys, and George A. Boyne. 2010. 'Better public services: the moral purpose of public management research?', *Public Management Review,* forthcoming.

Andrews, Rhys, George A. Boyne, M. Jae Moon, and Richard M. Walker. 2010. 'Assessing organizational performance: exploring differences between internal and external measures', *International Public Management Journal,* forthcoming.

Brewer, Gene A. 2006. 'All measures of performance are subjective: more evidence on US federal agencies', in George. A. Boyne, Kenneth. J. Meier, Laurence J. O'Toole, Jr. and Richard M. Walker (eds.) *Public Services Performance: Perspectives on Measurement and Management.* Cambridge University Press.

Carpenter, Daniel P. 2001. *The Forging of Bureaucratic Autonomy: Reputation, Networks, and Policy Innovation in Executive Agencies, 1862–1928.* Cambridge, MA: Harvard University Press.

Fernandez, S. 2005. 'Developing and testing an integrative framework of public sector leadership: evidence from the public education arena', *Journal of Public Administration Research and Theory,* 15, 2, 197–217.

Hargrove, Erwin C., and John C. Glidewell (eds.). 1990. *Impossible Jobs in Public Management.* Lawrence, KS: University of Kansas Press.

Heinrich, Carolyn. J., and Laurence E. Lynn, Jr. 2000. *Governance and Performance: New Perspectives.* Washington, DC: Georgetown University Press.

Hill, Michael, and Peter Hupe. 2009. *Implementing Public Policy: Governance in Theory and Practice,* 2nd edn. Thousand Oaks, CA: Sage Publications.

Ingraham, Patricia W., Phillip G. Joyce, and Amy Kneedler Donahue. 2003. *Government Performance: Why Management Matters.* Baltimore, MD: Johns Hopkins University Press.

Kelly, Janet M., and David Swindell. 2002. 'A multiple-indicator approach to municipal service evaluation: correlating performance measurement and citizen satisfaction across jurisdictions', *Public Administration Review,* 62, 4, 610–20.

Kuhn, Thomas S. 1962. *The Structure of Scientific Revolutions.* The University of Chicago Press.

Lynn, Laurence E., Jr., Carolyn J. Heinrich, and Carolyn J. Hill. 2001. *Improving Governance: A New Logic for Empirical Research.* Washington, DC: Georgetown University Press.

O'Toole, Laurence J., Jr., and Kenneth J. Meier. 1999. 'Modelling the impact of public management: the implications of structural context', *Journal of Public Administration Research and Theory,* 9, 3, 505–26.

Rainey, Hal G., and Paula Steinbauer. 1999. 'Galloping elephants: developing elements of a theory of effective government organizations', *Journal of Public Administration Research and Theory,* 9, 1, 1–32.

Ripley, Randell B., and Grance A. Franklin. 1991. *Congress, The Bureaucracy and Public Policy*, 5th edn. Pacific Grove, CA: Brooks/Cole.

Rourke, Francis E. 1984. *Bureaucracy, Politics, and Public Policy*, 3rd edn. Boston: Little, Brown.

Wilson, James Q. 1989. *Bureaucracy: What Government Agencies Do and Why They Do It*. New York: Basic Books.

Index

Printed in the United States
By Bookmasters